HELLGATE MEMORIES
— VIETNAM WA

A PATCH OF GROUND
KHE SANH REMEMBERED

* * * *

Michael Archer

Hellgate Press
Central Point, OR

A Patch of Ground: Khe Sanh Remembered

Hellgate Press
P.O. Box 3727
Central Point, OR 97502-0032
harley@hellgatepress.com *e-mail*

Editor: Harley Patrick
Assistant editor: Jan O. Olsson
Book design and composition: Constance C. Dickinson
Cover design: Chris Molé: In Cahoots Design
Cover photograph: David Douglas Duncan

Library of Congress Cataloging-in-Publication Data

Archer, Michael, 1948–
    A patch of ground: Khe Sanh remembered / Michael Archer. — 1st ed.
        p. cm.
    Includes bibliographical references.
    ISBN 1-55571-643-1
    1. Khe Sanh, Battle of, Vietnam, 1968. 2. Vietnamese Conflict,
1961–1975—Personal narratives, American. 3. Archer, Michael, 1948– . I.
Title: Khe Sanh remembered. II. Title.

    DS557.8.K5A73 2005
    959.704'342—dc22

                                                        2004027558

Printed and bound in the United States of America
First edition 10 9 8 7 6 5 4 3 2 1

♻ Printed on recycled paper when available.

We go to gain a little patch of ground
That hath in it no profit but the name.
　　　　　　　　　　 — *Hamlet, Act IV, Scene iv*

Contents

* * *

Preface   vii

Prologue   1

Alpha – Guadalcanal Redux   5

Bravo – Boot Camp   17

Charlie – War Games   27

Delta – Okinawa   35

Echo – Khe Sanh   41

Foxtrot – Slowly Surrounded   47

Golf – The Village   67

Hotel – Overrun   83

India – The Worst Place on Earth   103

Kilo – Incoming and Outgoing   131

Lima – We Gotta Get Out of this Place   151

Mike – Homecoming   181

Notes   189

Appendix – Official Letter of Condolence to Mrs. Patricia Mahoney   191

Presidential Unit Citation, 26th Marine Regiment   192

North and South Vietnam and the surrounding area   *Michael Archer*

Preface

* * *

I knew I would someday write about Khe Sanh from the first moment I stepped onto its puddled airstrip one drizzling December afternoon in 1967. My senses were crackling with excitement. Colors, smells, sounds, even a brisk gust of wind on my face, seemed more distinct and vibrant than any I had previously known. Soon, I would write letters home each day, filled with the particulars and peculiarities of the place and its inhabitants.

Three years later, as I sat down to write this story, I found myself agitated and unfocused after completing just the first few pages. The events were still too recent, some too painful, and all devoid of any perspective beyond my beleaguered consciousness. Therefore, I packed up all the notes, letters, logs, and other reference materials I had collected from my time at Khe Sanh, put them in a cardboard box, and stored them away at the back of a closet.

Seven years ago I opened the box and found among the contents a long-forgotten audio tape sent by a buddy of mine. While he was making the recording that day at Khe Sanh, I happened to be standing nearby with two other Marines. Suddenly, enemy shells began marching along the trench line toward us. We quickly dove through the hatch of an underground bunker, just as the last round exploded exactly where we had been standing. It was a close call, but by no means an unusual occurrence during those times. In his haste for cover, my buddy neglected to turn off his recorder, and for the next few moments the only audible sounds on the tape are the rattling of rifle slings and the scraping of boots and helmets against the hard earth as we struggled to untangle from one another. After a quick self-examination for shrapnel wounds, we all burst into a fit of up-roarious laughter interspersed with mocking arguments about who had been the first to hear the incoming, what size projectiles they must have been, and who moved so slowly they might as well go get measured for their body bag right then and there. Three minutes later we were outside in the trench once again, as if nothing had happened. It was not that we were unappreciative of the danger or testing our bravado like some "new guy." Rather, we were intensely familiar with the incessant danger, having survived thousands of incoming artillery and mortar shells during the previous two months of the siege.

As those voices reached me across the years, I could not help but marvel at the composure and audacity of these young men who just seconds before had escaped certain death. I heard my own voice among them, but it was no longer me. Now older, and much more cautious, I have lived the life they were yet to know—in the case of many, the life they would never get a chance to know. Now, I fully comprehend the preciousness of what we had risked, something I did not recognize at Khe Sanh or even later when I first set out to write about it.

The manner in which an individual faces mortal danger is the ultimate test of strength. And the men who fought at Khe Sanh and its outposts in 1968, began each new day calmly accepting, with enormous justification, that it could also be their last. Yet, somehow they found within themselves the courage to face that day and to endure. This is the story of a few of them. Everything in this book happened and, to the best of my recollection, happened in the way I describe, although I have changed some names to protect the privacy of individuals and their families.

I am very grateful for all the support I have received from my family, friends, and fellow Khe Sanh vets during the writing of this book, particularly Chaplain Ray W. Stubbe, chaplain for the 1st Battalion, 26th Marine Regiment at Khe Sanh, whose scholarship, encouragement, and friendship were a constant source of inspiration. In addition, thanks to Lieutenant Frank Ahearn and Captain Robert Black, formerly of Bravo Company, 1st Battalion, 1st Marine Regiment, for their unique perspective and insights into what took place at Khe Sanh after I departed, including what happened to Tom Mahoney. Also, my sincere appreciation to Jim Harris of Ketchum, Idaho, a Marine combat veteran of both World War II and Korea, who, when I needed them the most, pecked out words of encouragement to me on Ernest Hemingway's old "Royal Deportable" machine. And special thanks to the outstanding people at Hellgate Press for their invaluable assistance. And finally, deepest gratitude to my wife Becky, who patiently proofread the manuscript untold times and asked all the right questions.

Prologue

Khe Sanh Combat Base
Republic of Vietnam
February 1968

It was my first time back to where the tent had been located since an incoming enemy rocket touched off the adjacent ammo dump. Fires raged for several days amid the thousands of artillery shells stored there, periodically igniting tremendous explosions that rocked the area for miles, flattening every structure in that part of the base.

I found what appeared to be the right place. Remnants of the low sandbag wall that once encircled the tent now enclosed only a pool of mottled ash and tortured scraps of iron, the ground baked to a greasy brown crust. Nothing of practical or sentimental value remained. So I decided to find Ron Flagg, an acquaintance from radio operator school, who was nearby with 1st Battalion, 26th Marines.

Given his impulsive nature, I was not optimistic that Flagg had kept his head down low enough or often enough to still be alive—he would, in fact, be seriously wounded in the neck by mortar shell fragments a month later. My concern was unjustified, however, because I found him in his bunker along the trench line unscathed and proudly displaying a refrigerator he had just removed from the abandoned mess hall. I suspected someone would soon be missing an electrical generator. After a brief visit, I decided to return to my own area of the base.

On the way there, I stopped to enjoy a rare break in the overcast. Tepid rays of late afternoon sunlight touched my face—and made me think of rickets. When I was a kid, my mom often used that word to try and get me out from in front of the TV set. "You need to get outside more or you'll get rickets," she would call from the kitchen. Mom never provided enough information about this affliction to allow me to weigh its risk against an afternoon of not seeing the object of my undying ardor—the sparkly-eyed Mouseketeer, Annette.

I had a vague notion that exposure to sunlight could prevent rickets, so I would eventually, though reluctantly, heed her warning because the flinty little word sounded so lethal.

It nearly proved to be.

As I stood with my eyes closed and my chin tilted skyward, two artillery shells flew over and exploded fifty meters away. I had not heard the rounds approaching because I had not yet learned to identify the murmur of those distant enemy guns—a talent born of experience and the luck to live long enough to gain it.

Flopping forward onto the ground, I instinctively adopted what *The Guidebook for Marines* describes as a "creep." By definition, creeping is faster than crawling and, while that sounds like a good thing, it does have one serious disadvantage. The faster the creep, the more elevated the buttocks. Rapid creeping must have given rise to the peculiar admonition often heard from our drill instructors that we would someday find our "ass in a sling."

Yet at that moment, I was more concerned with the other end of my body, and could not force my nose up off the ground. In this position, reminiscent of a bloodhound hot on the trail, I blindly set off in search of cover. I soon fell into a small trench, the beginning of a new bunker being hacked into the hard, red scab of Khe Sanh. Just over six feet in length, and barely deep enough to fully permit all of me below ground level, it instantly had the disturbing feel of a grave.

Another incoming shell burst nearby with a sharp, ground-jarring crunch. A searing blast of air drove shrapnel fragments skittering past. Fist-sized clods of dirt rained down on my back. I clawed at the earth in front of my face in an absurd attempt to scratch out another inch of safety.

I was alone. We all dreaded this with unspoken anxiety. What if I get wounded? Or buried? Or wounded then buried?

There was another reason for apprehension, generally unrecognized, especially among those of us barely out of high school: we needed to act

Did you go only b/c you had to, or was there a personal mission?

brave. Left alone with our self-doubt and fear we might succumb to panic. At the very worst, this could leave you dead; at the very least, mistrusted— a pariah.

Eyes wide and unblinking, blood pounding at the base of my skull, a strange heaviness began to settle upon me—the creeping paralysis of terror. With great effort, I focused on my hands and willed them to stop ripping at the dirt. I then realized I wasn't breathing and forced myself to exhale.

A quick succession of shells shrieked over, their trajectories flat and impacts close. Each exploded with a great, resonant, ka-chunk sound. I began to pray, or more accurately, to bargain with God. I raced through the miracle stories I had heard during years of Catholic schooling, desperate to find one that corresponded to my current situation. Because I was not being crucified, ripped apart by wild animals, or burned at the stake, my choices were limited. I finally settled on St. Ignatius Loyola. Legend held that St. Ignatius had kept his vow to become a priest after surviving a fierce lightening storm alone.

Pressed for both time and relevancy, as I was at that moment, a lightening storm seemed close enough to what I was experiencing. I hurriedly solicited divine deliverance: "Please, God, let me live another day, just one more. If you do, I swear I'll dedicate my life to you. Just one more day, I swear!" I went on praying like that for several minutes, and then abruptly stopped. It was as if I could see myself at that moment from a kind of transcendental state—and I didn't like what I was seeing. I knew I wouldn't be keeping my end of the bargain. I was just lying to stay alive.

I later learned that other Marines, in similar situations, also prayed for "just one more day." I guess this was partly good salesmanship. By offering to accept just a single day, rather than, say, a week, it would appear to be less work for God; and consequently a better deal.

As if buying another day at Khe Sanh was worth all the chicanery.

Another shell wheezed lazily overhead, as if spent. It then punched the ground with a resounding thud, a pause, then a thunderous explosion. Dirt and splintered plywood peppered me. I became aware of the smell of smoke, and a taste like rotten eggs on the roof of my mouth. In the distance, a weak voice cried for a corpsman. My mind hurried along as the adrenaline churned. I thought of the prayer I had just attempted and wondered if anyone was listening.

The old saying that "there are no atheists in foxholes" is a compelling argument against atheism, the idea being that fear of imminent death brings a person around to God. On the other hand, as an atheist once pointed out to me, it may also be a compelling argument against the efficiency of foxholes. I knew I was not an atheist, as evidenced by the fact that I was currently engaged in a delicate negotiation with the Deity—the outcome of which was still uncertain. But, at the same time, the things I saw occurring each day at Khe Sanh seemed inconsistent with the handiwork of a perfect and merciful God described in my catechism. It was not so much the relentlessness of the killing that was exhausting my faith, as it was the randomness. I found it was just best not to think about it too often; but that afternoon I could not stop.

Suddenly, a mental image of my dad appeared. Already irritated with the enemy, God, and myself, I became infuriated with my dad. I could feel my lips moving in the dust and heard my voice, as if at a distance, ask, "How could anyone who has been through this shit, ever wish it on their own kid?"

A reply burst from me before I even realized what I had said: "Maybe he's never been through this." The answer shocked me for a moment.

All Dad's World War II stories about amphibious assaults on South Pacific islands, of death, disease, and fanatical "Japs," of toughing it all out—were they vicarious? If so, this little deception was likely to get someone killed. My older brother had already made it out of Vietnam alive. I was hoping to do the same. Though I had been a huge disappointment to my dad, I never quit seeking his respect. One of the few times I remember him ever smiling at me was on the day I came home from the Marine Corps recruiting office. I had always just assumed his anger and bitterness stemmed from some combat-related breakdown. Now, I wasn't sure.

At that moment, I underwent a profound change and knew it even as these doubts flooded my brain. My belief system was coming apart. Much of what I had learned at home, school, and church—intended to nurture and protect me—now seemed hazardous to my health. I felt cheated and angry, yet at the same time oddly relieved.

The last incoming shell sailed high overhead, a fluttering whisper followed by a sharp crack, like a heavy door slamming down by the runway. I listened intently for a full minute and then rose from that little grave, dusting off my hands and face. Had I been with fellow Marines, we would now have laughed a little nervously and acted a bit embarrassed. We would have made strident remarks about the "gook" not knowing "shit about shooting." Some of this bravado was the result of our training. Mostly, it was just behaving like the teenagers we were. In the peculiar world of boys at war, it was an embarrassment to act as if you wanted to live another day. But on this particular afternoon I had faced it alone and was never again the same.

Alpha

Guadalcanal Redux

$*\ *\ *$

The earliest memories I have of my dad involve the Marine Corps. Probably not a day in his life went by when he did not mention some aspect of it. When I was about five years old, I recall him taking his uniform out of the closet and trying it on. It would no longer button up due to the few pounds he'd put on since his discharge. I can still see the look of disappointment on his face, and hear Mom's mirthfully consoling voice. Despite the fact that he could no longer fit into it, that uniform hung in the closet beside his everyday clothes for the next forty-five years.

As the years went by, neighborhood kids would crowd into our little kitchen on Saturday nights. While Mom popped corn, Dad would thumb-tack a white sheet to the wall and show the silent 8 mm films he had made while overseas.

His memories involving his dad have to do w/ the marines

The first footage was of San Diego. It showed a long line of Marines slowly shuffling up the gangway of a troopship under the weight of their enormous sea bags. A truck then drove up the dock and stopped near the ship. Ten men without sea bags jumped from the back of the vehicle. Two armed guards then led the men up the gangway past the inquisitive Marines who had stopped to watch. "Not everyone wanted to go," Dad said without further explanation.

Next, we saw the tilted, scorched superstructure of the battleship *Arizona* jutting painfully from the cobalt colored water of Pearl Harbor. Almost certainly distracted by the emotion of that moment, Dad put the camera back into his sea bag without turning it off. The film ran on for

5

another few minutes in speckled darkness. It seemed like an hour to us kids, as we dutifully stared at the sheet. When a picture reappeared, it was of Dad tediously wading back and forth through a slimy tropical stream, installing a water pump.

Finally, we'd get to our favorite scene. There was my dad, standing at the edge of a jungle clearing on some sweltering island. He was shirtless, clutching a Thompson submachine gun close to his chest. He carefully re- connoitered for the wily enemy. Satisfied of his safety, he slowly moved to- ward a thatched hut, in front of which stood a seemingly unconcerned family of Melanesians—very dark people, with big hairdos. Dad gave the head of the household a long, robust handshake. Soon everyone, includ- ing the little kids, was smoking Dad's cigarettes. It never occurred to me to wonder who was running the camera during this one-man patrol. I was always too enthralled.

I saw these films so often I can close my eyes and still visualize the too- brilliant Kodachrome colors of the time. I can still hear the cadence of the clicking gears on the old black projector. Dad would begin narrating these scenes in his most serious voice, which by the end of the reel would change to sad and sentimental tones. He was unambiguous about his feel- ing for the Marine Corps. For most Marines, while their pride in having served in the Corps would continue to grow over the years, they never completely forget (what is traditionally referred to as) "the chicken shit." Dad, however, recollected it as a perfect experience, and his memories were unassailable.

My older brother Ed (who the family called Smokey) and I slept in military-style bunk beds. Our blankets were gray- green wool and stamped USMC. Dad trained us to make a per- fect hospital fold at each corner of our mattress. On Saturday mornings, in our pajamas, we stood at attention in front of our bunks while he inspected the tautness of our blankets by bouncing a coin on them.

As time went on, Dad would tell the same stories every week- end. Even when people came to visit, the conversation would

My older brother Smokey (left) and me play- ing "guns" in 1952

His dad treated them like military ppl

invariably get around to "The Canal," meaning Guadalcanal. To Mom's annoyance, he always seemed to reserve the dinner table for reflecting on how the bloated bodies of dead "Japs" would turn purple and black in the tropical sun, and could be popped with a bayonet "like a balloon." Over time, these no longer sounded like spontaneous recollections but became formulaic recitations, mantras.

In August 1942, for the first time since declaring war on Japan, U.S. forces took the offensive in the Pacific. This began with the landing of Marines on the Japanese-held island of Guadalcanal. After the Marines went ashore, the Japanese fleet drove off the U.S. ships supporting them. Despite this, the Marines held on for months. Although being heavily out-numbered, they repulsed every major Japanese counterattack. The fighting was often savage.

Guadalcanal put the Marine Corps on the front page of America's newspapers. By early 1943, reinforcements began to arrive on the island. Dad was among them. Guadalcanal remains to this day as, arguably, the most significant battle in Marine Corps history. Marines during that period wanted to be associated with the fighting there; just as twenty-six years later, Marines in Vietnam would want to be associated with the fighting at Khe Sanh.

Dad often told us how the Marines were tougher, braver, and endured more hardship than any other branch of the military. How when Marines watched newsreels in their makeshift outdoor theaters, Dad would join the others in booing U.S. Army General MacArthur. Louder boos, he would remind you, than they even gave the Emperor of Japan.

"Dug-out Doug" MacArthur, as he was referred to by the Marines, had, according to Dad, abandoned the 1st Marine Division at Guadal-canal. While the Japanese poured reinforcements into that battle, MacArthur held "a million troops" in reserve at nearby bases in Australia. To Dad, this was a perfect example of the unequal burden shouldered by the Marine Corps. *His dad was marine*

As such, I did not know the U.S. Army participated in the Pacific the-ater of war until I was in high school history class. I thought it was all "Marines versus Japs." I'm sure that's exactly how Dad remembered it.

No recitation of war stories was complete without him telling of how devastated he was when he received the telegram that his father had died. "I was never the same again," he would often say, still grieving forty years later. "After that, I was one mean son-of-a-bitch." It's hard to explain why his father's death had such a lasting effect on him. No one will ever know now and the likelihood of ever having truly known, even when Dad was alive, was slight. My mother speculated that my father's own father considered him undisciplined and unsuccessful. His father's death deprived him, forever, of the chance to return home to the praise and respect for which he longed—an aspiration of his own sons a generation later.

In December 1941, eight months after my parents married, the United States entered World War II. My father decided to enlist, even though they were not drafting married men and would not do so until 1944. He completed Marine Corps boot camp and trained as a water purification engineer. After three weeks of home leave, he left for the South Pacific.

It was the single most important decision of my father's life: one that would have a profound effect on his relationship with his wife and ultimately shape the course of his children's lives.

* * * *

I am the second oldest of five children, four boys and a girl. My mother, being a devout Catholic of the Irish persuasion, insisted that all her children follow in her family's tradition and attend St. Augustine's parochial school. The Catholic Church had a powerful influence on my early life.

The ritual was then in Latin and incomprehensible, although I always felt it added a sense of ancient mystery to it all. Religious instruction was always in English. This consisted of nuns coaching us on points of Church doctrine from the catechism, occasionally supplemented by stories of saints and martyrs who were tortured and executed in the most barbaric and bloody ways. The Stations of the Cross were much more violent than anything on TV, or even in the movies at the time, and were depicted with no sadistic detail left out. It was exciting stuff for a preadolescent boy.

As an altar boy I participated in many of the ceremonies. Being close to the action, I noticed the little things one could not observe from the pews: the heavy

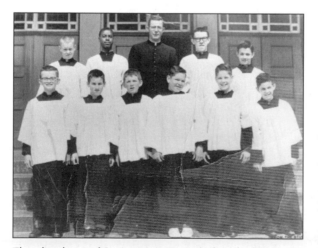

The altar boys of St. Augustine's Catholic Church, Oakland, California, in 1961 (I'm front row, second from the left). My friend Jack Mooseau is wearing the white shoes

*Altar Boy
@ catholic church* (handwritten)

vapor of molten candle wax, the soporific fragrance of incense, the smell of the sweet altar wine. How Father Grey, as I poured the wine into his chalice from a crystal cruet, would signal with swift jerks of his forefinger to keep it coming. Often, I would empty the whole thing into his cup.

The part of the ritual I most disliked was Communion. I would follow the priest along the altar rail as he placed the round wafer on each tongue. My job was to hold a gold plated dish under the chin of each communicant, in order to catch the host if it fell. By his second mass of the day, I was always a little concerned about Father Grey's aim.

I saw hundreds of beseeching tongues each Sunday, and it always gave me the same sense of revulsion. Some were pink and bubbled with saliva, others were dry and coated white as a bone. Some people stretched their tongues out so far that I could see their tonsils and hear a gurgling sound as they choked themselves from the effort. Even the prettiest girls looked hideous at that moment.

I was an excellent student throughout grammar school. I loved spending time in the public libraries, where I read every history book and biography I could comprehend. My first job was at age eleven, when I became an *Oakland Tribune* newspaper carrier. Besides learning the rudiments of business, I was exposed to an entirely new side of life. Some of the other paperboys, particularly the twelve- and thirteen-year-olds, seemed to have such immense wisdom, that I felt quite sheltered by comparison. The scope of their knowledge was limitless, and included such diverse subjects as which professional wrestlers did not "fake it"; what death was like; the best places to buy cherry bombs; and how to identify the space aliens living among us. *Exposed to Knowledge* (handwritten)

They were also experts on all matters pertaining to sex: "easy girls," anatomy, aphrodisiacs—in other words, information not provided by the nuns at St. Augustine's. They knew every swear word and curse that had ever been uttered. Their racial and ethnic hypotheses often matched Dad's in imagination, if not in animosity. There was no question an eleven-year-old kid could ask them for which they would not provide an immediate answer. It took me years to unlearn all that they taught me.

It was during this time as a young *Tribune* carrier that I became an avid reader of newspapers. I recall one unusual story in 1960 about two Japanese soldiers who finally surrendered on the island of Guam. Dad had been part of the invasion force on that island sixteen years before, and I could not wait to get his reaction. It was not what I expected. Rather than patiently reminding me, as he often had before, that "killing a Jap was like squashing a bug," Dad now seemed almost respectful. "Those Japs are tough little monkeys." This was, for Dad, an effusive display of admiration—and it confused me.

In fact, much about Dad confused me. When I was twelve, my favorite movie was *Invaders from Mars.* It was about a kid who had a telescope (like me) and wore blue jeans with big cuffs and T-shirts with wide horizontal stripes (like me). One night as the boy watched through his telescope, Martian invaders landed near his house. The aliens soon abducted his dad and surgically placed a tiny radio receiver at the base of his skull. After the boy's dad returned home, his personality had changed. He was now angry and short-tempered all the time. I remember peeking occasionally at the back of Dad's neck to see if there was an implant scar.

When the length of our hair began to approach nonmilitary proportions, in other words, noticeable, Dad would order my brother Smokey and me to ride our bikes over to Karl's barbershop for haircuts. On the wall above the big mirror, Karl had a series of sketches depicting examples of several haircut options. These included crew cuts, flattops, and comb backs (with a ducktail, if so desired). Dad, however, had given Karl orders to give us close, boot camp buzz cuts. Our hopes of someday having hair long enough to comb were still years from being realized. Boot camp hair

Karl and my father were political soul brothers. He would spend most of the time we were in the chair lecturing us about the way the country was "going to hell," and how the "spooks and the Kennedys" had wrecked everything. What concerned Smokey and me the most was that Karl's shop was just a few doors down from a small storefront that housed the Afro-American Association office (a precursor to the Black Panther Party). While in the chair, we would stare apprehensively out the window at passersby, praying that no associates, with their big Afro hairstyles, would walk by the window. Once, when my brother was in the chair, several did walk past. Karl cursed under his breath, his arm convulsed, and he inadvertently sheared a swath through Smokey's already scant fuzz.

The final phase of each haircut consisted of Karl shaving us around the neck and ears with a well-stropped straightedge razor. At these times, we would be particularly conscious of our carotid arteries, which pulsed rapidly in fear that Huey Newton or Bobby Seals would suddenly appear in the window.

My unfashionable buzz cut did not prevent me from being elected president of my eighth grade class, nor did the efforts of Sister Mary Assumpta to have my friend Gregory win. Sister's ineffective attempts to intimidate the electorate only incited them against poor Greg. On election day, I was swept into power along with Leslie, my running mate and the object of my affection. Vice-President Leslie, besides being intelligent, was also well endowed for a thirteen-year-old. No longer having my sagacious pals at the *Tribune* shack to guide me, I concluded that her "condition" resulted from carrying her cello nearly everywhere she went.

While in eighth grade, I went to hear President John F. Kennedy speak not far from our school, at Memorial Stadium, on the campus of the University of California at Berkeley. I believe the only reason Sister Mary Assumpta approved this was because the president was a Catholic—and Irish. God forbid, if he were Irish and not a Catholic.

Mom wrote a note of permission so I could go. Before handing it to me, she suggested that it might be best if I didn't mention to Dad that I was "going to be listening to a Kennedy." I nodded knowingly. Talking this bit of treason with Mom was fun, and so very Irish of us.

Because of its reputation as a haven for left-wing political extremists, the Secret Service considered Berkeley unsafe. Despite being a clear and warm October day, the president rode with a transparent bubble top on his limousine. Later, as he stepped to the podium in the center of the football field, I was surprised to discover he was a redhead—we did not yet own a color TV at home. After his speech, Kennedy departed through a nearby gate. I joined some other kids running up to the rim of the stadium to look down on his car. He looked back up toward us and waved through the plastic.

His assassination a year later had a destabilizing effect on me. It reinforced my growing belief in the bleakness of the future. My favorite doodles were nuclear mushroom clouds, and I doodled them frequently in class because I wasn't paying attention. I became depressed. In those days, adolescent depression was not treated medically, but was considered merely a symptom of juvenile delinquency. The only cure for this condition was escalating levels of discipline. I was sent to Saint Mary's High School in Berkeley, a private parochial school, whose Christian Brothers and lay teachers were not averse to employing corporal punishment on "head cases" like me.

Having failed several courses of study and continuing to be a disciplinary problem, I was finally asked not to return after my third year. The culminating event was a discussion I had with Brother Giles regarding my belief in the doctrine of predestination, which was at odds with the Church's teaching of free will. A highlight of our little debate was his accentuating a theological point by slamming my head into a wall locker on the way down the hall to the principal's office. This only reinforced my opinion that I was predestined to fail. In all fairness to Brother Giles, I was

Kicked out of school b/c belief in predestination

a truly disagreeable youth, who could conjure up the kind of smirk that made anyone over the age of thirty crazy with the desire to smack it off.

I spent my senior year in public school, at Skyline High in Oakland. There were girls there, and it was much less cliquey. Nevertheless, I did not improve scholastically, or otherwise, and nearly did not graduate.

His brother goes in marines

Two years earlier, Smokey had enlisted in the Marines. He was seventeen years and six months old, the minimum age for enlistment, so needed my parents' written consent. My mother was reluctant, but eventually acquiesced. Just two days after his graduation from high school, my brother left for boot camp. Dad was elated. Smokey went on to volunteer as a member of the Marine Corps' First Force Reconnaissance Company. He qualified in Parachuting, SCUBA, and Clandestine Tactics. He arrived in South Vietnam in 1966 and survived his tour, but just barely.

Shortly after my brother departed for boot camp, Mom became deaf in her left ear. "Nerve deafness," she claimed, although a doctor had not examined her. The car was Dad's favorite ranting place. There he was surrounded by an ever-changing panorama of things he despised—Blacks, hippies, and sundry bad drivers (many of whom he suspected of being Democrats) all of whom would be the recipient of what he referred to as his "one-fingered peace sign."

His mom... then him... start drinking

Mom had never learned to drive, so she was dependent on Dad for all her transportation. Because she lost her hearing in the left (driver's side) ear, I suspected this to be an instance of hysterical deafness brought on by a desire to tune him out. Mom's ability to do so, however, finally failed her and she began drinking frequently.

By age fifteen, I was drinking and smoking, too. In that way, I understood her. I also missed her. The Mom I had known—the well-read, intelligent, lively and loving Mom—was now gone. Even then, I had a sense that she was gone for good. There would be very few highs or lows for her ever again, just a kind of sedated indifference.

My brother's enlistment in the Marine Corps put an even greater strain on my relationship with Dad. Though certainly not his intention, Smokey was now the shining example Dad held before me. Interestingly, before my brother enlisted, he and my father rarely spoke; and Dad could find little good to say about him.

My father now hounded me constantly about what a failure I was. I moved out of the house several times, but could not make it on my own for very long. I spent a week living inside a storage locker in the underground parking garage of an apartment house—an ironic foretaste of bunker life at Khe Sanh two years later.

I never pictured myself in the Marine Corps. If anything, I gravitated toward opposing ideals. I resented authority. I owned all of Bob Dylan's albums with their lyrics of unhappiness, anger, and change. I spent my evenings on the campus in Berkeley, listening to sedition.

But there were other, more ingrained, forces at work on me as well. The book *Battle Cry* was making the rounds among my friends. It was a novel about Marines in World War II—loyal and brave young men. Things traditionally representative of manhood also appealed to me. Margaret Truman, daughter of the former president, once disparagingly called Marines "underpaid, over-sexed, teenage killers." Yet at seventeen or eighteen, most of us wanted to be just that!

The World War II movies we had grown up watching led us to believe that battle was tragic yet bittersweet. There always seemed to be a misunderstood character in these films who was never really appreciated until he was dead. The imagery of people crying over his grave, talking nicely about him, wishing they had treated him better—this was potent stuff for a despairing adolescent. *War was romanticized*

I didn't like myself and thought I didn't care about living. Yet at the same time, I had a dimly perceived longing to prove that I was not a failure. Even after years of Marine Corps indoctrination at home, and a brother whom I worshiped now in the Corps, it was still not enough to make me want to enlist. *Pat Haley enlists*

Then Pat Haley enlisted. Haley had been a hero of mine in high school. He was rebellious and daring. He never backed down from a fight, but seldom began one either. He had a reputation among the local juvenile population as being "a bad dude."

Doc Haley, Pat's dad, had been Mom's sweetheart in grammar school at St. Augustine's. Doc was the shortest boy in the class and was thrown together with my mother, the shortest girl, for the sake of line symmetry. While Mom stayed short, Doc grew in high school to well over six feet tall. He became a notable college football player, signed by the Chicago Bears. Before he could play professional football, the war started. Doc immediately enlisted in the Marines. He returned from the war highly decorated, and wounded just enough to prevent him from pursuing a career in professional football. He went to law school and practiced that profession in Oakland. Like my father, Doc was strict, mean, and unforgiving of mistakes made by his male children. This may have been the main thing Pat and I had in common.

Doc had Pat arrested on the first day of Christmas vacation in 1964. The charge was incorrigibility. He did this to prevent Pat from getting into trouble over the holiday. On Christmas day, Doc visited Pat in juvenile hall and gave him his Christmas present—a comb. Pat never admitted that any of this bothered him, but it did.

One night, when Pat was home on leave after boot camp, we went to a party and soon wandered over to the apartment next door where there was another party. Before long, he was in a fight. Ironically, the guy he was fighting turned out to be a recently retired Marine Corps gunnery sergeant who soon had Pat in a headlock out on the porch, intending to hold him there until the police arrived. I worried that Pat would end up in the Marine brig, so I began pulling his head out of the man's grip. It was comical in a way: Haley screaming that I was ripping his ears off, and me yelling at the gunny to let him go. Finally, as sirens approached, Haley's head popped out. We ran away moments before the police arrived.

This was the first time I had ever seen Pat Haley beaten in a fight. It was almost as if the Marine Corps had taken something out of him—his wildness, his indifference to the consequences. It seemed to have subdued him in a way I would later understand. I lost some respect for Pat that night. But it wasn't his fault. It was the illusion that was starting to let me down. Nevertheless, I was now ready to follow.

* * * *

Thomas Patrick Mahoney III was a fellow classmate of mine at St. Mary's High School. Tom lived with his mother, sister, and grandmother. When Tom was six years old, his father, an Air Force lieutenant, died during the Korean war. Buried in the National Cemetery at the Presidio in San Francisco, the family regularly paid their respects and Tom grew up treasuring the few memories he had of his dad.

In high school, Tom fell in love with a girl named Linda. After graduation, she left for an exclusive prep school in Rhode Island. Linda's parents were wealthy and socially prominent, and had only tolerated her fling with Tom in high school. But Tom's fatherless, middle-class circumstances required that he work after school as a supermarket clerk in order to help pay the household expenses, and so was not what they considered to be marriage material for their daughter. Tom was heartbroken when Linda left for the East Coast. Unfortunately, for Tom and those of us who cared about him, this would not be the last time he heard from her.

One April morning in 1967, I was traveling up Fairmont Avenue and saw Tom in front of his house working on his motorcycle. I stopped the delivery van I was driving to say hello. Tom told me that he was anxious to get away from Oakland and was going to enlist in the Marine Corps. He asked me if I wanted to come with him. Without giving it a moment of thought, I said, "Sure, why not?" The next day I took time off work and joined Tom at the recruiting office. I could not even do the ten "required" push-ups. The barrel-chested Marine gunnery sergeant was clearly anxious to meet his enlistment quota, so he just laughed it off. "The Corps will fix that problem," he promised me.

August 1966. Lake Tahoe, California. L to R: me, our friend Katie, and Tom Mahoney

"You'll be knocking off a hundred of them before long." I liked the sound of that. Within a few minutes, we had signed up.

I understood Tom's motivation for enlisting more than I did my own. Yet, certain practical considerations confronted me. I had no draft deferment available to me and would almost inevitably be getting a military induction notice soon. Yet, until that very day, I had no conscious intention of joining the Marine Corps. I did not realize how low my self-esteem had become until I experienced a distinct sense of surprise and gratitude at Tom's confidence in me. I had always regarded him as the kind of person I wanted to be. He was outgoing and unselfish. He dressed well and always drew lingering looks from the girls. Confident, idealistic, and willing to stand up for his principles—a guy could not have a more loyal friend than Tom Mahoney.

When I told Dad about our enlistment, he was delighted. I had suddenly become a great son. Though I did not enlist in a conscious effort to please him, I must admit that the respite from Dad's criticism was nice.

The two months between our enlistment and our departure for boot camp seemed like one long party. A house rented by some friends, which we christened "The Ranch," was filled with great people and endless drinking. Bill McGuiness, a former Marine, Vietnam-vet, and machine-gunner-turned-hippie, was a regular there. He knew our enlistment contract was legally binding, so tried to be as positive about it as he could.

One night, however, when the dope he was smoking made him melancholy, Bill told us about the war and "how futile" it all was. He described how the people in the countryside did not want us there; they just wanted to be left alone. Then Bill's face turned expressionless except for his eyes, which gazed upon us over the top of his rose-tinted, wire-rimmed glasses with a weary, pitying look. This unnerved us for a just moment. But Mahoney quickly recovered, chugging down the remainder of the beer he was holding, and in a fake Irish brogue he recited:

Here's to a long life and a merry one;

A quick death and an easy one;

A pretty girl and an honest one;

A cool pint—and another one!

Neither Tom nor I really cared much about Vietnam. We enlisted in the Marines for the adventure and to test our nerve, but certainly not to help a bunch of people we didn't even know. Yet, we were not against the war. We were Americans who loved our country and trusted our government to do the right thing. That was good enough for us.

Several days before Tom and I left for boot camp, a group of us gathered one last time to play some softball at the little park on Hampton Road in Piedmont. As the shadows grew long on that balmy June evening, I stood in left field looking at the guys and girls with whom I had shared so much of my young life; vaguely perceiving that we would never be the same friends again. I recall wishing I could stand there forever, within the sound of their laughter, smelling the freshly mown grass and absently socking at the webbing of my ball glove. As the sun slid behind the eucalyptus trees, my eyes began to burn. The game was over.

* * * *

Boot Camp

* * *

Marine Corps boot camp was one of the few things in my life that actually lived up to its reputation—and I hated it. My first day of basic training began four days after my nineteenth birthday at the military induction center in downtown Oakland. There were about fifty of us processing that day; fewer than half had enlisted, and even fewer were going into the Marines.

We sat on benches and completed numerous forms about ourselves, then stood in our first of many lines, for tests and medical examinations. Most of the group consisted of draftees. Although anti-war sentiment was only beginning in most parts of the country, in the San Francisco Bay Area it was already well established. In fact, there were a number of protesters picketing the building that morning as we entered, calling for us to "resist." Many in our group were not interested in going; some were quite vocal about it.

A shrill Army medic soon ordered us to stand along the walls of a large room and drop our pants, after which a doctor in a starched white medical smock moved along the line checking us for hernias. The young man to my right was a draftee with shoulder length hair and the scruffy beginnings of a beard. The doctor reached down to begin his inspection of the man and then let out a groan. I had been averting my eyes from the others, for the sake of decency, but couldn't help looking down just in time to see a considerable amount of peanut butter smeared all over the inductee's groin and buttocks. The doctor groaned again and then shouted, most unprofessionally, "Get this fucking animal out of here!" Two Army medics

17

responded, grabbing the man by his arms and leading him away in short, shuffling, steps—his pants still down around his ankles. We all laughed, and later discussed how it must have felt sitting for hours in all that peanut butter. I wondered aloud if it was smooth or chunky style.

Later that afternoon, about ten of us boarded a bus to the Oakland International Airport for our flight to San Diego and the Marine Corps Recruit Depot. On the ride there, one fellow boasted loudly for the benefit of us all how little "guff" he was going to put up with from his drill instructor (DI), and of this or that creature comfort he was going to insist on having. Mahoney shook his head and let out a short derisive chuckle. Both Tom and I had spoken to several former Marines about boot camp and were under no such illusions about our fate.

Also on the bus was a studious looking fellow with thick glasses and an overpowering impatience to talk. He pulled a little red book from his knapsack and waved it until he had our attention. This, he explained, was *The Quotations of Chairman Mao*. He had been reading it and was sure the DIs would appreciate him taking such an interest in the thought processes of our enemies. *One guy reading Mao's literature*

Later that night, that horrible night when we met our DIs, I watched as one pulled the "Little Red Book" from the kid's belongings. Upon realizing what he was holding, the DI flew into the most incredible rage. With his mouth an inch from the boy's ear he bellowed, "Are you really supposed to be here you little four-eyed son-of-a-bitch? It looks to me like you meant to join up with them godless gooks in the Red fuckin' Chinese Army!"

He accused the recruit of being a "spy," and threatened to have his "sorry commie ass" shot at sunrise. He only lasted in our platoon about a week. I guess he must have failed to watch the correct war movies while growing up. His recruiter should be ashamed for filling a quota with a kid who thought his mastery of Marxism would evoke praise from a Marine Corps drill instructor. Like me, he had enlisted at the time of the "Hill Fights" at Khe Sanh, when Marines were being killed and wounded in numbers not seen before in South Vietnam. The USMC, being a relatively small service branch, needed replacements quickly. It was no longer uncommon to find draftees in Marine uniforms.

I would soon learn that my fellow recruits were generally here for one of three reasons: they had enlisted of their own volition, they were draftees, or a criminal court had ordered them to enlist in the Marine Corps in lieu of a jail sentence. The latter was a surprisingly common occurrence in the 1960s. Occasionally, one of these "sentenced" Marines

Why ppl are there

would later die in Vietnam. This led to the morbid observation that in certain legal jurisdictions of the United States, shoplifting a six-pack of beer could get you the death sentence.

The next morning, after about two hours of sleep, a DI awakened us by shouting threats and banging on a trash can lid with his swagger stick. We all leapt from our racks and to attention. After a head count, he ordered us outside and introduced us to "The Pits" (short for sand pits), which were rectangular areas of sand in front of our Quonset huts. When not in use, they stood meticulously groomed. The Pits were where we did our push-ups. We were rarely told how many, but had to count each one, loudly, with a "Sir!" on the end. Often an enraged DI would order us, "to The Pits forever!" Then we would do push-ups until our arms went numb, and we were barely able to prop ourselves up on our elbows to keep our faces out of the sand. That first morning our DIs hurried us through the mess hall with barely enough time to eat. We then marched to the barber and had our heads shaved. Ahead of me in line was Tex Matthews, a nice kid from Amarillo; kind of quiet (for a Texan), yet possessing a fine sense of humor despite the acne, which had left his face and head a mass of scars and pustules. Our DI shouted instructions at the door, "When you maggots get in the chair, immediately identify any scars or moles on your head by placing a finger on it." Tex used all ten fingers. When he left the chair, he had rivulets of blood flowing from his head.

The next few weeks were a blur of marching, standing in lines, training classes, and drill instructors yelling in our faces. There were endless sessions in The Pits—either as a platoon or individually—for the most insignificant infraction, often for no infraction.

The Corps had pledged to tear us down and rebuild us in its image, yet it was not just a matter of pride that kept us from quitting. We had signed on and were going to stay, even if it killed us. Today the USMC will often discharge a recruit who is struggling. However, because of the recruiting exigencies in the late 1960s, the Corps did not accept mere failure as an excuse to be sent home from boot camp.

There were several ways to be removed from your platoon, none of them appealing. Overweight recruits, who couldn't keep up, were sent to what was called the "Pig Platoon." There, they underwent physical conditioning all day. The drill instructors stood over them in chow lines, directing the mess men just how much, and of what, went on the recruits' trays. They were virtually starved. When they had lost sufficient weight to join a regular platoon, they started again. These recruits were bed checked often throughout each night because of the high number of suicide attempts.

Recruits who balked at the intense discipline of boot camp were relegated to the Disciplinary Platoon. This was the worst place to be. The recruit worked endlessly, digging large holes and carrying the dirt in small buckets to a spot fifty meters away. When the hole met the DI's satisfaction, the recruit then returned the dirt, one bucket at a time, until the hole was full again. The next day, he would do it all over again. A high fence surrounded these barracks, but it wasn't quite a brig. The drill instructors there were the biggest and toughest in the Corps. Most of these recruits returned to a platoon to complete their basic training, and were no longer "head cases." The rest usually received medical discharges, typically for severe mental problems.

Another way out of your platoon was to commit a crime. This often landed you in the brig for a very long time. The last way to get out was to die. This happened on occasion, from either accident or suicide.

Regular boot camp was bad enough, and I like to think I had the fortitude to tough out this test of endurance. However, it was the thought of doing anything that would cause me to stay in that place for one minute longer than I had to, which drove me and kept me focused.

The only time we rested was on Sunday. Every Marine would have a religion. If you didn't have a religious affiliation, one was issued to you. The options were Roman Catholic, Protestant, and Jewish. On Sunday mornings we marched to a religious service. Later in the day, we sat on overturned buckets along the company street, cleaning our weapons or shining boots. Snatches of time were spent reading and writing letters.

Tom Mahoney and I would often sit beside one another. Mahoney was in a different squad than mine, and each squad lived in a separate hut. In the highly structured environment of Marine Corps boot camp, we had little time to speak to one another. Nevertheless, on these Sunday afternoons along the company street, we would share rumors and bits of information contained in our letters from home. Although Mahoney jealously protected the contents of letters he received from his girlfriend Linda, he would excitedly tell me each time one arrived. When he had not heard from her in a while, he would sit alone at the end of the line of our bucket-stools forlornly polishing a boot or belt buckle for hours.

* * * *

Two of our three drill instructors, Staff Sergeant Randolph and Sergeant Reed, were decent people. They were plenty tough, but you knew they were doing it to produce a particular result. They loved the Corps and wanted to make us worthy of the uniform. Randolph had great balance and intuition. We feared him, but he was a true instructor, always lacing his discipline with lessons: "You see why you're in The Pits son? Do you understand now?" He knew just when the menacing, cajoling, and demanding were about to cross the line from being a lesson to being destructive.

The first few weeks were particularly bad for me. I was scrawny, a smoker, and out of shape; and I had been cultivating a bad adolescent attitude for years. It took several weeks for me to, as the DIs constantly admonished, "get with the program." Hard for him to accept authority

One night, when I could not think of a single thing I had done right in the three weeks I had been there, I was called to the DI duty hut. Randolph was at his desk. "Come here, goddamnit!" he trumpeted, gesturing that I should come around the desk and look at the book in front of him. "Well," he barked, "read it. You do know how to read don't you?" The book was a progress report log on the platoon and was open to my page. On it, he had written, "Private Archer is showing improvement in all aspects of performance." I stared at the writing thinking it belonged to someone else. A smile suddenly crossed my face. "There will be no smiling in my house goddamnit, do you understand? You ain't made it yet, missy. Now get out of my face!" It was the moment my confidence was born, and Randolph knew it.

This kind of praise was rare in boot camp, and only the wise ones like Randolph used it. The only other time he said anything positive to me was during an odd occurrence on the pugal stick range. Pugal sticks are like wooden broom handles with plastic pads at each end. The pads are color-coded to represent the butt and blade ends of a bayoneted rifle. Bayonet fighting skills were important in World War I and to a lesser degree in World War II. The Corps, being traditional and slow to change, still dedicated hours to training us in this form of combat. I was cynical of this, and yet there would be a desperate night in Vietnam when my platoon was ordered to "fix bayonets." For most recruits, the thing they remember most about the training is the repetitive call of the instructor: "Put the leading foot forward. SLIDE, SLIDE, SLIDE!"

We were at the pugal range that day and had queued up on either side of a dirt quad. Upon reaching the front of the line, we paired off against an opponent on the other side. For protection, we received a football helmet equipped with a face guard. The instructor showed us how to parry our opponent's attack and then do damage.

My excitement really built up as my turn approached. By the time I put on the helmet and waited for the range instructor to blow the whistle, I was near blood lust. When the whistle sounded, I ran toward my opponent and, forgetting the technique I'd been taught that afternoon, kicked him in the groin—hard. As he bent forward and fell to the ground, I slid my hands down to the bottom of the stick, holding it like a baseball bat, and began to club him mercilessly.

The instructor walked over and picked up the man's fallen pugal stick. Taking a mighty swing at my head, he connected solidly sending me flying onto my back. "Get off of my range you motherfucker!" he screamed down at me. "Get off my range before I kill you!"

As I dejectedly jogged away, I passed the small platform on which the other drill instructors sat enjoying the spectacle and wagering cigarettes on the contestants. I expected Staff Sergeant Randolph to threaten me with some horrible punishment, but instead he leaned over and said quietly, "Nice work, son." One sergeant Randolph, was Father figure

Getting praise from Randolph was important to me. He was a father figure, whom I respected, who could do all the things he asked me to do and whose goal was to make me better. On graduation day, many of us asked to have a photo taken with Randolph, an unusual thing for recruits. He was an honorable man. I hope he survived all his subsequent tours in Vietnam and is enjoying his retirement pension.

The second of our three drill instructors was Sergeant Reed. Giant and rock-jawed, he looked like a Marine Corps recruiting poster. Reed was fair

August 1967. Graduation day at the Marine Corps Recruit Depot in San Diego, California. L to R: me, Mahoney, Drill Instructor Randolph, Woods, and Romans

in most of his dealings with the recruits, and the slackest of our three instructors. It did not take long for most of us to see through his tough-guy facade. He showed glimmers of compassion too often. However, when he sensed that we had detected this, he could be very tough, sending us to The Pits or on endless runs to the farthest reaches of the depot.

His favorite punishment was to run our platoon over to the fence that divided us from the Navy boot camp. In the distance we could see people moving about, but could not tell what they were doing. Sergeant Reed would fill in the gaps: "See those squids? They are lying around watching TV and eating pogey-bait (candy bars). They're going out on liberty tonight to drink beer and get laid—probably with your girl friends. They call their mamas and sweethearts every night on the telephone." We all roared for their deaths.

"Squid" was one of the many pejorative names Marines had for Navy personnel, which also included "swabbies," "deck apes," and "pecker checkers." The latter was a name ascribed to Navy corpsmen, who provided medical care for Marines. Because it was so insulting, we often used it for all Navy personnel.

Bidwell - 3rd instructor

The third drill instructor was Sergeant Bidwell. He had recently returned from Vietnam where he earned a Purple Heart. The only wound that was visible to us was a raw, liver-colored, shrapnel scar, about an inch in diameter, on his left cheek. This had damaged what he thought to have been his good looks, and he was clearly pissed off about it all the time. The DIs rotated night duty shifts and we all hated Bidwell's shift. He had the cruelest eyes of anyone I had ever seen.

Bidwell loved to punish the recruits. You could see it in his eyes and his sneer—the sadism. My worst day of boot camp came on rifle pre-qualification day at the Edson Shooting Range. A dozen of us recruits had not met the minimum prequalification score. Randolph and Reed had gone home and Bidwell grinned at us maniacally.

While the other members of the platoon sat in the shade waiting for the truck back to the barracks, he tortured us. First, we had to crawl on our bellies for 300 yards through the dirt. It was an extremely hot July afternoon. Next, Bidwell had us form a circle and start to do squat-thrust exercises. When a man faltered, he ordered him into the center of the circle. At Bidwell's command, we were to stop the exercise and run directly to the other side of the circle—right over the man in the middle. We obeyed. It was brutal. The squat-thrusts resumed, with more men in the center, more charges through the middle, more blood. Finally, after what felt like twenty repetitions of this, Bidwell had us form up and stand at attention.

He had deprived us of water throughout the afternoon and soon one of the Marines turned bright red and collapsed from heat stroke. His breath began to gurgle in his chest. I could see the panic start to show in Bidwell's eyes as he ordered someone to run for water.

I was kneeling next to the victim, trying to provide some shade, when Bidwell handed me his Smokey-the-Bear campaign hat and told me to fan the semi-conscious man. Just then, a canteen of water arrived. Bidwell began to pour it on the man's face in an effort to get his temperature down. Private Bedford, another concerned recruit, was now kneeling at the other side of the victim. We were both quite crazy from the heat and started talking back and forth about Bidwell, as if he weren't standing right there; remarking about how we hoped he would go to the brig for life if the kid died, and comments of that nature. I could tell from the expression on the DI's face that he clearly recognized our insubordination, yet he did not say anything. I no longer cared what happened to me. I stopped fanning the man with Bidwell's campaign hat and intentionally held the brim under the stream of water he was pouring on him, and then slowly I looked up into the DI's dead, blue eyes with a smirking grin that said, "Do something about it." He stopped pouring the water, but again said nothing. Bedford and I were so thirsty we began sucking moisture out of the stricken man's shirt collar. An ambulance eventually arrived and took him away.

I barely qualified the next day. So stiff and bruised from the prior day's exertion, I could hardly assume the correct shooting positions I had been trained to use. By the time I trudged out to the 500-meter line, I knew I was not doing well on my score and might not qualify. I assumed Bidwell would kill me.

At the 500-meter mark, I fired from the prone position, which was steadier and less painful to my battered body. The distant target shimmered in the afternoon sun. An image of Gary Cooper in the film *Sergeant York* came to mind, and I resisted the impulse to lick my thumb and rub it on my front sight—"to cut the haze." I recalled another line from the movie, when the rustic York was asked to explain how he single-handedly killed so many German soldiers. His reply was coolly unassuming: "Well, I jest kinda teched 'um off." I whispered that quote several times, slowly exhaled, and commenced firing. I scored eight out of ten shots—and qualified.

Bidwell didn't forget my abuse of his hat and got even with me just before graduation. It was a time when the other DIs were starting to treat us with some respect in preparation for our becoming fellow Marines. One night I came back from the shower and Bidwell was in our Quonset hut, standing by my footlocker. It was against the rules not to lock it up. I saw that my padlock was missing. Then, I recognized it as the object he was spinning around on his forefinger. This infraction usually got a recruit some time in The Pits, but not tonight. Bidwell commanded the other members of the squad to do a left face, so there would be no witnesses. Then, while I was standing at attention, he punched me fiercely in the gut. As I doubled up, he finished me off with a hammering right hand, which dropped me to the floor. I despised him for it, but I was less than a week from graduating, and nothing was going to keep me in boot camp a minute longer than necessary. So, I stayed down. He waited for several seconds, gave me one of his crazy smiles, and walked out of the hut.

I looked for Bidwell throughout my time in the Corps—in the States and out. Whenever I got to a new place, with new faces, I looked for his in hope that someday I could repay him for his "hands-on" concern about the contents of my footlocker that night. Our paths never again crossed.

* * * *

As we approached the end of basic training, we did not yet have a banner for our platoon flag. Platoons in each company competed for various banners to put on their flag. These large ribbons showed who had done the best in various categories, such as physical fitness, marksmanship, and drill.

Staff Sergeant Randolph decided we were going to win the drill banner. We marched and marched on the huge parade ground they called "The Grinder," often until past dark. We drilled much more than other platoons did. The idea behind drilling is to instill the sense of thirty-six individuals acting as a single unit. Nonpartisan DI judges would grade us on test day.

When that day came, we formed up and marched great: heels clicking, looking sharp. Near the end of the drill came a rather complex part of the *Manual of Arms* called "Stack Arms," in which three rifles are formed into a kind of tripod in precisely choreographed movements. During the movement, I tipped my head slightly more forward than necessary and hit the bill of my cover (hat) with my rifle barrel. The cover went askew to the right, but still balanced precariously on my head.

With the rifles now stacked, we were back at attention, and I could see the judging drill instructor straight ahead of me. As soon as he saw my cover out of place, he dramatically leaned forward at the hip, arms akimbo, and stared at me for what seemed like an hour. Eventually he turned and moved on down the line. When Staff Sergeant Randolph finally gave the command to unstack arms, I took a split second to tap my cover back into position with the tip of my rifle barrel.

We marched to the edge of The Grinder and were ordered "at ease" while the drill instructors conferred. I had no doubt that I was in big trouble. I pictured myself transferred to another platoon because I had screwed up the drill and lost our platoon's last chance for a ribbon. At the very least, I would be the guest of honor at a "blanket party" that night, an officially unauthorized ritual where several Marines grab the blanket a person is sleeping under and pull it tightly down as a restraint. Others then take turns hitting the blanket, typically with a bar of soap in a sock to leave no marks. Though never subjected to such treatment, I had seen it happen. I never participated, because no matter how much the recruit might deserve it, it was just too cowardly a way of dealing with the situation. I think most Marines felt the same.

Our drill instructors' conference with the judges soon ended. To my surprise, none of them were glaring menacingly at me; and none of my fellow recruits were whispering threats in my direction. No one seemed to have noticed my mistake. That evening we lined up on each side of the company street, facing inboard. Staff Sergeant Randolph harangued us about how hopeless we all were and how we did not belong in his Corps. When he finished, his face suddenly broke into a big smile, and from inside his utility jacket he pulled out the yellow drill banner. We had won. Everyone cheered.

I can pinpoint the moment when I made my first adult decision. It was during the stack arms drill when, faced with the difficult consequences of my inadvertent action I chose not to act impulsively, but rather deliberately; to act in a manner that would give us the better chance of achieving our collective goal. It sounds almost Zen-like but, in not fixing my hat, I finally understood what "it" was all about.

We graduated from boot camp in August 1967. The Archer and Mahoney families made the trip to San Diego for the ceremony. They were all nearly bursting with pride.

* * * *

War Games

✯ ✯ ✯

From boot camp I reported to 2nd Battalion, 2nd Infantry Training Regiment (ITR) at Camp Pendleton, California. Tom Mahoney was assigned to a different company within the regiment, and I would no longer see him regularly. It was while at ITR that I had my first liberty call since leaving home two months before. Because most of us were not old enough to drink in bars, we would often take the bus to Oceanside and aimlessly wander around or go to a diner and occupy a table for hours, drinking the same Coke until asked to leave.

Cabbies would offer group rates to deliver us down to Tijuana, Mexico, where liquor and woman were cheap and available to Marines of all ages. While still in high school, I had spent one night partying in Tijuana with my friend Pat Haley and another Marine, Jim Ritchie who was, at the time, also stationed at Camp

Jim Ritchie (Pat's buddy), Pat Haley, and me at a Tijuana, Mexico, bar in January 1966. I was 17 and still in high school at the time. Haley and Ritchie were both Marines about to ship out to Vietnam. Each returned alive, although Ritchie would be seriously wounded by a land mine

They would 27 go to Tijuana to party

Pendleton. We survived a drunken brawl between Marines and sailors at The Jockey Club, somehow avoiding arrest as the *policia* herded nearly every other ambulatory patron into the paddy wagons parked out front. Early the next morning, we even got into a fight on the bus back to the U.S. border. In between, we were accosted, it seemed, by every prostitute, beggar, con man, watch salesman, and drug dealer in town. I had no desire to return.

In Oceanside, some Marines went straight to tattoo parlors for a "Globe and Anchor" or a "Devil Dog," usually on the bicep or forearm. Others went to photo studios to have pictures taken in borrowed dress blues and unearned medals to titillate the girl back home. Pimps, religious hucksters, and con artists struck up conversations with us on the street, preying on the naiveté of the recruits, many of whom were away from home for the first time.

There were fistfights nearly every night in ITR, and you had better be prepared to fight. Because I was skinny, other Marines often tested me to see how much abuse I would take. I learned that even if I had no chance of winning a fight, as long as I hurt the other guy or at least made him look bad while whipping me was often just as effective. Soon, they stopped picking on me. During my time in the Corps, I had two teeth broken and a few minor concussions from fighting. It was all part of it.

Regional peculiarities and race were often the cause of these fights. If you were from California, you would frequently have your masculinity questioned: "California is the land of steers and queers, and I don't see any horns on you, boy." Texans constantly ridiculed Oklahomans. You had better smile if you called a Mexican a "beaner" or "greaser." New Yorkers considered everyone a hick and never passed an opportunity to verbalize that belief. Racial insults were a common cause of fighting between blacks and whites.

Daily life was a lot like prison, except we got out on weekends. In one odd respect, it was the opposite of prison because the institution intentionally cultivated anger and violence. They trained us to kill and hoped to channel it toward the enemy at just the right moment. In Vietnam, however, there were fewer fistfights. Preoccupied with getting home safely, few indulged in unnecessary violence. The exception to this was the occasional spontaneous race riot.

Normally, a Marine would go on home leave at the completion of ITR. To my dismay, I was randomly selected for a month of mess duty at Camp Pendleton's Las Pulgas area mess. Washing pots, ladling food into trays, and wiping down tabletops was not what I had joined the Corps to do.

Compulsory mess duty tended to dull the impact of all the high-powered training we had been receiving up to that point and was a breeding ground for malcontents. I could not wait to get away from there. Once mess duty ended, I was finally able to take home leave. Unfortunately, because of this delay, I missed seeing Tom Mahoney, who had already been home and returned to Camp Pendleton.

Mom's cooking tasted better than I remembered; and Dad took me around to as many of his friends and business acquaintances as he could, to show me off. I did not need to visit his barber Karl though, as the USMC had provided me with a "high-and-tight" cut, which I'm sure, Karl would have considered a masterpiece. In return for being displayed around town like a carnival attraction, Dad let me use the family station wagon at night to carouse. I went immediately to The Ranch. Though welcomed out of past loyalty, I could feel the discomfort my presence caused among some of my old acquaintances. I had changed, and my new demeanor had a lot to do with it.

His dad proud of him when he's on leave

Late one night, shortly before my leave expired, I arrived drunk and in a bad mood. A man with long hair and wearing hippie clothes was sleeping on the couch. I grabbed him and after a short fistfight, threw him out of the house. I later discovered he had just gotten out of the Army after a tour in Vietnam—and here I had not even been there yet. I met him again years later and apologized. We laughed about the incident and agreed that those were extremely confusing times.

I never returned to The Ranch after that night. The premonition I had that evening on the softball field in Piedmont came true in just four months!

When my home leave ended in late October 1967, I reported for Schools Battalion at Camp Pendleton to train as a Field Radio Operator. There was a definite "social" pecking order among the communication specialties taught at the school. The lowest "life forms" were the wiremen, then came radio operators, radio teletype operators, and finally, radio technicians (the latter generally being noncombatants). It was felt that the wiremen were the least intelligent and technicians the most. I personally think it had more to do with how well you did during a written aptitude test in boot camp under the pressure of a drill instructor threatening to "kill you if you don't hurry it up!" If a Marine flunked out of radio school, he became a wireman. It was great incentive not to fail when you stood in the chow line each day alongside wiremen trainees. Invariably, there would be one wearing huge gauze and tape bandages on his hands and face, to cover the enormous slivers he had received from sliding the length of the old wooden practice poles—after missing a step.

The atmosphere at radio school was much more relaxed than I had previously experienced in the Corps. Sergeant "Ski" (the unofficial Marine Corps name for nearly everyone Polish) taught the class on radio theory. Ski's lessons were a mixture of the principles of electromagnetism and front-page tabloid press. For example, he would enthrall us with lectures on how radio waves theoretically travel through space for eternity. This gave us a vague sense of immortality. We were grateful for this, especially since we had recently learned that radio operators had one of the highest mortality rates in combat. The enemy, knowing damaged radios cannot be used to call in bombers or artillery on them, often sought out radiomen as primary targets.

After describing the infinite character of radio waves, Sergeant Ski would then expound upon a personal theory. He adamantly believed that he was able to receive incoming radio transmissions in his mouth, by rubbing a piece of aluminum foil on a gold filling. Try as he might, and despite the painful electric current it produced, it never seemed to work when others were around.

We learned radio procedure mostly outdoors at the foot of a steep hill called "Sheepshit." If you did not take good care of the radio equipment, screwed up, or the instructor just didn't like you, you spent a good part of your day running up and down Sheepshit. I somehow managed to avoid this treat, although I heard the view was great.

* * * *

I first met Steve Orr at radio school. We would later serve together in Vietnam and become close friends. However, in those days I could not stand him. He came into the barracks the very first night with his drinking buddies, shouting, falling into wall lockers, and waking nearly everyone up. One night Private First Class (PFC) Sherwood, a member of this group, recognized an acquaintance named Lowery, sleeping in the rack next to mine. Sherwood began chatting with Orr about how Lowery talked in his sleep and would frequently call out the name of his girlfriend, Marie.

With that, Orr tiptoed over to Lowery's rack, put his face close to the sleeping man's ear and began whispering in a low, hypnotic voice, "Low-er-y. Low-er-y. Marie is out tonight banging sailors." Steve repeated this several times in that soothing monotone, until Lowery began thrashing around in his sleep, crying, and shouting fitfully—a source of great amusement to Orr and his friends. It was something like that every night with Orr. And although we had a lot of studying to do, he never cracked a book, and yet passed the tests just the same as those of us who worried constantly about being sent to wireman school, or even worse, basic rifle-man training.

Orr's girlfriend was attending school at the University of California, Santa Barbara. Orr hitchhiked there from Camp Pendleton to see her on weekends. As a private, his pay was only about $125 per month, so he was always short of cash. My first conversation with Orr occurred when he stopped by my rack one morning and tried to sell me a sweater. I refused to buy it, or loan him the money, which I suspect was his real intention. I wondered then if it actually was his sweater.

* * * *

After completing radio school, we went to Staging Battalion at Camp Pendleton, where we received advanced infantry and special weapons training. This was our last stop in the United States.

One morning after chow, the Staging Battalion instructors herded us all into a small warehouse that served as an administrative office. Against the far wall was a long counter with several windows; behind each window sat a clerk. We queued up in front of the windows, obeying our natural in-stinct to seek out the shortest line. Because of this random sorting, Steve Orr and I ended up standing in line together. We, like all the other Marines, expected to get orders for either 1st Marine Division, or 3rd Ma-rine Division, either of which would result in a thirteen-month tour of duty in South Vietnam. As we reached the counter, the clerk found three orders for the 9th Marine Amphibious Brigade (9th MAB). He handed Orr and me each one, and our platoon sergeant, standing behind me, the third. The sergeant immediately let out a hoot. "Boys," he said, "fate has been kind to us. We're going to Okinawa instead of Vietnam."

About a week earlier, Tex Matthews and I had gone to PFC Woods' house in Oceanside to drink beer and watch two Texas college football teams play on TV. Woods had been in our boot camp platoon, and was a friend of Matthew's by dint of their Texas citizenship. Woods had some-how gotten orders for a stateside billet, and not Vietnam. The more he drank, the more he bragged about his good fortune. As I had decided by this time that I would prefer not to go to Vietnam myself, I found his boasting to be increasingly annoying.

Yet now I knew how good it felt to have orders elsewhere. If ordered, I would have gone to Vietnam, but my perspective was changing with each day of training. Our Staging Battalion instructors walked us through mock ambushes, patrols, and defensive perimeter situations; all the while re-minding us that even the best-trained troops ended up dead in "The Nam."

He has orders to Okinawa, not Vietnam

The cynicism of the instructors, enlisted men, and combat veterans was clear. It was after the lessons on field tactics were completed, and the smoking lamp was lit, that the reality began.

I did two tours there. Don't recall anything that was worth dying for.

Watch for Bouncing Betties (anti-personnel mines). They don't usually kill you, but they'll most definitely take your balls off.

Don't panic if you take a bullet in the lung, you've got two of them after all. Just plug up the hole air-tight with some cellophane from your cigarette package, and try not to breathe too much. [The irony of having cigarettes handy in order to save a lung was not lost on me even then.]

By the time the official lesson plan was completed, and all the not-so-obvious land mines and booby traps were pointed out, my adolescent day-dreams of heroics on the battlefield had been significantly eroded. And so, I received the news of my impending tour of duty on Okinawa with secret relief.

* * * *

In early November, I met Tom Mahoney in Oceanside for dinner. He was with Beford and Egan, both of whom had been in our boot camp platoon and were now with Tom in another Staging Battalion company. All three had trained as basic riflemen. They were leaving for Vietnam within a few days. Egan chattered on about this or that daring deed he was going to perform just as soon as he got a chance at "Charlie." He told us of an appointment he had made with a professional photographer in Oceanside, intending to have his picture taken while posing in a casket with the Medal of Honor around his neck. Egan was positive he would earn the Medal, but wasn't sure how good he'd look when it was over. "Jumping on a live grenade," he glumly explained, "can really fuck you up!"

Tom was preoccupied and humorless that evening, although he seemed to perk up briefly and was genuinely happy for me when I told him I had received orders for Okinawa instead of Vietnam. But, he almost immediately lapsed back into a distant stare. I sensed that the reality of the situation, particularly the recognition that he would not be seeing his girlfriend for at least another thirteen months, had him downhearted. I didn't ask.

Later, we slapped backs all around and said our good-byes, but there was a palpable air of forced optimism about it all. I guess I had expected it to be more like partings in those World War II Marine movies I watched so often as a kid, where William Bendix shouts something like, "See you in

Tokyo, Mac!" and Lloyd Nolan one-ups him with, "I'll give your regards to the Emperor." Nothing audacious or witty like that came to mind as we stood in front of the diner in Oceanside that night. The best I could do was, "Keep your head down." And even that came out sounding more like golf advice.

A couple of weeks later, I flew home for the weekend to visit my family. On Sunday evening, as Dad was preparing to drive me back to the airport, Mom said she wanted to go along. She had never done this before. Because she so disliked driving with Dad, I knew that she must have had a premonition that this would be my last time home. At the airport I hugged her and said goodbye. She couldn't talk because of the emotion, but just kept nodding her head up and down. It was her way of saying she loved me. I shook Dad's hand as he sputtered a string of last minute advice to me. It was generic stuff like "Don't believe everything you hear," and "Go with the flow"; yet I knew it was as close to a display of affection as Dad was capable of, and I appreciated the attempt.

I boarded the airplane and sat on the terminal side, so I could see Mom through the window. She was staring back at the plane, actually at a window farther forward, where she must have guessed I was sitting. She looked so tiny, sad, and tired. As the plane rolled away from the gate, I thought I'd never see her again and started to cry.

* * * *

Okinawa

★ ★ ★

On Thanksgiving Day, 1967, I had dinner with Tex Matthews at a coffee shop in Oceanside. I don't recall many details of our pathetic little feast, only that it is my last memory of being on liberty in the United States. The next morning our staging company took an early bus to El Toro Marine Corps Air Station then boarded a Continental Airlines Boeing 707 bound for Kadena Air Force Base, Okinawa. *Orr + he become companions*

Steve Orr and I sat next to each other during the flight. Thrown together with him by fate, I decided to make the most of it. I soon discovered Orr to be much saner than I had earlier imagined. He had been born and raised in Mobile, Alabama, but lived the last few years in Sacramento, California, which was only about 100 miles from Oakland.

Orr looked like he was about fourteen, with pink cheeks and curly blond hair—the kind of looks most women find adorable. Later, in Asia, the young women would often giggle when they saw him, exclaiming in pidgin, "Oh! You baby-san." I noticed the rapport he was soon achieving with the stewardesses on our flight and figured that knowing him could be a real asset in Okinawa. So far, in my young life, I had not had much success attracting girls on my own.

The flight lasted eleven hours. We arrived at Kadena on the afternoon of the following day—a consequence of crossing the International Dateline. It was raining, but not particularly cold. The coastline and hilltops were largely weathered outcroppings of old volcanic rock. I could detect no signs of the horrendous combat fought there twenty-two years earlier.

During the drive to Camp Hansen, I peered continuously from the back of the truck. My great adventure was beginning and I didn't want to miss any of it.

Camp Hansen was the transient facility for all Marines going to, and returning from, South Vietnam. Orr and I also had to pass through this facility to get our orders for the 9th Marine Amphibious Brigade (MAB). At Camp Hansen, Marines stored a second sea bag with belongings that would not be required in South Vietnam such as dress uniforms and civilian clothes. The sea bags were then stored in large warehouses to be reclaimed on the return trip. Those Marines would receive their equipment, including weapons, when they reached their units in South Vietnam. This differed from procedure used by the Army, which generally equipped its soldiers in the U.S. and flew them directly to that country.

The routine at Camp Hansen was the same each morning: reveille, chow, and a formation consisting of several hundred Marines and Navy personnel. A staff sergeant stood in front of the formation reading the list of names of those who would be "going south" that day. Those whose names weren't called would then be assigned to work details around the camp. These work details, although not arduous, were incredibly boring and to be avoided if possible.

It did not take long for Orr and me to figure this out. We noticed that between the announcements of those going to Vietnam that day, and those selected for work details, the staff sergeant commanded others who had not yet received all mandatory inoculations to wait behind after he dismissed the rest of the troops. Orr saw this as our window of opportunity. Each morning we pretended to need our shots, and marched with the others to sickbay. The non-commissioned officer (NCO) in charge of our group would usually leave us standing in front of the building while he went inside. At this point, Orr and I would slip away and spend the rest of the day as we chose. Since we had very little money, one of our favorite pastimes was to go the music room in the camp library. There we would choose an album, slip on the big padded headphones, and nap.

On occasion, after marching us to sickbay for shots, the NCO would not go into the building, but merely knock on the door. At those times, it would be necessary for us to assume the identity of the world's two dumbest Marines. "We're not here for our shots," Orr would plead, raising his eyebrows in his classic portrayal of a dimwit. "We thought we were coming here to see that hygiene film about meeting the lady in front of the bus station and then having to get the penicillin shot." The Navy corpsmen, most of whom were inclined to think of all Marines as imbeciles anyway, would scornfully wave us through the line. On one occasion, however, they did not believe us, and gave us our (second) gamma globulin shots. This produced a golf-ball sized knot in my hip, which took nearly two days to rub out. As time went on, our plan began to look less clever.

The enlisted men's club at Camp Hansen, called the "Animal Pit," could have been considered an extension of our combat training. One night Steve and I were there talking with a Marine who was returning from Vietnam. He was very serious and direct, willing to answer our questions with apparent honesty. As our conversation proceeded, a melee raged around us. Furniture flew and people punched complete strangers without provocation. It was like a saloon brawl in a John Wayne movie. A big bottle of Orion beer sailed past us, missing our heads by inches, shattering against the wall in an explosion of foam and shards of brown glass. I thought it was all very exciting.

Orr and I stayed at Camp Hansen for several days and then transferred to our parent unit, the 26th Marine Regiment, which was further north on the island at Camp Schwab. The camp appeared nearly deserted, and we bounded up the steps of the headquarters building with high hopes of spending the next year in this delightful place. Our elation was short-lived. The headquarters company clerk immediately informed us that the only reason we had been sent to Camp Schwab was to pick up our orders to join the rest of the regiment. I reluctantly asked the clerk where the "the rest of the regiment" was located and I can still vividly recall the fleeting, sardonic grin that seemed to change the shape of his mouth—but not his eyes. He clearly enjoyed that question. The clerk slowly rose from his desk and strode, almost theatrically, to a large wall map of South Vietnam. Using his pencil as a pointer, he gradually swept up the country from south to north, farther and farther, until the tip of his pencil stopped at a point in a remote corner of the country. *They learn they will be transferred to Vietnam*

From where I was standing, I thought he was actually pointing to a spot inside the Demilitarized Zone between North and South Vietnam. But upon moving closer to the map, I could see a small red pin protruding near a place called Khe Sanh; an inch to the right of Laos, and about two inches below North Vietnam. We were disappointed, but not surprised. If we had learned anything from our short time in the Corps, it was that we had not learned anything.

Though disappointed, we learned that we would be staying at Camp Schwab for another three days so tried to make the best of it. We shot pool and played Ping-Pong during the day. At night, we drank thirty-five-cent scotch and soda at the enlisted men's club. Unlike the Animal Pit at Camp

Hansen, the few people who visited this club refrained from breaking glass and furniture.

Living the high life at Camp Schwab, we soon ran out of money. One morning Orr and I went to the payroll office. Just PFCs, the second lowest life form in the Marine Corps, the payroll clerk quickly rejected our request. I began to rant and pound my fist on the desk. I shouted that we were on our way to Khe Sanh and asked him if he knew where that was on the map. No? Well I did! It is way up there by the goddamn DMZ. The goddamn pencil was almost in North Vietnam! Did it sound to him like we were coming back alive? Well did it?

My act worked. A lieutenant who was standing nearby intervened on our behalf, and we were each given an advance of twenty-five dollars.

We were soon returning to Camp Hansen, and it would be only a matter of days until we shipped to Vietnam. So that night, we took our twenty-five dollars to the enlisted men's club to commiserate and consume numerous thirty-five-cent Zombies (that evening's drink "special"). A local Okinawan band imitated the Beach Boys. The more we drank, the less phonetically acquired their English sounded.

Later that night I took a walk outside. The club was located next to the ocean. An ancient sea wall constructed of irregularly carved stone blocks, barely protruding from the surface, meandered about 100 yards out to sea. It was a dark night, and I was feeling the tremendous buzz from the Zombies. I carefully walked the entire length of the wall and stood for a long time at the end, looking out into the blackness toward home and reflecting disconsolately on my fate.

Eventually, I turned to go back and discovered that tidal forces had been at work. The only spot not now underwater was where I was standing. I started to make my way back toward the distant lights on shore, probing with a submerged foot, before laying down a step. The chilly waters of the Pacific were often knee-deep. I was wearing civilian clothes, including a pair of floaters (a kind of high-topped leather shoe, fashionable at the time), which I soon discovered did not actually float. I finally made it back to shore, foolishly explaining my wet clothes above the scornful laughter of the club's patrons.

After the enlisted club closed that night, Orr and I staggered toward our barracks. Soon disoriented, we decided to just find the nearest barracks with empty racks and sleep it off. We thought the entire camp was deserted except for a few administrative personnel and us.

Two hours later, at about 0430, the dark and angry face of a Marine sergeant rudely awakened me. He was screaming for me to "Get up and on the road NOW!" We had fallen asleep in the middle of a Marine battalion embarking by ship for Subic Bay, then on to Vietnam. People were scrambling all around; packing last minute items; shouting and cursing.

After rolling out of the racks, we stood there in our civilian clothes, swaying back and forth. Orr tried to explain to the sergeant that we had orders for the 26th Marines, and that we had accidentally fallen asleep amongst them. Of course, this is exactly the kind of thing that someone who really did not want to go to Vietnam would say.

We asked everyone within range if they knew us or had ever seen us before, but all we got back were looks of disgust. The sergeant reluctantly admitted that he did not recognize us. Soon a captain came and looked at us with great loathing. He began yelling that we had better get into our utilities, get our gear on, and be outside in five minutes or he'd have the Shore Patrol take us aboard "in irons." He then hurried off. We implored the sergeant again, and this time he acquiesced, shaking his head twice in the direction of the doorway and bidding us farewell with an almost kindly, "Get the fuck out of here."

It is almost axiomatic that once an officer gets involved in a situation, the empathy level among enlisted men rises. If that captain had not interrupted the sergeant, we may have ended up AWOL from the 26th Marines and on our way south with another unit. On the way back to our own barracks, we swore we would never drink again. I slept all that day and night; and the following morning our orders were ready and we headed back to Camp Hansen. Once there, Steve and I resumed our habit of avoiding work details by joining the inoculation group and then running off to the library to read the newspaper.

The major news story at the time was about the fighting at Dak To, a U.S. Army base in the Central Highlands of South Vietnam. Earlier that week, the North Vietnamese Army (NVA) had slammed rockets into the base igniting a thousand tons of ammunition and destroying two C-130 cargo planes on the runway. Later, the enemy launched a ground attack from the plantation orchards at the end of the runway. According to the news story, the battle lasted most of the day, with the enemy so close at times that U.S. forces had to lower the barrels of their howitzers and skid artillery shells down the runway at the attackers.

Trained to fight an enemy who lurked in the shadows and shot you in the back, this news of pitched battles with large, well-equipped, and fearless enemy forces surprised me. I would recall the battle at Dak To two months later, after witnessing a replication of this tactic by the enemy at Khe Sanh. It was hard not to see a pattern developing.

On December 2, the staff sergeant reading the list at our morning formation barked out Steve Orr's name, and he was soon gone. Three days later, my name finally made the list, along with about twenty others. After the formation, we shuffled silently off to our barracks to finish packing our sea bags. Later, we boarded a bus for Kadena Air Force Base and sat near the runway in a driving rain until well past midnight. I was already suffering from bronchitis exacerbated by my cigarette habit, that caused periods of coughing so severe I could barely catch my breath. A compassionate corpsman gave me a vial of tetracycline capsules as we boarded the plane that night, and wished me luck. We were both going to need it.

* * * *

Khe Sanh

$\star \ \star \ \star$

The flight to South Vietnam was quiet, in contrast to the one from California to Okinawa. It was late and we were wet. Most of us were scared. Few of us even thought to flirt with the stewardesses.

As we approached the coastal city of Da Nang, an ivory sun crept out of the Pacific behind us and the flight crew put on flak jackets (body armor)—not an encouraging sign. I had a window seat on the right side of the airplane from which I could see the approaching coast of South Vietnam and the black peaks of Hai Van protruding from the yellow-green mist. I could not really see the city, which soon sprawled below us in the gloom.

We landed without incident. Leaving the plane, we walked past a line of servicemen, mostly Marines waiting to take our seats for their flight back to Okinawa—they were heading home. A few sang out the traditional "You'll be sor-r-r-r-e-e-e," and other exaggerated expressions of mock condolence. Most were silent, their sidelong glances containing a look of mild disappointment, as if they had expected us to be wiser than we were. A few gazed more strangely, their half-closed lids hiding something I did not yet recognize—a weariness, a torpor, a disturbing indifference. A year later, I would be standing on that exact spot waiting to board a plane. Although I did know it at the time, looking into those faces was like looking into the future.

A Marine enlisted man then came by and instructed all the radio operators in the group to follow him to a nearby shed. Once inside, we lined up against a wall. Despite our printed orders, there were particular units that always needed men—dangerous outfits with high casualty rates. That day, an officer from a reconnaissance battalion was looking for two radio operators. After not getting any volunteers when he asked, he began walking slowly down the line, carefully examining us for suitability. My brother had been in Recon, I knew how hazardous it was, and did not want to go. A sudden fit of coughing shook my frame and seemed to dissuade the officer from considering me further. He eventually decided on two other radio operators, who ruefully followed him out the door of the shed. At that moment, I resolved not to begin taking the Tetracycline I had been given by the corpsman that morning in Okinawa for my bronchitis, until I had figured out what was going on around here.

With the news of battle at Dak To still uncomfortably in the back of my mind, and now seeing this shanghaiing of replacements to fill depleted units, I had a vague, troubling sensation in the pit of my stomach. Looking back, the closer I got to the war (even in those pre-Tet Offensive days), the more it appeared that things were not going so well.

After rejoining the rest of the new arrivals, we boarded a bus to the in-country flights terminal located in another part of the sprawling air base. The bus had metal screens welded over the windows to keep out enemy grenades. This trip required us to drive briefly through part of the city. The filthiness of the place appalled me. Okinawa was primitive by U.S. standards, but had a certain charm. Da Nang did not. However, I would return to Da Nang six months later, after living in the more rural parts of the country, and it would seem clean and cosmopolitan by comparison.

We eventually arrived at the in-country terminal, although the word "terminal" gave it a propriety it didn't deserve. It was actually a large tin-roofed shed, completely open on the side facing toward the runway. To my surprise, Steve Orr was standing at the door of the bus as I came down the steps. So far, he had managed to avoid flights to Khe Sanh Combat Base.

Of course, I gave him a bad time about it, accusing him with mock disappointment of wanting to spend the entire war in the relative safety of Da Nang. The truth, however, was that monsoon clouds in the mountains had prevented any planes from landing there that week.

Once inside the terminal building, Orr directed me to the correct counter, where I handed my orders to a ruddy, perspiring Air Force enlisted man. He pointed to several large handwritten signs on the wall behind him. The signs were covered in acetate, on which grease pencil numerals denoted the departure times for various flights. The flight to Khe Sanh was scheduled to depart within the hour. I sat on the floor, leaning on my sea bag and talking nervously with Orr and a few others we had just met who were waiting for the flight. I felt jumpy inside, wanting to go and not wanting to go in alternating waves of excitement and apprehension. My unfamiliarity with tropical humidity, now bathing me in sweat and making me light headed, only heightened the sensation that some invisible and irresistible current was sweeping me headlong toward an unknown fate.

After waiting for nearly an hour, Orr left to find a piss tube. Moments later, the Air Force clerk called our names and pointed us toward the runway where other Air Force personnel were loading a C-123, a large, twin-engine cargo plane with pallets of C-rations and mortar ammunition. I ran aboard, stowed my sea bag, and strapped into a folding nylon seat attached to the interior wall of the plane. This seating configuration had me facing inboard toward the cargo, which was about three feet from my face.

Soon the plane was airborne and heading north. It was obvious that Orr had missed yet another flight to Khe Sanh. I could not help laughing aloud at the thought. I wondered if he missed this flight by accident, or if it was merely a variation of his inoculation scheme on Okinawa. That last possibility made me laugh even harder.

I sat on the left side of the plane, near a small window and could, if I craned my neck far to the left, view the countryside as it passed below. Dense, gray clouds quickly enshrouded the plane, but I kept staring out the window anyway. Through occasional breaks in the cloud cover, I could see damp jungle, steep mountain slopes, and bits of streams glimmering here and there from shadowed ravines. There were great stands of tall trees, in stunning shades of dark green and near blue. I noticed no signs of human habitation, except the bombed ruins of a large metal bridge. Rusting pieces of its roadbed lay partially submerged in a slow, brown river. I had no idea where I was.

I did not even know how long the flight lasted. As we neared the airfield, a gap in the clouds opened, seemingly not much larger than the plane itself, and we plunged through it in a steep left bank. My first glimpse of the Khe Sanh Combat Base appeared in my little window amid vapor swirling in the propeller wash—a mile-long red scrape in the greenest green imaginable. The landing was smooth and we rolled to a stop at the Logistical Supply Area (LSA) near the center of the base. With a sea bag hoisted on my shoulder, I ran down the rear ramp and onto the runway. There I was, just about as far north as I could be in that country and still be in it. The pencil had not lied.

* * * *

The plateau on which the runway stood had formed during volcanic activity about one hundred centuries earlier. As the lava cooled, basalt formed near the surface. The site had been chosen for an airstrip in large part due to its proximity to an abundance of the hard rock, which was quarried and crushed for the runway foundation. Thousands of monsoon seasons had dissolved the other volcanic material into red laterite clay, resulting in the distinctive red-orange dirt that left its stain on all who would later come to live here.

But the geologic feature that would most influence the history of this area was located nine miles west of the airstrip, near where Highway 9 crossed from South Vietnam into Laos at a place called Lao Bao. The rugged and densely forested Annamite Mountains form a natural impediment along the western border of Vietnam, extending hundreds of miles from China, south to Cambodia. Lao Bao, one of the few passable gaps in the chain, provides a narrow corridor from the interior of Indochina to the coast of the South China Sea and served as a trade and invasion route for thousands of years.

Since the first of the kingdoms rose to power in the ninth century B.C., the Vietnamese have engaged in near constant warfare to repel invaders. An American general could have just as easily written the third century B.C. Chinese general's military report to the emperor in 1967: "The Viets are extremely difficult to defeat. They do not come out and fight, but hide in their familiar mountains and use the jungle like a weapon."[1] The Chinese armies were eventually driven out in A.D. 39, but later returned. It would be another 900 years before they were forced out again, completely and permanently. In their wake, a succession of warlords ruled the land. Yet, resistance to foreign military occupation would remain deeply ingrained in their cultural memory.

In 1262, the Chams, then occupying an independent kingdom in the area of what is now Da Nang, repulsed a Mongol invasion at Lao Bao. A reminder of this event remains on maps of the area, where the location of the Khe Sanh airfield is named "Xom Cham," or Village of Chams.

North and South Vietnam began a separate political existence in 1620. The Nguyen of the south constructed two enormous walls near the center of the country to protect it from the Trinh armies of the north. The Trinh never succeeded in breaking through these barriers, despite several major military campaigns. The Portuguese and the Dutch, great European trading powers of the day, struggled to keep the other out of South East Asia. The Portuguese supported the Nguyen, while the Dutch supported the Trinh. Each side received modern weapons from Europe. This conflict portended a future superpower rivalry; one in which the cold war between the United States and the Soviet Union would turn hot in the land of the "Viets."

Fighting at Lao Bao persisted for the next 200 years as the Vietnamese drove back a series of Siamese invasions. In 1836, forces of the Vietnamese Emperor Minh Mang finally reasserted sole authority over the mountain pass. It was not until the 1830s that the first non-Asians arrived in the Khe Sanh area. In 1834, a Franciscan missionary priest, starved to death in the infamous prison at Lao Bao.

That priest was undoubtedly the first westerner to die in the Khe Sanh area. But, as history has shown, certainly not the last.

* * * *

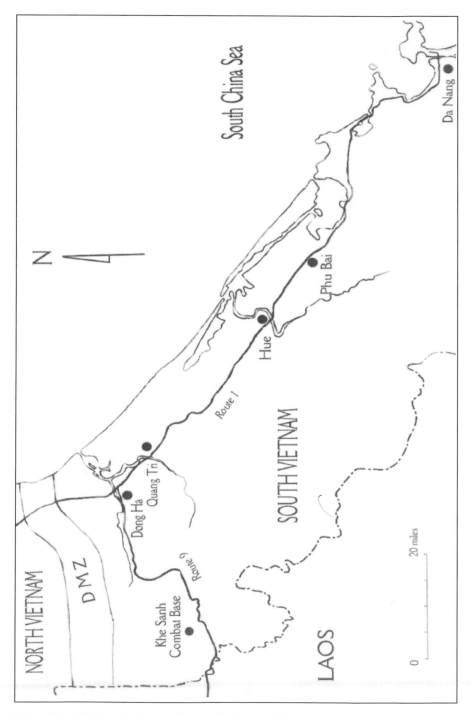

Map of the DMZ and Northern I Corps in January 1969   *Michael Archer*

Foxtrot

Slowly Surrounded

★ ★ ★

Excerpt from the 26th Marines After Action Report:

The area of operations, consisting of some 403 square miles, is located in northwestern Quang Tri Province. Bordered on the north by the DMZ and west by the Laotian border, the area of operations generally encompasses all of Huong Hoa District.

The area is thinly populated, rugged, and mountainous. Heights over 500 meters (above sea-level) are common throughout the area. Terrain is severely dissected and thickly vegetated with dense undergrowth, broad-leaf evergreen forests, and bamboo thickets. Trail networks are plentiful, but trafficability to vehicles is almost uniformly restricted to National Route 9. Excellent cover and concealment exist throughout most of the area of operations and provide both friendly and enemy forces numerous covered approaches to attack positions and protection from enemy fire.

The heavy vegetation throughout the area of operations consists of a 60-foot-high jungle canopy, elephant grass, and dense areas of bamboo and vine thickets, which, combined with the steep slopes, create an effective natural obstacle to cross-country movement and greatly reduce long-range observation. In general, cross-country movement is restricted to existing trails and streams. Periods of steady heavy rainfall also make many of the streams in the area of operations difficult to impossible to cross.

Dong Tri Mountain, the highest peak (1,015 meters) in the area of operations dominates the Khe Sanh Valley. Hill 861 controls the approaches from the north and northwest. Hills 881 South and 881 North, and Hill 918, dominate the approaches from the west. The [hill masses] south of Route 9 are important as they dominate the eastern approaches of Route 9 into the area of operations.[2]

* * * *

My first impression of Khe Sanh was the way it smelled, as if someone had just turned over a large, wet rock: a sour blend of standing sewage and sodden, decaying textiles. I got my first whiff of shit smoldering in diesel fuel (the standard method for disposing of human waste), and reflexively placed the back of an index finger to my nostrils to keep from gagging.

It was the middle of the monsoon season. Although it was not raining when I got off the plane, it had rained recently and a lot. I felt excitement, like a gnawing hunger in the pit of my stomach. But mostly I was feeling dumb, real dumb. Conspicuous in my stateside utilities and boots, I asked directions and was soon slogging up a muddy road toward the 26th Marine Regimental Headquarters Company area. At the intersection of two roads, near the main mess hall, there was a large hole filled with mud, a trap for new guys and entertainment for everyone else. I did my part, dropping one leg knee-deep in the muck, to the derisive shouts of my audience.

I checked in at the regimental administrative office where they assigned me to Communications Platoon, Headquarters and Support Company. Once the paperwork was completed, a clerk showed me the way to my new quarters—a tent just south of the runway next to the base's huge ammunition dump. Inside were twelve cots, six on a side. Because I was the new guy, my cot was by the door flap. Khe Sanh base was 1,400 feet above sea level and always cold and wet that time of the year. Consequently, the cots nearest the tent opening were the least desirable. At night, it was so cold I put on every bit of clothing I owned—including my boots—and then got inside a sleeping bag (I'd stored my cold weather clothes in Okinawa, believing Vietnam's climate was always tropical).

The next day I went to the company supply office and received my gear: M-16 rifle, webbed gear, and new jungle boots and combat utilities, which I hoped would stop me from looking so obviously like a new guy. A Marine in my tent convinced me I had to go to Graves Registration to be measured for my body bag. I regret to say I believed him. It gave the sergeant at the base morgue a good, long, pitying laugh as well as the chance to talk to a live Marine.

Another tent mate asked me to go to the communications supply office and bring back a can of "zero beat." Zero beat, I would come to find out, is a name given to the sound made by a PRC-47 radio when calibrating its frequency. Once again treated like a buffoon by the clerk, I returned empty-handed to the laughter of my new tent mates.

The members of my new platoon were, for the most part, friendly. Sergeant Richardson was a good man, and sympathetic to those who had just arrived. He only had a few weeks to go on his second tour of duty in Nam. The day after I arrived, Richardson led some of us new men out past the east end of the runway in order to familiarize us with our M-16 rifles. Surprisingly, it was the first time I had fired an M-16, having trained only with the M-14 and M-1. We fired a few hundred rounds across the runway. I remember thinking how incredibly beautiful the country was. Hill 1015 (hills are named for their elevation in meters above sea level) was a spectacular pinnacle, covered in dense, verdant rain forest of hues I did not even know existed. Its lower slopes broadened slightly into a plain of yellowish-green elephant grass, six feet high. As it neared the Rao Quan River gorge, the slope disappeared into a thick tangle of vine and bamboo.

In the tranquil magnificence that afternoon, it would have been difficult to picture an enemy camped atop that mountain, vigilantly recording our every move. More impossible to believe, would have been that a few weeks later, the very place we were now standing would be securely in enemy hands. Yet that would not have been the first time.

The Khe Sanh Combat Base lay astride a jumble of footpaths used by local tribesmen for hundreds of years. These mountain trails ran roughly parallel to the borders of Laos and South Vietnam. Viet Cong, North Vietnamese soldiers, and civilian laborers, began construction of a roadway capable of truck traffic into the area in 1959.

The road started in the North Vietnamese city of Vinh, crossed the mountains into Laos, and ended near the South Vietnamese-Cambodian border. It consisted of an interlocking system of paths and roads thirty miles wide and 300 miles long, through some of the most densely forested terrain in the world. The North Vietnamese called the trail system the "Truong Son Route," but the soldiers who walked its tortuous length called it the "10,000 Mile Route." Before long, the Americans had dubbed it the "Ho Chi Minh Trail."

The Central Intelligence Agency knew the gap at Lao Bao was a favored corridor along the Trail for NVA troops and supplies moving into South Vietnam, so decided it wanted a U.S. presence in the area to monitor the movement. The site selected was the same place the French had chosen decades before, for the same reason.

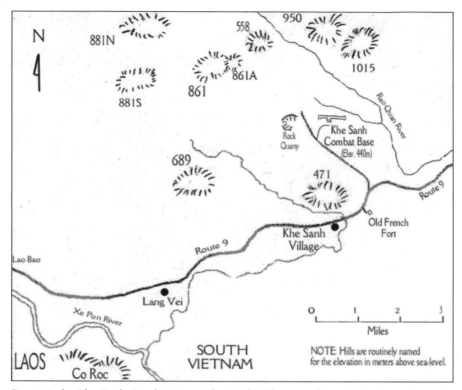

Route 9, the Khe Sanh Combat Base, Khe Sanh Village, and Lang Vei where the main force of Special Forces was located   *Michael Archer*

On July 4, 1962, a U.S. Special Forces team, under CIA control, moved into the abandoned, old French fort on the eastern edge of Khe Sanh Village. Sixteen days later, representatives of the United States and the Soviet Union signed the Declaration and Protocol on the Neutrality of Laos in Geneva, Switzerland. In the document, Russia pledged to keep North Vietnam from conducting operations in Laos. However, the building of truck roads along the Ho Chi Minh Trail in Laos continued. By the end of November, operational control of the Special Forces team at Khe Sanh passed from the CIA to Military Assistance Command Vietnam (MACV). This "officially" allowed the team to begin patrolling and engaging the enemy. An ARVN engineer unit upgraded the dirt airstrip about two miles north of the old French fort.

The Special Forces team battled a company-size enemy unit near Khe Sanh in October 1964. The presence of such large units of NVA operating in the area caused the team to abandon the fort and relocate to a more defensible position near the airstrip. Here they constructed concrete bunkers, the same ones I would inhabit about three years later.

*Laos-
neutral*

The following year, in an effort to answer the North Vietnamese abrogation of the Declaration and Protocol, President Johnson approved the creation of MACV-SOG (Studies and Observations Group). SOG would lead reconnaissance teams into Laos. These teams were comprised primarily of local troops, called the Civilian Irregular Defense Group (CIDG). Their mission was to observe traffic along the Trail and, when possible, direct air strikes. These operations were highly classified and directed from a special office in the Pentagon. Because SOG was created for the specific purpose of circumventing the accords, the State Department gave reluctant approval, but only after insisting that Americans going into Laos, or North Vietnam, not carry any form of identification. This gave the State Department the "plausible deniability" it sought in order to protect itself as signatory. Consequently, SOG advisors could not risk capture and would eventually have the highest per capita mortality rate of any unit in the war.

In December 1966, the U.S. Army Special Forces/SOG unit moved from the airstrip to a small base camp near the village of Lang Vei, several miles down Route 9, and closer to the Laotian border. Five months later, a large enemy force overran this camp. Two Viet Cong sympathizers within the CIDG helped the NVA troops enter the camp. Twenty loyal CIDG forces were killed in the attack along with the American Special Forces commander and his executive officer, who were blown up in an act of internal sabotage. More than forty others were wounded and taken out by helicopters the next morning. The CIDG turncoats, who ironically wore no shirts that night in order to be recognized by their comrades in all the confusion, evidently escaped. By late 1967, Special Forces had constructed a new camp about one half-mile farther west of the old camp. This new location was on a small hilltop overlooking both Route 9 and the border with Laos.

However, it was not just the Army Special Forces who were losing men in battle at Khe Sanh. In April 1967, during some of the fiercest fighting of the war, two Marine battalions engaged a large enemy force on Hill 861 and on two nearby hills about a mile apart, both designated 881. Hill 881S (South) was captured and held by the Marines after a bloody four-day battle against the NVA forces occupying it. Hill 881N (North), though briefly occupied by the Marines, would thereafter remain in enemy hands. The Marine assaults on these three hills effectively disrupted the NVA's plan to attack and destroy the Khe Sanh Combat Base in the spring of 1967. This series of battles became known as the "Hill Fights," and later, the "First Battle of Khe Sanh." When it ended in May 1967, 170 Marines were dead and 500 wounded.

Did you keep a journal, or you have good memory?

Monsoon rains calmed attack

Lead elements of Regimental Landing Team 26 (later to reorganize as the 26th Marine Regiment) arrived at Khe Sanh during this time. I would join them about six months later. On June 6, 1967, the day I went to boot camp, rockets pounded Khe Sanh Combat Base. Simultaneously, the enemy assaulted the communication relay station on Hill 950, about two miles to the north. Hill 950 had extremely steep slopes around its summit and was considered nearly unassailable. The enemy overwhelmed the surprised Marines, but some of the defenders were able to escape. After enduring a night filled with the screams of a captured Marine being tortured to death by the NVA, the surviving Marines rallied and drove the enemy from the hilltop. By the time a relief force was airlifted from the base to aid them, only five Marines were left standing.

With the arrival of the monsoon rains in the autumn of 1967, an unusual calmness settled over the area.

* * * *

After I completed checking in, Staff Sergeant Allen, my new platoon sergeant, assigned me to work in the underground Regimental Combat Operations Center, or COC (pronounced see-oh-see) bunker. My radio was located in the main room, where the regimental staff officers pondered tactical matters on a giant wall map. Working in the COC was an eye-opening experience for a newly arrived PFC. I had never even spoken to an officer higher than the rank of captain. I soon discovered that field grade officers (majors and above) generally treated lower-rank enlisted men more courteously than they did NCOs and junior officers.

My first "official" duty was to fetch water. Because I had seen the movie *Gunga Din* many times, I knew that this was a task assigned to the lowest person in a military group's social order. Nevertheless, I saw this as an opportunity to prove I was cooperative and a team player. I wanted to do a good job. The task was simple: take the empty five-gallon water can to the water point down by the airstrip control tower, fill it up, and bring it back. And yet, I found a way to complicate the process by inadvertently taking Lieutenant Colonel Hennely's cover (hat), instead of my own, from a peg on the wall. Within minutes, a nineteen-year-old PFC with only a few days in country was strolling with a water can down the main road of Khe Sanh Combat Base, the silver oak leaf of a lieutenant colonel shining on the front of his cover. I noticed people staring at me, but thought it was because I was still so obviously green. While I stood filling the can at the spigot, an enlisted man actually saluted. Never quite knowing what was going on at any given time, I kept silent and simply nodded my head slightly in recognition. This seemed to work, so I adopted the technique for the walk back.

Upon returning to the bunker and removing the cover, I discovered what I had done. Word of my gaff eventually got back to the lieutenant colonel. He waited until the room was full of people and then, in mock seriousness, confronted me about taking his cover. He accused me of trying to usurp his command and said there was not a yardarm in the fleet high enough for the hanging that would befit a mutinous dog like me.

Lieutenant Colonel Hennely was in his late forties, possibly even early fifties—when you are nineteen years old, everyone over thirty looks approximately the same age. He was the commanding officer of 1st Battalion, 13th Marine Regiment, which provided our artillery support at Khe Sanh. I had immense respect for him. Eventually, the stress of the siege and the enormous responsibility of his command affected his health, and he was flown out of Khe Sanh for medical attention.

Nine months later, near Da Nang, I met him again and was able to tell him how much I appreciated his brilliant work in the defense of Khe Sanh. Surprisingly, he was the one who initiated our conversation, even remembering my name. I include this insignificant fact here only because, after all these years, it is still a source of great pride.

* * * *

Steve Orr arrived at Khe Sanh a few days after I did. I never let Steve forget that he was "a boot to the bush," and he never missed the opportunity to remind me that he had been in Nam longer than I had. It was good to see him.

Orr was immediately assigned to mess duty, which lasted two weeks. It was long hours of tedious work, and he hated it. One benefit of his mess duty assignment, however, was his proximity to chow all the time. He brought back food at night from the mess hall to our tent, which made him an immediate favorite. Because of this, he was spared much of the early harassment that I—the foodless new guy—had to endure.

During this assignment, Orr became acquainted with Bill the Messman. Bill had survived the fighting on Hill 950 the previous June, and participated in the now legendary counterattack that drove the NVA back off the hilltop. Considered by everyone to be a bona-fide war hero, Bill the Messman was an unassuming and friendly guy, happy to remain on mess duty until his tour of duty in Vietnam ended and he could go home. Since he was so widely respected, we new guys watched and listened to him carefully, using him as a kind of a gauge to judge how we should act. By the end of December, Steve Orr had gotten out of mess duty and onto the radios down in the COC.

In early January 1968, I went to the Tactical Air Control Party (TACP), which we referred to simply as the "air team," and moved to the Fire Support Coordination Center (FSCC) in another part of the COC bunker. There, in addition to the TACP personnel, were officers and radio operators of the 13th Marines, our artillery battalion. In a small adjacent room, the regimental intelligence officer, Major Hudson, had set up shop.

Being an air team radio operator was desirable duty. This was because we worked for the Air Officer—typically a pilot doing his ground duty. Since the Marine Corps had more pilots than aircraft, it expected each pilot to perform six months of duty on the ground with a Marine unit—coordinating helicopter resupply and close-air support bombing. Pilots were often less "formal" than other officers, consequently the atmosphere on the air team was generally more relaxed.

I worked an all-night radio watch with another radioman, Raul "Oz" Orozco. Oz hailed from San Antonio, Texas, and had been at Khe Sanh

since the Hill Fights the previous spring. He immediately dubbed me "Nicky New Guy," which I considered a step up from the usual moniker applied to new arrivals— "FNG" (Fucking New Guy). Oz was helpful, easy going, and had a fine sense of humor. If he had a fault, it was his obsession with Patsy Cline, the famous country singer. He had only one tape of hers, Patsy Cline's "Greatest Hits," and he played it constantly. Oz spoke of her often, in the present

Raul "Oz" Orozco standing on the porch in front of Orr and Steve "Tiddy" Tidwell's bunker

tense, as if she were his sweetheart. I never asked him if he knew she had died five years earlier, and he never mentioned it.

Before the siege began, the air team radio operators worked closely with the helicopter pilots stationed at Khe Sanh. We tracked flights in and out of the area, and advised the aircraft in what part of the sky they would be in danger from our artillery fire. We coordinated the resupply of the hill outposts and dispatched medical evacuation choppers (medevacs). It was interesting work that provided us with a broad picture of what was going on in the countryside around us.

I recall how angry the U.S. Army SOG patrols would get when our aircraft would spot them. These patrols consisted mostly of indigenous forces, Montagnards or "mountain people," a primitive and tribal population who had lived until recently in the virtual isolation provided by their remote mountain homes, and Nung mercenaries, a Vietnamese minority group of ethnic Chinese descent with a reputation as fierce fighters. Our pilots often mistook them for the enemy and made passes in an attempt to strafe them. Occasionally, they actually attacked.

This problem grew worse through December and January, as their reconnaissance patrols pushed further into Laos to spy on the enemy build-up. Our aircraft would often broadcast the precise coordinates of these patrols back to us at the TACP in order to determine if they were friendly forces. We did not have this information because the Army would not tell us where they were operating. The danger to them was exacerbated because the enemy also had radios and carefully monitored our frequencies. Even if our aircraft did not fire on the SOG patrol, the NVA now had their exact location, and usually went after them.

There had been enmity between the Marines and Army since the first Marine units had arrived in Vietnam in 1965. Marines generally felt Army troops were undisciplined and pampered. The Marines had a saying in those days that an Army infantry soldier was "guaranteed three things when he got to Nam: a seat on a helicopter, a hot meal each day, and a Bronze Star." The latter rankled many of us, who returned home to see so many Army uniforms festooned with Bronze and Silver Stars. Among Marines, particularly enlisted men, it was rare to see such medals, and when they were awarded, it was often posthumously.

In the summer of 1967, as the new Lang Vei camp was under construction, the Army flew in high quality building materials from the United States for the project. Yet, back up the road a few miles at the Khe Sanh base, Marines had to build their own bunkers with green and bug-infested local lumber, and even that was subject to availability. This added to the animosity between the Marines and Army.

General Tompkins, commander of the 3rd Marine Division, was in charge of the entire area of operations, which included Khe Sanh and Lang Vei. He felt the conflict between the Army and Marines went deeper than jealousy over building materials. Tompkins commented that the SOG people were "hopped up" that is to say, on drugs. "There was something mysterious about these wretches," said Tompkins. "[They] were a law unto themselves."[3]

Despite the fact there were more Army troops than Marines in Vietnam, Marines died in higher proportions. Many Marines felt that if they had access to more modern equipment, as did the Army, they would have sustained far fewer casualties. Many in the Army, including General Westmoreland, who commanded all the U.S. forces in Vietnam, felt the Marines were over-rated and inefficient. They thought Marines died foolishly, employing high-risk tactics, such as frontal assaults on heavily fortified enemy positions, in order to show bravado. They thought it was our lack of imagination, rather than the often-limited supporting arms and aircraft that was the cause of such disproportionately high casualties.

This rift only deepened when Westmoreland called upon the Marines to dig in and defend the base at Khe Sanh. Most of our training was geared to the assault; we were neither psychologically nor materially prepared for defensive warfare. As a result, we were not always good at it.

Nearby, the enemy was patiently observing and incrementally moving more than 30,000 troops into the immediate area. Colonel David Lownds, the commanding officer of the 26th Marine Regiment, was growing desperate for intelligence information on their exact whereabouts. All indications pointed to the fact that they were now closing in on the base.

As early as November 1967, SOG patrols and Marine recon teams were reporting numerous signs of a large NVA presence in the area. They often found fresh elephant dung along the Xe Pon River. Both Montagnards and the NVA used elephants to transport heavy loads along the trails. The elephants often wallowed in the streams and rivers, and the iron-rich reddish mud would dry on their bodies. It was not uncommon to hear a chopper pilot hovering above some slow moving stream exclaim to an air team radioman, "I haven't had a drink in days, and yet I'm still seeing pink elephants!" Sadly, our pilots had orders to kill any elephants in the area that were not clearly the property of local civilians.

In late 1967, we radio operators began to hear Vietnamese chatter on several of our frequencies from the increasing enemy military radio traffic. As enemy troops in Laos began staging for battle, just a few miles to the west, thousands of Montagnards began to cross the Xe Pon and move closer to the base at Khe Sanh for protection. The modern machinery of war was about to forever change the way of life of these primitive people.

On January 18, 1968, General Westmoreland decided that the impending showdown at Khe Sanh was so important he would use his secret intelligence-gathering weapons: electronic sensors. These devices were so highly classified that only one officer in our entire regiment had ever even heard of them.[4]

Electronic
Sensors
show
enemy
movement

The development of this sensor technology came about as the result of a plan, championed by U.S. Defense Secretary Robert McNamara, to build an electronic barrier system across the width of South Vietnam, just below the DMZ. Rising Marine Corps combat casualties and the inability to stop enemy infiltration distressed the Secretary, causing him to lose confidence in the military. Perhaps he was also aware of the historical precedent set by the 17th century Nguyens, who had successfully used a wall across this part of the country to impede invaders from the North. McNamara envisioned Marines pulling back from their forward outposts along the DMZ, and letting electronic equipment monitor enemy movement. Once detected, the infiltrating forces would be easily annihilated by American artillery and air bombardment.

Before becoming secretary of defense, McNamara had been head of the Ford Motor Company and believed running a successful war was much like running a successful business. His conviction that technology could replace troops on the ground was matched in naïveté only by his confidence in the statistical certainty that a consistently favorable body count ratio was an indication of victory. The Pentagon eventually convinced McNamara of the defects in his plan, such as the ability of the NVA merely to walk around the "McNamara Line" in Laos, which they eventually did anyway.

Now that his plan was scrapped, the sensors were available for the impending defense of the Khe Sanh Combat Base. Air Force operatives had already been testing some of the sensors to monitor southbound truck traffic on the Ho Chi Minh Trail. The equipment was so good that Westmoreland received reports showing that 1,116 enemy trucks rolled past Khe Sanh in October 1967, 3,823 in November, and 6,315 in December.[5]

Spike-tipped seismic sensor devices dropped from helicopters stuck in the ground near precisely mapped locations along trails and roads. Whenever the enemy marched or drove by, the sensor picked up the vibration and transmitted the data. Acoustic sensors floated on parachutes into the trees near NVA base areas. Air Force technicians, in specially equipped airplanes high overhead, could turn these on by remote control and listen to enemy conversations. On one occasion, they picked up the excited voices of NVA soldiers who had spotted an acoustic sensor in a tree, the sound of a man climbing the tree to the encouraging chants of his comrades, and then his screams as he slipped and fell to the ground. The electronics within the sensor self-destructed if anyone tried to open the device.

Helicopters and low-flying, fixed-wing aircraft sowed more than 300 sensors around Khe Sanh in mid-January 1968. Because there was little time to train the Marines on this complex equipment, the Air Force continued to operate the detection system. A specially equipped Air Force EC-121 was always on station above Khe Sanh to receive signals from the sensors and transmit the information to a top-secret Infiltration Surveillance Center in Thailand. There, computers compared the incoming signals to data already on file in order to determine what caused the sensor to activate. This information was then relayed by encoded teletype to the Target Intelligence Officer (TIO) in the Fire Support Coordination Center at the Khe Sanh Combat Base.

Once seeded, the sensors immediately began broadcasting reports of enemy movement west and north of Khe Sanh. We then switched from our standard harassment and interdiction (H&I) artillery fire to artillery fire aimed at sensor-identified targets. I always thought that H&I fire was a curious thing. Typically, the artillery team at the FSCC desk would "guess" a likely spot along a trail or road, and randomly shoot some artillery at different times of the night. They were literally shooting in the dark hoping to hit something. Often the shells carried propaganda leaflets encouraging the enemy to surrender. I became increasingly amazed at our huge expenditure of ammunition, even before the siege began. About this time, I read an article in *Time* magazine reporting that it was costing the U.S. taxpayer $350,000 for each confirmed enemy killed. I believed it.

Expensive to engage in fighting

* * * *

During December and early January, Staff Sergeant Allen was sending the radiomen out on work details, despite the fact that we had been up all night on twelve-hour radio shifts. We were preparing for a major attack, there was much to do, and as such, our complaining was relatively subdued. One work detail involved removing debris from the old mortar pit across the road from the COC (The Pit, as it was called, would later become my home). It had been a dumpsite for several years.

As we removed one large piece after another, big, dark brown rats would scurry away. Sergeant Richardson stood with his entrenching tool at the ready, trying to smack them as they ran by. He was successful once, and as the stunned rat lay twitching on the ground, a Bru (pronounced Brew) tribeswoman came along and in sign language asked for the rat. She put it in the pocket of her thin, black quilted jacket, and took it home for dinner. Some of the Bru, a tribe of Montagnards that lived in nearby hamlets, were frequently trucked up to the base to do menial tasks. I was disgusted at the thought of someone eating rat, then a few weeks later, while living in the village and seeing how abjectly impoverished these people were, I understood better.

As Christmas approached, our intelligence reports were indicating a growing NVA presence in our area. The feeling of impending danger heightened my sense of homesickness. I wrote a letter to my parents that contained the latest rumors, one of which was that Soviet IL-28 heavy bombers had been flying close to the DMZ in preparation for a bombing run over Khe Sanh.

During this time, I often had to walk guard duty in the tent area. One of the things I was guarding was the mysterious "tropo" van, which contained sophisticated and highly classified communications technology capable of scattering radio waves into the troposphere (hence its name) for less distortion. A radio operator, always one with experience, sat inside it during the day. I only saw the inside once, but the one thing that stands out in my memory is that it had an old, dented electric coffeepot plugged into an array of otherwise high-tech electronics. It was kind of a secret place, even to the radio operators privileged to work within its cramped confines. The only information about it they would ever divulge, and this was unclassified, was that they could pick up stateside rock radio stations.

This type of guard duty was incredibly tedious, certainly not as interesting as guarding the south perimeter, in front of the garbage dump. There, at night, rock apes (so named because they would throw rocks at us when they were frightened) would troop in to scavenge for food. These lively primates had the habit of being noisy and looking, in silhouette, like diminutive humans. Their antics were amusing during the safer days, before the enemy began probing closer to our perimeter. Soon, however, it became no longer prudent to assume it was a merely rock ape out there pitching a stone and not an NVA soldier throwing a grenade. After sentries fired on the apes for a few nights, their visits to the dump became less frequent.

On Christmas Eve, I walked guard duty in the rain and mud, my poncho being of little help because the wind was whipping it up around my head. Later that night, during a break in the rain, our mortars sent red and green flares up above the base, illuminating everything in pale Christmas colors as they drifted on little parachutes down through the low cloud cover. It went on for several minutes, and it was beautiful. I wondered what the enemy nearby was thinking about it.

That night, Zeke, a fellow radio operator, ingested a variety of substances containing alcohol, including a couple of bottles of mouthwash. Sometime later, he fell into a refuse pit filled with discarded coils of barbed wire. The wind and rain that night prevented me from hearing his cries for help, and after struggling for a while he passed out. I discovered him the next morning, like a large, green elf ornament dangling in the tinsel.

Zeke has alcohol problem

Zeke's alcohol problem led to many such tribulations. The most famous, at least in the lore of the 26th Marines, occurred a few months before while he was at Camp Schwab on Okinawa waiting for his orders to Khe Sanh. One afternoon Zeke got drunk at the enlisted men's club and then staggered over to the camp recreational office and signed-out a two-man rubber raft. Dragging the raft down to the shore, Zeke boarded it and started rowing home, which as I recall was Chicago, Illinois. By the time he sobered up, Zeke was too far off shore to return. He drifted with the current overnight and well into the next day before a commercial fishing boat rescued him. Upon his return to Camp Schwab, the commanding officer chose not to take disciplinary action against Zeke; however, his orders for Khe Sanh were processed with curious expediency.

Christmas dinner at the Khe Sanh mess hall was not special, despite Bill the Messman's best efforts. I vaguely recall, though, liking the flavor of the Kool-Aid that day. Later that evening, I spent a lot of time weakly reassuring my parents in a letter home that I would be "just fine," with an occasional reminder that things "might get rough soon." I encouraged Mom not to worry. I'm sure that did the trick.

Bob Hope did not come to Khe Sanh that Christmas. In late December, however, General Chapman, the new Commandant of the Marine Corps, was supposed to visit us. He canceled at the last minute. All the regimental officers, including the commandant's son, a captain with 1st Battalion, 26th Marines, were down at the runway waiting for him when the radio message came in to the COC that General Chapman was not coming. I wish I could have been the one to deliver it—just to see everyone's "restrained" reactions. Many of us viewed his "no show" as an ominous sign; that the area was becoming too dangerous for important people.

An excerpt from a letter I sent home at the time relates my feelings about this.

> The commandant was supposed to be here yesterday but he canceled out at the last minute. The weather was the reason he gave. His son, Capt. Chapman, is stationed here at Khe Sanh with the 1st Battalion, 26 Marines. His daddy, however, told him to fly down to Dong Ha to meet him. How touching! The father is worried about flying in this weather so he has his son do it instead. Mrs. Chapman must be real nice, too.

Hanoi Hanna, the Vietnam War's version of Tokyo Rose, broadcasted on a civilian radio frequency out of North Vietnam. Between the jazz quartets and the marching bands, which her "un-hip" Marxist program manager evidently decided would keep us American boys glued to our transistor radios, Hanna dispensed defeatist propaganda in the confident, soothing, and slightly provocative manner of a Miss America contestant.

On New Years Eve, she played *Auld Lang Syne*, dedicating it to the "men of the 26th Regiment," then informed us that, "Ho Chi Minh will be celebrating Tet in the Khe Sanh mess hall." I think Bill the Messman, secretly took this as a compliment of his cooking ability. We all made our usual obscene comments about how we would go about shutting her up if we ever got the chance; but the personal nature of this threat made us all slightly uneasy.

Midnight was a repeat of Christmas Eve, with illumination crackling above the base. The next night, however, things got far more exciting.

In the early hours of January 2, 1968, a listening post, essentially a Marine hiding in the bushes, called the base to say that his scout dog had picked up a scent. A platoon from Lima Company, 3rd Battalion, 26th Marines was dispatched to investigate. After reaching the listening post, about 400 meters west of the runway, the platoon leader learned that six men had just walked past. The platoon followed in the direction the men had gone and soon came upon them standing together. The Marine platoon commander challenged them in English, but received no reply. When one of the men apparently raised a weapon, the Marines opened fire. The platoon moved back to the base to wait for sunrise. At dawn, they went back to the area and found five bodies. It appeared that maps and identification documents had been taken from the bodies, probably by the sixth man who was only wounded. Using the dog, they followed blood into a nearby tree line, but lost the trail after going about sixty meters.

Rumors spread that these men were wearing green U.S. Marine utility uniforms. Later, word was that they were wearing brand new NVA uniforms, probably indicating that they were recent arrivals in the South. North Vietnamese soldiers were usually issued new green or khaki uniforms when they were staging to go south. They seldom got new uniforms after that. After a while, you could almost tell the length of time an NVA soldier had been in South Vietnam by how bleached-out and uncoordinated his uniform looked, and by the quality of his last haircut.

One body was particularly tall and appeared to have different facial features than the others. Rumors abounded that he was Russian, Cuban, or East German. The body was flown to Dong Ha for a physical and dental examination. We never heard officially, though most people who saw the body believed he was Chinese. Nearly twenty years later, in May 1989, the China News Service reported that during the mid-to-late 1960s the People's Republic of China sent 320,000 troops to assist the NVA.[6] This is a huge number of soldiers and, if the report is accurate, they may have been regularly fighting against us.

It is likely some of the men killed by Lima Company on the morning of January 2 had been officers, and one of them may have been a regimental commander. There was no hard evidence to prove this, such as insignias of rank or identification documents, but the SOG indigenous troops, who routinely monitored nearby enemy radio frequencies, told our intelligence officers that the North Vietnamese network around Khe Sanh erupted in numerous and unusually anxious calls in the minutes after the shooting occurred.

Why would a high-ranking officer risk death or capture, and what kind of information did he think he could obtain by standing a few hundred meters from the end of our runway in the dark? The NVA were very careful in planning even the smallest action. They rehearsed specific attacks for weeks or even months in advance; meticulously pondering every detail, including the reaction time of our artillery and air support and the time it would take our reinforcements to reach the fighting. Given the inflexible chain of command in NVA units, these killings could not have had anything other than an adverse effect on their plan of attack.

A few days later, a Marine reconnaissance patrol made contact with the enemy near Hill 950. They captured one NVA soldier and moved quickly back to the LZ (landing zone). The prisoner was trying desperately not to keep up, so they dragged him much of the way.

Colonel Lownds and Major Hudson, the regimental Intelligence Officer, went to the airstrip to watch the prisoner arrive. They desperately needed first-hand information on enemy troop strength in our area. Just before the chopper arrived, the prisoner "fell" to his death from the door of the helicopter. We all knew he had been pushed. Colonel Lownds was furious about losing this potentially important source of intelligence, yet, as far as I know, ordered no investigation or disciplinary action against any of the recon Marines.

I recall laughing pitilessly with others about the fate of this NVA soldier. It was murder, of course, but we were arrogant—not only because we were Americans but because we knew we were going to win. Their pathetic attempts to fight us, their pointless sacrifices, all seemed a bit conceited to us. They asked for it.

It would not be long, however, before we would be on the receiving end of the enemy's often-superior firepower, and it would be a humbling experience. Humbling, not only because we could not stop them from shooting at us, but because, in a vague and annoying way, it was becoming

Do you believe U.S. should have been in Vietnam?

evident that we might never be able to stop them. Despite our clear technological advantages, they might still win the war.

There was little information in early 1968 about the structure of NVA units and their field operations. It wasn't until the early 1970s that a complete picture began to emerge, largely due to Rand Corporation "think tank" studies based on interviews with deserters and interrogations of POWs.

According to Michael Lanning and Dan Cragg, in their book *Inside the VC and NVA*, by 1967 most NVA soldiers were draftees. Draft deferments were granted for the physically disabled, only sons, and individuals who could prove they were the principal support of families. Party officials, students, and technicians with special skills could also be deferred. The children of Communist Party officials often received student exemptions, and in many cases were sent to the safety of another country to study. North Vietnamese Army soldiers trained in conventional small unit infantry tactics and weapons training. Their basic training, like ours, lasted about two months, with some of them going on to specialized schools such as radio communications.

Although Hanoi's propaganda would later depict all the soldiers who went south as being volunteers, POWs and deserters told a different story. Most did not want to leave their homes and families. Their superiors often told them they were going to a staging area or on a training mission. Only after they were far from familiar surroundings did they learn that they were on the way to South Vietnam.

Comparison between NVA + U.S. soldiers

NVA troops were subject to intense indoctrination regarding the reasons they were going. Political cadres told them that the Americans had occupied South Vietnam, that they were going there to liberate their countrymen, and that if they did not fight the Americans now, they would have to fight them in the North. This was not very different from what the American servicemen were told: it is better to stop communism in Asia than closer to home. Once an NVA soldier arrived in the South, he could expect to be there for the duration of the war. Now dependent on his fellow soldiers, he had a different outlook than did U.S. troops, who knew exactly what day they would be returning home.

Supervision of NVA soldiers was intense. The basic organizational unit was the "cell," which consisted of three people. Political cadres were assigned at every level. The close brotherhood established by this bond, plus the pervasive criticism and self-criticism, usually kept the correct behavior. Three cells comprised a squad, three squads a platoon, three platoons a company, and so on up the line.

The NVA ate mostly rice, supplemented by what they could forage, hunt, and buy or appropriate from the locals. Contrary to the popularly held American belief that the NVA were natural jungle fighters, most recruits came from the metropolitan Hanoi/Haiphong area or from the rice farms along the Red River and South China Sea. The average North Vietnamese had no reason to enter the jungle.

Most of their difficulties occurred from disease and obstacles of nature. Of all the dangers in the jungle, snakes perhaps received the most notice for the least cause. Although poisonous snakes were common in the jungles and rice paddies, none were aggressive, and practically all species did their best to avoid humans. Accounts of soldiers on either side being bitten by snakes were rare; yet fear of such attacks was a real danger in itself. It was not uncommon for the NVA and VC to imprudently light torches while on night marches, often tipping off their location to our recon teams.

Besides American bombers, the most threatening danger along the Ho Chi Minh Trail was mosquitoes. Although issued malaria pills containing much of the same ingredients as those used by the Americans, NVA soldiers contracted the disease more frequently. This was largely due to shortages of the pills, which had to be taken regularly to be effective.

Many of the infiltrators who made it the length of the Trail were surprised to find that much of the propaganda to which they had been exposed was incorrect and that the South Vietnamese people were ready to fight them when they arrived. Instead of being welcomed as liberators, they quickly had to adjust to the truth of the situation: that there was a high risk they would be wounded or killed and that it might be years before they could return to their villages and families.

Despite this, the NVA continued to fight. Some areas of the Trail were reported to be two feet deep in *chieu-hoi* (amnesty) leaflets, dropped there by U.S. aircraft. Their political officers, of course, ordered their people not to read the leaflets. Those who did learn about the surrender program were generally not interested. Many feared reprisals against their families in the North, but most stayed out of loyalty to their fellow soldiers.[7]

We grudgingly considered the NVA soldier to be a worthier opponent than the Viet Cong, who we referred to as "Charlie" (from Victor Charlie, the phonetic alphabet letters for VC). For the NVA, we often used the more respectful "Charles," or "Mr. Charles." If time and experience embittered you enough and the naïveté of your friends and family aggravated you more with each passing mail call, you might one day hear yourself talking about "Charles" as if he was one of the few people in the world who really understood you. You still wanted him dead, of course, but there was no satisfaction. It was simply a requirement of survival.

There was little mercy shown on either side. One of the few documented instances of interaction on the battlefield occurred near Pleiku in 1967. Although it resulted in saving lives, this incident appears to be more an example of exhaustion than of mutual respect. On a steep mountainside, a company of the U.S. 25th Infantry Division was battling an NVA unit of similar size. A driving monsoon rain prevented the Americans from calling in air support. The intense fighting resulted in heavy casualties on both sides. During a brief moment of relative calm, one of the Americans shouted, "Hey, you sons of bitches, you quit fucking with us and we'll quit fucking with you!" Someone on the other side apparently understood English and shouted a quick translation to his comrades. Without further word, the shooting ceased. Both sides gathered their dead and wounded, and withdrew.[8]

Late one night in early January, Colonel Lownds could not sleep and came into the COC. He lit up a cigar, sat down in his old, canvas lawn chair and stared at the Big Map. Soon the colonel was absently twirling one end of his handlebar moustache. There was no one else in the room but Orr and me, dutifully sitting at our radios. Suddenly, as if some hidden yet obvious fact had miraculously become clear, the colonel announced to no one in particular, "We're slowly getting surrounded."

We both heard him. I glanced sideways at Orr and rolled my eyes in an effort to mask my anxiety. Lownds, I would later learn, had survived the nightmare of Iwo Jima, so had no illusions about how bad things could get. On

Colonel Lownds entering the Combat Operations Center (COC)

the other hand, I could not imagine just how bad things were about to become. Still, for months thereafter, during the worst of times when we
needed a good laugh at the irony of our situation, Orr and I would lam-
poon the colonel by twirling our imaginary mustaches and grimly muttering, "We're slowly getting surrounded."

* * * *

Steve Orr sitting in his chair and twirling his imaginary
mustache in imitation of Colonel Lownds. Over his
right shoulder is the Khe Sanh Officer's Club. Over his
left shoulder is the "state-of-the-art" bunker he shared
with Steve "Tiddy" Tidwell

Golf

The Village

★ ★ ★

At 0600 on January 12, 1968, as I was preparing to end my radio watch, Staff Sergeant Allen ordered me to pack my gear and prepare to leave for the Combined Action Company Oscar (CAC-O) in Khe Sanh Village. I put some items in a duffel bag and said my good-byes. By 0900 I was in a Jeep that had joined three vehicles including a large truck heading down to the village.

This little convoy was part of the Medical Civil Affairs Program, or MEDCAP, designed to bring regular medical attention to the villagers as part of the rural pacification strategy. One Jeep contained a medical team, including a doctor. The MEDCAP convoy also brought supplies and mail to the CAC Marines.

With us was Steve "Tiddy" Tidwell, a fellow radio operator from the Headquarters Company. An Alabaman, Tiddy was an honest, easy-going guy who always seemed to be in a good mood. He had a pronounced lisp, so he was always easily identifiable on the radio. It wasn't an effeminate lisp, more like Daffy Duck. Doc Topmiller, the Headquarters Company corpsman, loved telling the story of how Tiddy came to him, once, with what turned out to be hemorrhoids. "Thay Doc," said Tiddy, "I've got thum bumpths on my ath."

The 26th Marines had been supplying the CAC with radio operators who rotated back to the base every two weeks. Only one radio operator went to the village on the last trip, and it had not worked out very well. In fact, the CAC commander had sent the man back to the base. One night a few weeks earlier, the NVA and VC attempted to sneak into the district headquarters compound with the help of a local insider. The plan was for the enemy to lob several mortar rounds into the compound. While everyone scurried for cover, the traitor would remove his clothes so the attackers could easily identify him. He would then open the front gate to let them in.

The mortar shells exploded in the compound right on schedule and the naked man pushed open the gate and waited. Inexplicably, the enemy did not show up and the turncoat was quickly arrested. I never found out what happened to him. I did ask a Marine who was there at the time, whether the man was just shirtless or completely naked. The Marine insisted he was stark naked and speculated that he may have discarded additional clothing in an effort to "insure" that the NVA attackers were clearly aware "he was their man."

Most of the CAC Marines found the incident amusing, but a radioman on loan from the base did not. Believing they were under attack, he suffered what one Marine described as "a nervous breakdown." The radio operator was medevaced back to the base. Because of his behavior, some members of the CAC would immediately mistrust Tiddy and me as soon as we arrived.

After departing the base by the main gate, our convoy proceeded down past the garbage dump. The road was extremely rutted, the ride slow and bumpy. The ruts did not diminish much even after we intersected with Route 9, the national "highway" across this part of Vietnam. I was sitting on the passenger side of the third Jeep worrying about mines and ambushes. I knew that there was increased enemy activity throughout the area. The base was "slowly getting surrounded" and I had no idea when or if I would ever get back. I was scared.

I had my M-16 rifle across my lap, diddling the safety. As we entered a coffee plantation, I caught some movement out of the corner of my right eye. Standing beside the road, less than six feet away, was a Bru woman with a large, dark red bandanna wrapped around her head. She was holding a machete. A tree had blocked my view of her until she was almost beside me. It was lucky for her that my reaction time was so slow. I was so jumpy I could easily have blown her away before I realized she was a civilian.

A little farther down the road, we passed the "Frenchman's" house. It was an old, two-story villa with yellowing plaster walls partially obscured by black, creeping vines. The Frenchman, Eugene Poilane, had settled in the area in 1918. Born in France in 1888 just five years after French Colonial rule in Indo-China began, Poilane began military service in that region in 1909. Later, as a botanical explorer, he traveled by foot to the far regions of the Vietnam-China border and returned with thousands of botanical specimens.

Poilane established the coffee plantation at Khe Sanh in 1922 as well as an experimental garden where he planted various fruit trees and vegetables to test their suitability in the soil there. In January 1954, a guerrilla army established by the charismatic Vietnamese nationalist Ho Chi Minh, annihilated a large force of French Legionnaires moving against their stronghold at Lao Bao—less than ten miles from the Poilane plantation. About that time, Poilane received serious shrapnel injuries during a Viet Minh mortar attack but survived.

By the early 1960s, the inhabitants of the Khe Sanh Valley knew Poilane simply and affectionately as "Papa." His coffee trees were now abundant and though his advancing years had slowed him down, he still would go out and inspect the orchards daily. In so doing, he discovered that defoliant sprayed in nearby Laos by the CIA seemed to be causing certain fruit trees to cease producing. He filed a claim for which the Americans paid damages, but corrupt South Vietnamese officials kept it all for themselves. ~~Story of Frenchmen~~

In 1964, the seventy-six-year-old Eugene Poilane was assassinated by the Viet Cong, gunned down one night while driving on the same stretch of road I was now bumping along on my way to the village.[9] His estranged widow, Madame Bordeauducq, and their son, Felix, continued to operate the plantation. Madame Bordeauducq, a rugged and independent woman, married Eugene in the 1920s, but refused to take the Poilane name. Now in her nineties, she was regarded as a fearless pioneer. It was said that she had shot more than forty tigers over the years, often by hiding in a tree at night. "I don't like to shoot the tigers," she once explained, "but they eat up my peasants."[10]

Our MEDCAP convoy continued down the road for another several hundred meters toward a narrow bridge, which crossed the river on the east side of the village. About 250 meters to the south was the old French fort, which immediately excited my curiosity. Almost entirely walled in, the ponderous mass of dark-colored concrete sat on a slight rise and appeared to be something from another age.

As we crossed the bridge, I viewed the village for the first time. To my right was a soccer field partially surrounded by stone structures for seating. The dwellings near the field and back along the river were mostly wooden shacks. About one-half mile away was a small hamlet on the side of Hill 471. It was quite scenic with nearly all the thatched dwellings on stilt

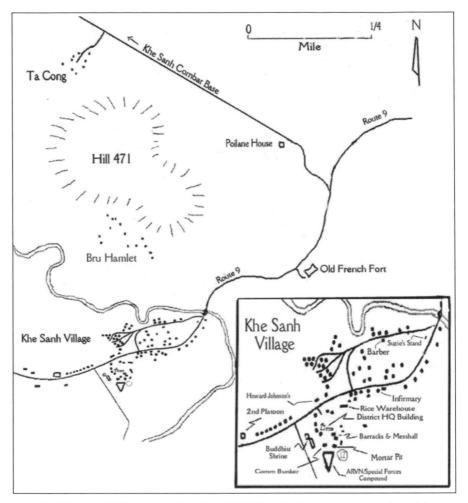

Detail of Khe Sanh Village, Bru Hamlet, AVRN Special Forces compound, and the old French fort in relation to Hill 471   *Michael Archer*

foundations. The hillside, unlike the surrounding area, was clear of most tall vegetation and completely covered with light-green grass.

After crossing the bridge, the road turned to the right into the main part of the village. There, a young Vietnamese woman named Suzie operated a small wooden kiosk that contained magazines, newspapers, and soft drinks. Suzie could not walk, so she lay on a pallet behind the stand. Rumor had it that she had been paralyzed as the result of an exploding land mine placed in the road by the VC. She was friendly, fluent in English, and quite attractive in her flowing pastel *ao dai* dress, a body-hugging, floor-length gown with high side splits over wide billowing trousers.

The Huong Hoa District Headquarters compound on Route 9 in the Khe Sanh Village prior to the NVA attack of January 21, 1968

Courtesy Ray W. Stubbe

The main street of the village, actually a dusty stretch of Route 9 about three city blocks long, was comprised of mostly single story stucco or cinder block buildings, many with wooden awnings. Our destination, the district headquarters compound, known more formally as Huong Hoa District Headquarters, was located at the west end of the village. Across the street from the district headquarters sat a long wooden shack. This was the local brothel, amusingly referred to by everyone as "Howard Johnson's."

The district headquarters complex was roughly triangular shaped with one side along Route 9 and one side parallel to a Buddhist shrine and school just to the west. The base of this triangle, about 200 meters in length, ran southwest from a rice storehouse on Route 9 to the end of the Army Special Forces compound. Stacked coils of razor wire and beds of low-strung barbed wire called "tanglefoot" surrounded the district head-quarters compound. Bunkers and covered fighting holes were located at intervals along the perimeter.

As we drove into the compound, a large courtyard of pounded earth was to our left. Upon it was a platoon of Bru Provincial Forces (PF) arranged in a semblance of a military formation. The district headquarters building was directly in front of the driveway. It was a massive construction of stone blocks and stucco in the French colonial style, with high ceilings and a large verandah. In front of it was a twelve-foot-high sandbag tower, on top of which stood a .50-caliber machine gun. Next to it was another large building with a long portico. This building housed the administrative offices and barracks of the Provincial Forces.

Although most of them had family near the village, the Bru PFs trained here during the day. Some stayed at night to be available for patrols and ambushes or to stand guard duty. The CAC at Khe Sanh Village was the only location in the entire country where Montagnards were organized as a military unit. It was as much a social experiment as a military one.

Once out of the Jeep, I walked down an alleyway between two large buildings that led to the area behind the headquarters. There I found several other structures: a small barracks for the Marines, mess hall, mortar pit, and showers. Behind these was a small helicopter landing zone. The comm (communications) bunker, where I would stand radio duty, was located directly behind the district headquarters building and about twenty meters from the barbed wire fence forming the west side of the compound. Only half of the bunker was below ground, and it was topped by a corrugated metal roof. The interior was divided into two rooms separated by about ten feet of empty space. The room to the left was for the Army Special Forces radio operators, the one on the right for the Marines.

Contiguous to the south side of the Marine compound was the U.S. Army Special Forces compound. There, two platoons of the ARVN 915th Regional Forces Company lived with Captain Clarke and three other American soldiers. This compound, self-contained and more heavily barbed-wired than the Marine's, was surrounded by a shallow trench filled with *punji* stakes (sharpened bamboo spikes). One entered the Special Forces compound by passing through a narrow opening in the barbed wire next to the comm bunker.

The Special Forces main force was located four miles farther down the road at Lang Vei. In addition, Forward Operations Base Three (FOB-3), another Special Forces group, had moved out of the old French fort in November and was now located just outside the main gate of the Khe Sanh Combat Base. Colonel Lownds did not trust the indigenous troops the Special Forces led, believing some might turn on us as had been done the previous May at Lang Vei. So, he ordered the repositioning of several Marine tanks to an area between FOB-3 and the rest of the base.

The animosity between the Marine and Army personnel in the village was immediately apparent. You could clearly read the look of disdain on their faces when crossing paths with them. To complicate things, the Vietnamese Regional Forces (RFs) despised the Montagnards. The village defense personnel were riddled with cultural, ethnic, and, in the case of the U.S. forces, interservice enmity.

The Marine presence consisted of three platoons of the Combined Action Company Oscar (CAC-O). They had arrived the preceding February with the mission to train civilians and indigenous troops to defend their village from the Communists and in the process win their "hearts and minds" for the government of South Vietnam.

It fell upon the CAC 1st Platoon (CAP-01) to defend the district headquarters compound. The CAC 2nd Platoon (CAP-02) established a small perimeter of its own just west of the Buddhist shrine on the north side of the highway. The CAC 3rd platoon (CAP-03) was located at Ta Cong hamlet, near the main gate of the Khe Sanh Combat Base.

I had expected the village fortifications to be as good or even superior to those back at the base. Lance Corporal Mike Reath, a fellow air team radio operator at Khe Sanh base, had been on several truck convoys from the base to help guard Naval Construction Battalion workers who were building the new Lang Vei camp in the summer of 1967. He had often regaled me and the other new arrivals with stories about Lang Vei, which he and many others considered the most impregnable fortification in Vietnam. Deep, reinforced concrete bunkers ringed the new camp. Minefields,

tangle-foot, and piles of coiled, razor-sharp, barbed wire confronted a potential attacker who, if he made it past all of that, would then have to scale
a ten-foot-high chain link fence. They installed powerful generators and
electric lights flooded the perimeter each night. Reath once summed it up
in his most colorful New Jersey hyperbole. "The place could survive a
fuckin' atom bomb," he said.

Yet, the district headquarters compound was nothing like Reath's description of Lang Vei. There seemed to be less preparation for an attack in
the village than back up at the base. A few additional sandbags were filled
and occasionally the barbed wire was inspected to see if it had been "pre-
cut." The mood was almost relaxed in comparison to the base; yet even to
me, a new guy, the defenses seemed inadequate. For example, the gate
used each night to block the driveway into the district headquarters compound was nothing more than a ten-foot-long wooden sawhorse with
some barbed wire wrapped around it.

The Marine CAC commander was Lieutenant Stamper. He had recently arrived to replace Lieutenant Elmore, wounded during the mortar
attack a few weeks earlier. This wound was his third since arriving in Vietnam and, according to regulations, he could be sent home. Ironically,
Lieutenant Elmore was sent to the CAC at Khe Sanh Village after receiving his second wound—because it was considered a quieter place!

With the arrival of Tiddy and me, the 1st Platoon had three radio operators. Lance Corporal Wolverton, the permanent CAC radio operator,
took the morning radio watch. Tiddy stood watch from 1400 until 2300.
Because I was lowest in seniority, I got the graveyard watch from 2300 to
0600.

Things were quiet for our first nine days. Most mornings Tiddy and I
would walk around in the village—always well armed. One day we went to
get haircuts in the marketplace down by the river. The shop was merely an
open-air wooden booth with a wobbly stool in the center. I became a little
nervous when the barber started giving me the "deluxe" treatment, which
included putting a sharp bamboo skewer into my ear to remove the wax.
Concerned that he might be a VC by night, I told Tiddy to shoot the barber if he saw the stick coming out the other side of my head.

One morning we set out on Route 9 to explore the old French fort at
the other end of the village. Halfway there we saw a group of young Vietnamese men standing on the road ahead of us. They became visibly nervous as we approached. Just then, several kids came running up behind us
begging for food and cigarettes. I often carried some graham crackers
from the mess hall to give to them. This distracted Tiddy and me for a

moment and when we turned back around, the men had vanished. The whole sequence of events gave us a creepy feeling, so we immediately returned to our compound, looking back over our shoulders the entire time.

Most of the dwellings in the village were small shacks constructed of stone, wood, tin, thatched reeds, or a combination of these materials. The houses near Route 9 were solidly constructed, clean, and well lit. Down the side streets leading to the river, the dwellings were shabbier and less sturdy. The interiors were often dark single rooms containing mangy dogs, crying children, and bad smells. The numerous cooking fires smoldering within these little houses enveloped the neighborhoods in a perpetual haze.

Khe Sanh Village was the largest population center in this part of the country. About 1,300 Vietnamese lived there. In addition, approximately 20,000 Montagnards of the Bru tribe lived in the vicinity. About two million Montagnards inhabited the Annamite Mountains chain, which extended from China south to the low foothills near Cambodia. The Bru tribe of Montagnards consisted of only about 30,000. Ten years earlier, the new South Vietnamese Army went into the mountains and rounded up all the Bru they could find, forcing them to resettle in hamlets near the village. Montagnards, whose dark skin was considered a social stigma in Vietnamese society (both South and North), were looked upon as racial inferiors. Consequently, the Vietnamese would not allow the Bru to live within Khe Sanh Village.

The Bru historically subsisted by practicing a primitive slash-and-burn form of agriculture, clearing patches of jungle to grow rice and vegetables. When the soil became exhausted after a year or two, they would simply move. Because fish and game were so abundant in the region, they never faced starvation. But once resettled, the Bru were largely dependent on the French growers in the valley for employment. The Vietnamese shopkeepers routinely cheated the Bru out of the rice they earned on the coffee plantation. Montagnards were simple, trusting people who had difficulty understanding the reason for this behavior. Their conclusion was that "the Vietnamese have two gall bladders."[11] Now squeezed into this confined area by the mounting dangers of war, they struggled to survive. Despite the fact that many Bru now had rifles, it was common to see them still out hunting with their traditional crossbows.

The relocation of the Bru was ostensibly to protect them; but a major concern of the South Vietnamese government was to keep them from aiding the North. Although they had never known national borders before, the Bru ancestral lands were now divided into parts of three separate countries: Laos, South Vietnam, and North Vietnam. Straddling what had come to be known as the Ho Chi Minh Trail, the Bru homeland would eventually suffer the most concentrated destruction of the war and near extinction of the tribe.

It had already been a bad year for the Bru. Nine months earlier, on March 2, 1967, two U.S. Air Force fighter-bombers inexplicably attacked the village of Lang Vei with napalm. One hundred and sixteen Bru died, 200 were wounded. Some walked all the way to the base, about six miles, with pieces of burned flesh hanging from them. Bodies lay on the runway for two days. "That's another Khe Sanh smell that will never leave me," said a Marine who was there.

Private First Class Whiting, the CAC cook and grenadier, would occasionally take some of the Bru down to the river for hand grenade fishing. He would find a wide, slow spot in the river and toss in a hand grenade. A few seconds after the muffled explosion, big dun-colored fish would slowly rise to the surface and the Bru men would run excitedly into the water after them.

Whiting did not live in the small barracks with the rest of the Marines. Instead, he resided alone in a tiny sandbagged cell adjoining the west exterior wall of the comm bunker. He was a friendly guy, mostly a loner and slightly crazy. During the mortar attack a few weeks earlier, Whiting, whose little bunker doorway faced directly across from the Buddhist shrine, stepped outside and launched a couple of M-79 grenades onto the roof of that building. The shrine, one of the largest structures in the village, was perhaps twenty-five feet high with a large sloping tile roof. Whiting's grenades blew off some of the tiles. The congregation immediately lodged a protest with the District Advisory officials. Upon his arrival, one of Lieutenant Stamper's first duties was to reprimand Whiting and formally apologize to the priest. Whiting chuckled after telling us this story. He said he knew the NVA would put a machine gun up there some night and had just been using the enemy mortar attack to adjust the grenade launcher's range to the shrine's rooftop.

Whiting told Tiddy and me about another strange event that had happened on a night patrol a few weeks earlier. Less than two miles southeast of the village, in an otherwise uninhabited area, an electric light, much like a vehicle headlight, came on right in front of the patrol. They began shooting at the light, which he believed to be about fifty meters away. None of the shots or Whiting's M-79 grenades extinguished it. Whiting was sure he had heard numerous metallic sounds—like hits on metal and ricochets. The patrol immediately returned to the district headquarters compound and sent a report to the base commander about what they believed to be an enemy tank in the area. As far as Whiting knew, no response to this intelligence information came back to outposts. Three weeks after Whiting told us this story, the NVA launched a surprise attack just four miles down the road against the Special Forces camp at Lang Vei—with ten Soviet-made tanks.

* * * *

On January 14, 1968, the Oakland Raiders, my hometown team, played the invincible Green Bay Packers in Superbowl II. I was out not only of TV range but beyond the range of Armed Forces radio, as well. I lamented this in a letter home.

> I'll be back at the base in another week. It'll be better. I like it more when there are 1,100 Marines instead of just 11. Not that I don't trust the ARVNS, just that blood is thicker than water.
>
> P.S. I had to reopen this letter. It's 0430 on the 15th. I'm on radio watch now and my friend (Orr) up at the base is relaying the score of the Superbowl game over my network. The score is 3 to 0 Green Bay. I don't think I want to hear anymore. At least I know what you're doing right now.

The next night, I made a terrible mistake. I fell asleep while on radio watch. I remember trying hard to stay awake, but there was little space to walk around in the poorly ventilated, eight-by-twelve foot radio room. The last thing I recall was reading aloud from a book, hoping the sound of my own voice would keep me alert.

The next thing I knew, I was awakened by the shout of an angry corporal rushing through the door. He had just returned from a night patrol and had radioed to advise me they were coming into the district headquarters compound. It was a very dangerous situation for them, and I should have been awake to acknowledge the call. He chewed me out for several minutes and then left the bunker. I had no excuse for what I had done and felt awful.

When my radio shift ended, I went to the mess hall for some chow, then to the barracks to get some sleep. As I slid into my sleeping bag, I felt something round, hard, and metallic touching my bare toe. When I reached down and took hold of the object, I knew immediately it was a hand grenade. Fortunately, the pin was still in place. It was a message I understood at once. I had played right into the distrust the CAC Marines already had for the radiomen from the base. Never having been accepted by the group anyway, except for the obsequious Bru houseboy and Whiting, who was slightly crazy, my life in the district headquarters compound did not change appreciably after this event—though I slept much more lightly.

Three days later, on January 19, I completed my radio watch and did not even stop by the mess hall for morning chow. This was the day Tiddy and I were scheduled to return to the base. I went directly to the barracks to pack my gear. Tiddy was lying on his cot, his belongings still scattered about on the shelves and pegs above him on the wall. I excitedly reminded him that the MEDCAP convoy would be heading down here soon and he had better start practicing his good-byes. Tiddy was, like me, a recent arrival in Vietnam, but had been in the Corps about a year longer, so was more tuned into the subtleties of our current situation. He asked me if I had been listening to the red alert drills coming from the base each night that week over the base defense radio network, or if I had noticed the increased frequency of the CAC and Army patrols. He wondered if I had seen the number of Bru PFs sticking around the district headquarters compound each night to staff the perimeter. I told him I had not.

Then he made a point so compelling that even I immediately understood it. Why did Staff Sergeant Allen send two of the newest guys in the regiment (rather than more experienced radio operators) to the village at a time when enemy activity in the area was clearly increasing? Before I could answer, Tiddy did. "Because," he said, "he knew it was going to be the last convoy."

Tiddy then put his boots on and went to the mess hall for breakfast. Unnerved but undeterred by his negative take on our predicament, I packed up my belongings, walked the short distance to the main gate, and waited. I looked up that road for several hours, but the convoy did not appear; in fact, no vehicles of any kind came by. I finally picked up my gear and trudged over to the comm bunker, where I borrowed the radio handset from Wolverton and contacted the base to find out the status of the MEDCAP convoy. About twenty minutes later, I received a brief response to my question. "The convoy has been cancelled." There would be, I knew now, no more trips to the base. Immediately, I recognized that I had never been faced with a problem quite this serious before in my young life.

That afternoon, a young Bru man walked into the district headquarters compound wearing only red shorts. He informed us of an NVA platoon that had recently crossed the highway only a few hundred meters to the west. They had taken almost everything from him, including his clothes and sandals. It was unusual for the enemy to expose themselves in broad daylight, especially so close to a U.S. position. Everyone was nervous.

Lieutenant Stamper ordered the big truck loaded with Marines and PFs, then raced off down the road. It seemed quite reckless to me at the time, as it could have easily been a set up for an ambush.

The front of the compound was now deserted except for PFC Brown and me. It was ominously quiet and we were feeling defenseless. The driveway into the compound was wide open; any number of enemy troops could have easily walked in. I cursed Stamper for his impetuousness. Suddenly a bugle sounded from somewhere in the village. I had never heard it before, nor had I recalled the use of a bugle by any of the local forces in the vicinity. Again, the foreboding silence prevailed.

We decided to go over to the sandbag tower in front of district headquarters building. We climbed the ladder up to the top and sat behind the .50-caliber machine gun, which pointed straight out the driveway at the Howard Johnson's. Nothing happened. Eventually the truck returned. They had not made contact or even seen any evidence of NVA troop movements. Stamper began questioning the validity of the young Bru's story.

Reports from the base would soon make him a believer. An hour later and less than two miles from the spot where the enemy soldiers had crossed the road, the NVA were engaged in a skirmish with a Marine patrol from India Company, 3rd Battalion, 26th Marines. The next day, the men of India Company would find themselves fighting even more enemy—an entire NVA battalion. A dozen Marines and about 125 NVA died in those two days of fighting. Yet, even this was just a warm-up for bigger things to come.

About an hour after Lieutenant Stamper and his truckload of Marines and PFs returned to the district headquarters compound, I returned to the front gate to see if anything new was happening. PFC Brown was still there, standing near a truck with its engine idling. I did not recognize the three men in the cab, but they all appeared to be Americans. One of them told me they were heading up to the base and would take my mail if I went and got it quickly. They were in a big hurry to get there before dark. The events of the day, including the presence of these slightly agitated men in the truck, made it clear to me just how desperate our situation was becoming. Though I sensed this was going to be the last truck out of the valley, a feeling of despair suddenly weighed me down and prevented me from penning a quick, and possibly a last, note to the folks.

As the truck began to pull away, PFC Brown ran after it and jumped on the back. The act seemed driven purely by impulse, but he must have immediately recognized he was deserting us because he never looked back. I watched the truck accelerate through the village until it disappeared in a dusty cloud and continued to watch until the cloud of dust disappeared, as well. I had mixed feelings watching him go. Part of me wanted to be on that truck, too.

The battle India Company had just fought that day, less than two miles from us, finally prompted more serious defensive preparations around the district headquarters compound. We set out a dozen more Claymore mines. Each of these devices fired 700 steel balls in a fan shape toward the enemy, detonated by an electrical plunger held by a defender. The mines were set in close to the wire because enemy sappers (soldiers specially trained to undermine defenses) often snuck in and turned them around so they would shoot back into the defenders. We did not put any of these mines out in the front of the compound, to avoid civilian injuries on the other side of the street.

On the afternoon of January 20, many of us assembled at the edge of the LZ to test fire our weapons. The CAC had one 81mm mortar. The mortar man was a tall, easy-going black guy whose name I never learned; so we simply called him "Mortarman." I was sitting in the mortar pit while he was attempting to see how close to our barbed wire he could place the rounds. The wire was only about thirty meters away. He said he was "pretty sure that Mr. Charles would be close tonight" and that by the time we knew he was there, "I won't have time to do no aiming." So, he kept turning the elevation dial until it appeared that the mortar tube was pointing straight up. He seemed a little apprehensive as he dropped a shell down the tube, saying, "Well here goes nuthin'."

Because I was right next to the mortar, I could clearly watch the projectile launch out of the tube. It appeared to be going straight upward until it disappeared against the pale blue sky. The trajectory made me believe that the shell was going to drop right back down on the tube. Still, I didn't want Mortarman to think I had no confidence in him, so I waited uncomfortably for a few more seconds. Mortarman suddenly took off running for a nearby bunker. With that, I started running too. The round exploded about forty meters away, in the center of the LZ. "Just where I aimed it!" he exclaimed with total confidence as he reemerged from the bunker.

After Mortarman completed the adjustments on his weapon, the rest of us fired our rifles and pistols. We stood in line in the LZ, leisurely shooting out into the woods. The South Vietnamese RFs and Montagnard PFs had an assortment of old weapons, some dating from World War II, like Browning Automatic Rifles (BARs) and M-1s. These old rifles had been designed for soldiers of larger physical stature than the Vietnamese and

Montagnards who were generally not much over five feet tall and quite lean (though surprisingly sturdy). It was amusing to watch them lugging around a fifteen-pound BAR or trying to shoot an M-1 whose stock always seemed too long for their arms.

An RF standing next to me was shooting an M-1 carbine, which is a smaller and lighter version of the M-1 rifle, coveted by the indigenous troops. I was familiar with the M-1 rifle because we had used them in ITR, but this was the first time I had seen the carbine version of the weapon. Using pidgin and hand gestures, I told the ARVN I liked it. He immediately wanted to trade it for my M-16. I really wanted that old carbine, but the deal he proposed was preposterous. Perhaps the Bru were right: maybe the Vietnamese do have two gall bladders.

Whiting was there with his M-79 grenade launcher. This weapon looks like a stubby shotgun and shoots an explosive round shaped like a large, fat bullet. The M-79 grenade launcher acquired the nickname "Blooper" because the trajectory and range are similar to the type of hit in baseball called by the same name. We all had fun shooting it, until Whiting put things in perspective. "That pea-shooter," he said, "won't stop no tank."

As much as I came to respect Lieutenant Stamper, I could never understand why he let us expend so much ammunition that afternoon. Looking back, I find it amazing how calmly we went about our business that day, fully cognizant that hundreds, maybe thousands, of enemy soldiers were rapidly closing in on our tiny force.

Later in the afternoon, Corporal Verner Russell showed Tiddy and me where our fighting positions would be if we were not on radio watch at the time of the attack. I was to man an old World War II vintage, .30-caliber machine gun located in a small bunker on the east side of the district headquarters compound. Russell gave me a cursory explanation of how the machine gun worked and how the ammo belt was loaded and removed. I didn't practice firing it, however, because some houses in the village were about fifty meters in front of the gun position. With so few men available to defend the perimeter, no one would be assigned to assist me. About twenty meters outside the wire, and directly in front of that bunker, was a fifty-five gallon drum of aviation fuel mixed with naphtha (essentially homemade napalm). Russell instructed me to wait until the enemy was near the drum and then shoot at it. The hot tracer bullets from the machine gun would ignite the contents.

After Corporal Russell completed my instruction on the old machine gun, he took Tiddy to the west side of the compound, which adjoined the little cemetery that lay between the Buddhist shrine and our barbed wire perimeter. I sat alone in the little sandbag bunker for about twenty minutes, fiddling with the gun bolt and nervously opening and closing the metal ammo boxes nearby. I stared out over the gun sight, past the piles of coiled of barbed wire, into the village. The longer I looked, the more houses I noticed among the trees and undergrowth. I was soon overcome with the childish and irrational notion that, if I just sat there and did not move from that safe and quiet spot, nothing bad would happen.

I might have tested that theory longer, but I had to go on radio watch. As luck would have it, I was on radio watch when the attack began.

* * * *

Overrun

★ ★ ★

As I walked to the comm bunker that evening, I saw a young Vietnamese man squatting in the four-foot by four-foot barbed wire cube that the local troops used as a jail. He had a sad and submissive look on his face. Two RFs stood by, heckling him. A third came up and began to urinate on the prisoner, much to the merriment of the others.

I relieved Wolverton of radio duty at about 1800. Lieutenant Stamper had used Tiddy that day to work on strengthening our defensive positions around the perimeter, so he had missed his shift. Wolverton and I would now split the radio watch duty into two, twelve-hour shifts—except if we were attacked. In that case, as senior radio operator, he would immediately assume that duty once again.

Defending the village that evening were about thirty Americans and 140 indigenous troops dispersed at several locations in the vicinity, with the bulk of them at the district headquarters compound. I spent most of that night reading a paperback book about Bob Hope's previous USO tours and chuckling intermittently at his jokes. I radioed my hourly situation report to the base with a brief, "Intrigue, this is Mutter. Sit rep all secure. Out." (Intrigue was the call sign of the 26th Marine Regiment; Mutter, the call sign for CAC-O.)

I checked to see where they kept the spare batteries for the radios and eventually found a couple. The three-volt batteries were the size and shape of a brick. They had a life of only an hour of actual transmitting time, so I was glad I had a couple of extras. We had two radios, one belonged to the

83

On duty; he finds they are under attack [handwritten margin note]

CAC and one was a backup I brought from the base. I was surprised at how relatively relaxed I began feeling as the night wore on, fooling myself into believing that each passing hour of peace was a positive sign that the enemy might not come.

At approximately 0500 the following morning, January 21, I heard a radio transmission from the Khe Sanh Combat Base putting all forces in the area on red alert. This was not the usual drill. I recognized the voice on the radio as that of PFC French. French had been a tent mate of mine when I was up at the base. A big guy who kept to himself and slept with his eyes open, French scared the hell out of the rest of us. Yet that morning his voice was so calm and controlled, it gave no hint of the fact that they were under a sizable enemy rocket attack.

I left the radio bunker and crossed the thirty meters to Lieutenant Stamper's room. He occupied what had been servant's quarters in a small apartment behind the headquarters building. I banged on the door and went in. The lieutenant sat up in bed, taking a moment to shake off sleep.

Stamper then ordered me to wake the troops who were not already guarding the perimeter, then return to the radio. I walked the short distance to the barracks. Everything was dark and quiet. When I arrived there, everyone was already awake, dressing, and putting on gear. The muffled rumbling explosions coming from the base two miles away had awakened some of them. I had not heard those distant sounds, perhaps because I had been in a sandbagged bunker. I then walked back to the comm bunker to await further instructions.

About 0530, automatic weapons fire erupted from what sounded like the south and west sides of the district headquarters compound. Sound can be misleading when you are in a bunker because everything appears to be coming from the direction of the largest opening, in this case the doorway. The gunfire soon encircled the compound and, mixed with our outgoing fire, created an unbelievable racket. The deafening roar in the center of a pitched battle nearly defies description: a seamless earsplitting blend of chattering bursts of semi-automatic rifles, the oscillating knock of machine guns, teeth-jarring detonations of rocket-propelled grenades, and the deep, reverberating thump of exploding mortar shells. At times, the sound would shift away and then return, like waves on a beach. At other times, the volume would decrease in intensity on one side of the compound for a few seconds, but long enough to have me anxiously wondering if the defenders had been overwhelmed.

Alone in the bunker, fear cramped my neck muscles and tremors shook my head like a seizure. Tears filled my eyes and I started to repeat the same question aloud, "What am I gonna do? What am I gonna do?"

Do you feel training
your prepared
you for battle?

Hotel – Overrun 85

Just then, Wolverton staggered through the doorway. He was clearly in shock. Blood flowed from his right hand, which he was holding carefully with his left. A piece of shrapnel had nearly ripped off his middle finger, which now clung to his hand by a half-inch wide flap of skin. A fractured stick of bone protruded through the translucent fat. I quickly wrapped his hand with a large bandage from a first aid kit and laid him down on the cot across from the radio desk. He stared up at the ceiling, panting and frightened. Though he had made his way back to the comm bunker to relieve me of radio duty, he was clearly in no condition to do so.

With great effort, I forced myself to breathe normally, to get calm. What to do? What to do? A few days before, I had received prearranged artillery fire coordinates to transmit to the artillery battalion back up at the base, in case the enemy overran us quickly. I had written them on the acetate-covered map with a black grease pencil. Then I saw my scribbling, down in the lower right-hand corner: AT110, AT111. These codes targeted both the Marine and Special Forces compounds with variable-timed (VT) artillery. This meant the shells were timed to explode in the air about twenty feet directly above the compound. The idea was to create a shower of shrapnel deadly to anyone caught out in the open. If I radioed these target codes back to the Fire Support Control Center at Khe Sanh base, hundreds of these artillery shells would be unleashed upon us. No other authority was required to start the barrage. Nevertheless, I continued to wait—a minute, perhaps two.

As I rested the radio handset against my cheek, still trying to decide whether it was time to make that call, Lieutenant Stamper burst through the doorway. He was out of breath and had a large wet stain on the front of his trousers. My first thought was that he was wounded and didn't yet realize it. He started yelling for artillery, "Arty! Arty! Arty!" I squeezed the button on the handset and began transmitting as calmly as I could, but realized I could not hear my own voice over the din. Although I'd been taught that this radio handset would both amplify my voice and filter out background noise, I was too much a novice and too scared to accept that as fact. So I took a deep breath, re-keyed the transmit button, and shouted the prearranged artillery fire codes as loud as I could into the mouthpiece. Miraculously, PFC French, the radio operator at the base, was able to understand my request and passed it quickly on to the Fire Support Coordinator.

Little of the enemy gunfire had yet penetrated the narrow window in the bunker that faced the Buddhist shrine, but I wasn't sure what the shrapnel from our own artillery airbursts would be like. I immediately took clothes, books, whatever loose items I could find, and stuffed them into the slit, which was the only opening in the bunker other than the doorway.

During the interval, Stamper and I remained speechless. We anxiously glanced at each other, both knowing that it was now a race between the arrival of the artillery shells and the rapidity with which the overwhelming enemy force could push past our perimeter defenses and reach the shelter of our covered fighting holes and bunkers.

Although it was less than five minutes, it seemed like an eternity. The first shells exploded overhead with an extraordinary sound, like thunder reverberating in a narrow canyon. Part of the bunker window was still unblocked and through it I could see the white-orange splashes of flame against the still dark morning sky. Once the artillery support finally stopped, it was deathly quiet for several minutes. The airbursts caught much of the 66th NVA Regiment out in the open, decimating them. Sporadic NVA small arms and machine gun fire soon resumed, along with an occasional flurry of mortar rounds, but with nothing of its previous intensity.

At first light, we were able to see just how close we had come to being completely overrun. Enemy dead littered the ground right up to our fighting positions. Near Tiddy's dugout, an NVA soldier slumped dead on his knees in a mess of concertina wire. The enemy may have concluded this was a weak spot in our defensive line because in the first minutes of the attack, Tiddy shot and killed five of them just a few feet in front of his position. Some of the surviving attackers now dug in close to our barbed wire and continued firing at us.

Despite our successful defense of the district headquarters compound, the NVA had taken the rest of the village. They set up one machine gun on the roof of the rice storehouse just outside our wire to the east and another one on top of the Buddhist shrine, just as Whiting had predicted. Though they had briefly taken part of our compound near the LZ, the enemy had been repelled by sunrise. Approximately twelve defenders were dead and twenty-five wounded. Nevertheless, we had held.

Lieutenant Stamper then told me what had happened to him after I woke him up. While checking on the Marines around the perimeter of the compound, Stamper realized that he had not relieved himself yet that morning, so he went up to the LZ where the piss tube was located. As he was urinating, he happened to glance out across the LZ. There, twenty meters away, he saw a squad of NVA soldiers stealthily advancing toward him from out of the morning gloom. They were directly under the ARVN machine guns in the adjacent Special Forces compound, yet no one had noticed. Stamper turned and dashed back through the narrow opening in the barbed wire fence, yelling the alert—the stain on his pants as testament to his interrupted mission. The enemy opened fire on him but missed.

Despite the fact that we were anticipating the enemy's arrival, nearly 500 of them silently entered the village that morning. In fact, they had almost walked through the backdoor of the district headquarters compound undetected.

After sunrise, I went outside to take a leak and look around. I kept low because of the sniper fire. I noticed the jail cage was empty. The prisoner from the previous night probably would not have survived our artillery airbursts, so someone must have either let him out before the attack or had already taken his body away.

Our first close air support arrived about 0800. An air observer in a single engine airplane, call sign "Covey," circled above us directing flights of fighter-bombers. The precision of the bombing was often remarkable. I watched as a napalm bomb tumbled from the bottom of a Phantom F-4, which was traveling at over 400 knots. The bomb was aimed at a sniper who had dug-in close to our barbed wire. It actually nicked the top of the barbed wire, causing it to jiggle slightly, before going on to explode just a few meters on the other side.

Later in the morning, the air observer radioed me that he had spotted about 100 NVA moving out in the open approximately one mile southwest of the compound. He requested permission to target them, rather than continuing to work on the enemy troops dug in around us. I was the only one in the comm bunker at that time, but readily gave him approval. He radioed back a few minutes later, in a clearly excited voice, that the napalm had run right through the column, killing all. I later learned that these were not NVA reinforcements, as I had assumed when giving the air observer the approval, but rather a column of wounded being evacuated from the field.

In the morning, after Lieutenant Stamper had guardedly radioed Colonel Lownds about our extreme shortages of ammunition—particularly machine gun ammunition, mortar shells, and grenades—the colonel ordered a relief force sent to us. By early afternoon a platoon from Delta Company, 1st Battalion, 26th Marines, had moved from the Khe Sanh base to the north edge of the village without incident. Although less than a mile from us, the platoon had halted because they suspected an NVA ambush ahead. Lownds radioed the platoon commander of the relief force to advance no farther and await his orders.

About midday, a helicopter came on my radio frequency. The pilot advised me that he was currently above the district headquarters compound with boxes of machine gun ammunition for us. He could not land because he was taking sniper fire. I grabbed the radio and ran outside. There, hovering about 100 feet above the headquarters building, was a silver and white UH-1E helicopter (commonly referred to as a "Huey") with no discernable military service markings. I later learned that it was an Air America chopper. Air America was a commercial airline company whose helicopters and fixed wing aircraft provided civilian air transportation throughout South Vietnam. The company was also owned and operated by the CIA and used for a variety of clandestine purposes as well. I'm not sure why they called me on the Marine radio frequency and not the Special Forces radio operator next door.

I was holding the radio set in my left hand and the handset in the other, pleading with the pilot to drop the ammo on to the roof of the headquarters building. He refused, believing there was a good chance it would fall outside the wire and into the enemy's hands instead. From where he hovered, the line between the NVA and us was nearly undistinguishable. I tried to convince him they had all the ammunition they needed and could get more—but we couldn't!

While the whopping of the chopper blades drowned out other sounds around me, I could distinctly hear the occasional ping of a sniper bullet striking the chopper's fuselage. Both the pilot and I were now shouting into our microphones at the same time. I picked up the last few words of his transmission (". . . out of here!") as he sped off toward the east—without dropping a single bullet.

Corporal Russell had manned the bunker that would have been my responsibility if I had not been on radio watch during the attack that morning. The doorway into the little dugout was directly behind where the machine gunner would kneel and was screened by a low blast-wall. Rocket-propelled grenades and hand grenade concussions knocked Russell completely back out of that bunker doorway—twice. Both times, he shook off the effects and went back in. He continued firing that ancient machine gun until it ran out of ammunition. For his heroism in stopping the enemy from overrunning the east side of the district headquarters compound that morning, Russell was later awarded the Silver Star.

Now suffering from numerous shrapnel wounds, Russell lay bandaged and resting on the floor of the comm bunker. In the early afternoon, I went over to check on his condition and offer him a cigarette. I asked him if he had tried to hit the drum of "napalm," as he had instructed me to do. He shot the big can several times, he replied, but could not get it to explode. He speculated that we had probably failed to stir the mixture often enough or perhaps the locals stole the fuel when no one was looking.

Russell then told me that he had been listening to the work I was doing on the radio, calling in artillery and bombing strikes and continuously
prodding the regiment for reinforcements; he wanted me to know what a
good job he thought I was doing. His words lifted my spirits, as by that
point I had been talking continuously on the radio for over twenty hours
and was wearing down a bit. But, more importantly, his words represented
a kind of vindication. Earlier that week, Corporal Russell had been on the
patrol that I failed to acknowledge on the radio because I had fallen asleep.
He was the one who subsequently put the hand grenade in my sleeping
bag. What poetic justice, I thought—atonement for having fallen asleep
then by not falling asleep now.

Throughout the afternoon, we continued to take enemy mortar and
automatic weapons fire. Our air observer reported that the NVA had put a
mortar tube in the village infirmary, about a block to the east, and torn a
hole in the roof through which to fire at us. He called in an immediate artillery strike on the clinic and silenced the mortar. I hoped no civilians
were in the clinic waiting for medical treatment at the time, but never
found out.

With only an hour of daylight left, Stamper took my radio handset and
made a personal plea to Colonel Lownds to have the Marine relief force
advance the rest of the way to us. Several minutes later I received a radio
call back from the base. It was Colonel Lownds' voice, rather than a radio
operator's. I knew it couldn't be good news. He asked for Lieutenant
Stamper. Lownds then advised Stamper that, because of the high likelihood of being ambushed while moving through the village, he was ordering the platoon to return to the base. Stamper gave it his best "Yes, Sir,"
and ended the transmission.

I knew how little ammunition we had left and that we had taken about
forty casualties already. I believed that without reinforcements we would
not make it through the night. I could not fathom them forsaking us and
desperately searched for an explanation. Then it occurred to me that the
platoon commander of our relief force was Captain Chapman, the son of the
Commandant of the Marine Corps. If Chapman died unnecessarily, it might
be bad for Colonel Lownds' career. This had to be the reason. A surge of
anger gripped me, intensified by a stinging sense of betrayal. Marines never
left other Marines behind. You would risk your life to save your buddy,
that was the code. I stood by the radio bench stiff and silent, trying to
come to terms with the potential consequences of this abandonment.

Within a few minutes, Captain Clarke came charging over from the
Army side of the comm bunker. He had just learned the relief force was

not coming and was furious. Clarke snatched the handset from me and called Colonel Lownds. Once Lownds was on the radio, Clarke demanded that the colonel send back the platoon. He went on about how the Marines had guaranteed the safety of the Special Forces troops and that it was Lownds' duty to meet that obligation. Clarke complained at length in unencrypted language about our lack of grenades and mortar and machine gun ammunition.

I knew the NVA were monitoring this radio frequency. In fact, they had been trying to jam my radio all day, blowing a shrill whistle and screaming at me in what I took to be, from their rather hysterical tone, Vietnamese threats and obscenities. At first, this was annoying and ominous. Despite the fact that they were nearby, judging from the strength of the transmissions, I was always able to override them due to the relative superiority of my own radio's output. (In situations when it was obvious the enemy was listening, radiomen often employed a simple method of encryption when discussing numbers or radio frequencies. This included expressions we hoped the enemy would not understand. As an example, if we were saying the number ten, but wanted to mask that information we would say something like, "Mickey Mantle's uniform number, up three." If we wanted a helicopter pilot to meet us on radio frequency 34.5, we would tell him to go to "a perfect bowling score, up forty-five." I don't know if it fooled the NVA, but it made us feel secure and clever.)

I felt that Captain Clarke's careless language was providing the NVA with too much information, that he was compromising our security. Stamper could see my concern and thought I was going to grab the handset away from Clarke. I was, by that point, so witless from fatigue that I might have tried something that stupid. Stamper was standing behind the captain. As I looked from Clarke's face to his, Stamper held my eyes in his gaze and with a slight shake of his head, silently instructed me to "let it go." Clarke was the senior officer at district headquarters and, despite the fact that he was Army, was in command of us all.

Having yelled himself out at Lownds, Captain Clarke left the bunker with Stamper following. It was quiet outside now. I sat on the floor with my back up against the radio bench. Wolverton was asleep on the cot from a morphine injection administered an hour before by a short-tempered Army medic who had been making the rounds of the wounded and had not passed up the opportunity to scold me for how poorly I'd bandaged the hand.

Through the narrow window, the setting sun cast a warm ray on my face. I soon felt a great sense of peace, as though some enormous weight

[handwritten margin note: He is prepared to die; they are out of ammunition]

had lifted. This was due in part to the exhaustion of having already been on the radio continuously for nearly twenty-four hours. I thought of my family and friends and how they would react to word of my death—and the lack of a body to bury. I pictured each of them for just a moment, as if checking them off some private list in my heart. By the time I finished, I was resigned to my fate. There was no help coming, we were nearly out of ammunition, and the NVA, now that they knew all of this too, would be coming back at dark—maybe with a tank or two.

As darkness approached, I envisioned the end. I had kept one fragmentation grenade under the radio table. If still alive when enemy soldiers came through the doorway, I would have the pin already pulled and the grenade pressed to the side of my head; painless, I thought. No capture, no torture, maybe even make a "dink" or two bleed a bit for the cause. It wasn't the best idea I had ever had, but at least it was a plan. I was relieved to have an alternative to simply not knowing what I would do. In reality, however, no one can be sure what they will do until the instant they actually face death.

Sitting there on the floor of the bunker, I looked down near my boot and saw something shiny pressed into the damp, packed earth. After scratching it out with my finger, I saw that it was a brand new Kennedy half-dollar. It was illegal to possess U.S. currency in Vietnam, but even more unusual was to find it in such a remote place as this. I put the coin in my pocket. Maybe it would bring me luck.

With the Marine relief force now returning to the base, the Army took action. By 1730 that evening, ARVNS and U.S. Army Special Forces advisors in a dozen helicopters manned by U.S. crews were enroute to reinforce us. The hastily adopted plan was to blast a landing zone in Felix Poilane's coffee trees just northeast of the village, then march the half-mile to the district headquarters.

An Army air observer was assigned to direct the bombers that would create the LZ. However, he had trouble making radio contact with the Marine air observer who was flying near the village to direct the air support bombing around us. Worried that this lack of communication might lead to a collision with the other aircraft, the Army air observer radioed the lead assault helicopter, advising them of the need to delay the air strike.

U.S. Army Lieutenant Colonel Joseph Seymoe, the officer commanding the rescue operation, was in the lead chopper. Believing the mission was about to be cancelled and not wanting to abandon us in the village, Seymoe ordered the pilots to land instead at the old French fort.

Earlier that morning, just after the attack on the district headquarters had been stalled by the blanket of artillery fire from the base, I briefly heard anxious radio transmissions from another American unit operating in the area. They were evidently an Army SOG patrol. They described themselves as "down by the bridge," which probably meant they were in the vicinity of the old French fort, east of the village. With our district headquarters surrounded and hundreds of enemy soldiers now installed in the village, the SOG patrol was certainly in a precarious position. By late morning, their radio traffic stopped and I didn't know what became of them. Their sudden radio silence may have been a hint of the tragedy about to unfold.

Unknown to those of us in the village or, more disastrously, to Lieutenant Colonel Seymoe and his men, the fort was now occupied by a platoon of NVA ordered there for the express purpose of preventing relief forces from landing. An enemy RPG hit and destroyed the lead chopper. As the remaining choppers landed to drop off their troops, they too came under intense enemy fire. Within minutes, it was over. Twenty-seven Americans and seventy-four Vietnamese soldiers lay dead.[12]

Captain Clarke, next door in the Army side of the comm bunker, learned about the failure of the mission almost immediately, possibly from ARVN survivors of the ambush who had eluded the enemy and made it to the district headquarters. I had mixed feelings when I heard the news. I was grateful for the attempt they had made to save us, yet angry they had failed. Mostly, however, I was filled with dread. For it now seemed as if there were thousands of enemy soldiers between the Khe Sanh Combat Base and us.

At about 2000, Lieutenant Stamper had me call on the landline telephone from the comm bunker to tell those in the district headquarters building he was coming over. Despite the fact that the building was only fifty feet away, it was now dark outside and there were many nervous trigger fingers within our compound. He then left the bunker.

Stamper returned an hour later holding a nearly empty bottle of Johnny Walker Red Label scotch whiskey. My first thought was that he had decided to get drunk at this crucial time, and I began to seethe with anger. He soon explained that he had gotten the bottle from his room and taken it around to the Marine positions on the line, giving each a gulp before advising them we were nearly out of ammunition and ordering them to fix bayonets. No soldier or Marine in any war likes to hear that particular command because it means you will likely be ending your life in a one-sided knife fight.

[handwritten margin note: NVA are occupying to prevent supplies from coming]

Swirling the remaining contents of the bottle for emphasis, he said to me, "I can't give you any, radioman, because you have to keep your head clear. But when we get out of this, I'll buy you a whole damn bottle." I replied that I would hold him to that.

As the evening went on, enemy automatic weapons and mortar fire increased. A C-143 flare ship arrived in the sky over us at 2100. It remained on station for about four hours, dropping flares at regular intervals over us. The illumination it provided took away the cover of darkness from our attackers and made them reluctant to attack. Occasionally, when there were long delays between flares, the exchange of gunfire became more vigorous, but with the next flare burst, it quickly diminished. I watched through the little window to make sure the flares were dropping over us regularly.

After the first flare ship left, we were visited by Spooky, a flare ship enhanced with several electrically-fired Gatling guns that could generate an amazing six thousand bullets per minute. Stamper and I climbed on top of the comm bunker, staying low against the corrugated steel roof because of snipers in the nearby Buddhist shrine. In whispers, we directed Spooky to fire to the south about 1,500 meters. This was the direction from which we believed the main NVA force had come, which might indicate a troop staging area in that vicinity.

As it slowly circled, a curved, nearly continuous stream of glowing tracer bullets flowed from the left side of the aircraft. "Like pissing molten steel," someone once described it. But the real "spooky" part was the sound. The groaning of those guns was fearsome, almost animalistic, like the lament of a dying bear. It gave me chills to hear it echoing out of the night. I can imagine the terror it must have instilled in those it was targeting.

After Spooky departed, we went back inside the bunker and soon another flare ship arrived. Stamper and Sergeant John Balanco sat in the comm bunker with me, taking turns finishing off the remainder of the scotch. They soon nodded off.

Balanco was a recent arrival to the CAC, joining us just the day before, but he acted like a veteran of this kind of combat. He refused to wear a helmet, despite Stamper's constant shouting at him to do so, and moved confidently through the sniper fire. Balanco seemed to be everywhere at once and his optimism was infectious. He would say things like, "We're getting out of this, easy" and "We're walking away from here, no sweat." We soon began to believe him. He seemed to be everywhere. Two CAC Marines would win Silver Stars for their actions during the defense of the village (an unusually large number for such a small unit). Balanco would be one of them. During a conversation with him in the comm bunker that night, I learned that he was from my hometown and had gone to Oakland High School. We even had mutual acquaintances.

As the night wore on, my lack of sleep really began to catch up with me. I could no longer remember the call signs of the flare ships. One had the call sign "Basketball." I soon was calling it "Baseball," then "Beach ball," and finally just "Ball." Occasionally, I would press the transmit button and forget the call sign entirely, broadcasting "uh . . . uh . . . uh" for a few moments while I tried to remember it.

The pilot, who could tell how exhausted I was, tried to keep me awake by talking. He asked me questions about myself and, upon discovering I was from the Bay Area, actually found an old copy of the *San Francisco Chronicle* on board the plane. Letting the copilot take the controls, he began to read me the local news and sports sections. I couldn't believe my good fortune. I started feeling homesick and consequently less resigned to the idea of dying there. When he left, the pilot told me to look him up when I got to Da Nang, so he could buy me a beer. I liked the sound of that "when," but was almost too tired to care.

I tried staying awake by rocking back and forth and slapping my own face. I didn't want a repeat of the last time I fell asleep on radio watch, particularly now that I had finally been vindicated. About 0200, however, I dozed off for a few minutes and suddenly all hell broke loose. Furious small arms fire and grenade explosions erupted all around the perimeter. Our troops responded with long nervous bursts of precious ammunition. Some PFs had already fired all their rifle ammunition. Two Bru were killed by the searing back-blast of a bazooka-like anti-tank weapon, which one of them fired from the confines of their tiny dugout. Other, less enterprising PFs could only lay low with empty rifles and watch. It was pitch dark outside, and the battle was underway again. I had let the flare ship drift off course and did not know the direction it had gone.

I ran outside with the radio and crouched in a shallow trench, poking my head up in quick jerks amid the gunfire, desperately looking for flares. I asked the pilot to keep dropping them, which he said he was doing. The plane was already too far away, I couldn't even make out a glow in the sky. Nor could the pilot see the flashes of the weapons and grenade explosions around us. I went back into the bunker and called Mortarman on the landline telephone. He had a couple of illumination rounds left, our last, but fired them anyway.

The flare ship, now several miles away, spotted our last mortar illumination flare as it floated down over the compound and was back over our position within a few minutes. The shooting subsided. This last flare ship departed at approximately 0430, which left us with about ninety minutes before first light. The NVA did not attack again. At dawn, it seemed apparent that most of the enemy had moved out of the immediate area. A Marine helicopter gunship soon arrived, circling low to see if it would draw enemy ground fire. It did not.

Sergeant Balanco asked me to cover him while he went to collect some intelligence information—identification cards, maps, orders, and such—from the bodies of the dead NVA in the cemetery on the west side. Later, Lieutenant Stamper arrived and ordered me to take the radio up to the LZ and direct the medevac choppers.

As I talked the first choppers into the LZ, Tiddy came by. Seeing how badly I needed sleep, he relieved me on the radio. I lay down on the cot in the comm bunker, covered myself with pages from a Stars and Stripes, and immediately fell into a deep sleep.

About 1030, Tiddy woke me to ask if I had called any artillery fire missions into our area lately. He had stepped out for a few minutes to find some chow and heard some unusual incoming. I told him I had not made any calls while he was out. Just then, there was a huge, resonant explosion. I jumped up, went over to the radio, and called the base. The Fire Support Center radio operator there advised me that they were not firing any artillery in our direction. Tiddy and I looked at each other with exactly the same expression: let's be on the next chopper out of this place!

The enemy was now shooting at us with large artillery. We did not know it then, but this was the first use of the 152mm guns the NVA had hidden in Laos, six miles to the west on Co Roc Mountain. I was incredulous that they had such weapons.

Now wide-awake, I left the comm bunker and went over to the barracks to get my gear. The back of the building was gone, completely blown off, and shrapnel had extensively perforated the corrugated metal roof. Sunlight streamed through the shrapnel holes, dappling the interior. For the first time that morning, I noticed how quiet the place was now.

I had come to the village with my belongings in a green duffel bag, which I eventually found in the debris, still packed from my anticipated departure two days before. Picking it up, I headed back to the comm bunker. Villagers were now frantically crowding into the district headquarters compound. Some had broken the lock on the small supply bunker next to our barracks and were carrying off cases of C-rations.

Down the alley between the administrative buildings, I noticed our big, 6 × 6 truck was still parked in the front of the district headquarters. I wondered if we were going to leave it and if so, should someone destroy it before the NVA returned? I soon lost interest in the problem and moved on. As I walked past the back of the district headquarters building, I noticed it was horizontally stitched, at close range with automatic weapons fire from the direction of the LZ. I looked in that direction and realized the person who fired that burst must have been inside the compound. Yet, I did not see any bodies there.

Upon reaching the comm bunker, I encountered Gunny Boyd (actually a staff sergeant, but everyone called him "Gunny"), the senior enlisted Marine in the CAC. I asked him what we should do with the radios. "Leave 'em," he barked, then headed for the LZ. Tiddy and I were rather fresh out of radio school at Camp Pendleton. We tried to remember what Sergeant Ski told us to do in this situation. The answer soon came to me: thermite grenades.

Thermite grenades were not designed to explode like fragmentation grenades, but rather to burn with an intensity that would melt metal. Sergeant Ski had instructed us to use these to burn the radios in a hopeless situation in order to keep them from falling into the hands of the enemy. I remembered there was one grenade stashed at the back of the radio table.

I located the confidential radio code booklet, put it in my pocket, then stacked the two radios on top of each other. I tore the map off the wall and laid it on top of them. Pulling the pin on the grenade, I set it on top of the map. It erupted with a bright flash and a great, thick cloud of green smoke.

Of course, the correct procedure would have been to take the radios with us. They weighed just twenty-five pounds each and were quite portable. It was the logical thing to do. However, I was too weary to reason. Staccato pieces of my radio school course work from two months earlier were the only tunes playing in my head at that moment.

Outside the comm bunker, I began searching through my duffel bag, doing a calm inventory while troops and civilians ran about in soundless pandemonium. I took each item out of the bag, looked it over as if I had never seen it before, then threw it away. I tossed everything: my extra clothes, rain gear, webbed gear, personal effects, and gas mask. Finally, when the bag was empty, I threw it away, too. It was as if I were sleepwalking.

I picked up my rifle, a bandolier of ammo, and my helmet. About this time, Tiddy told me that the last chopper was coming in and we should get up to the LZ right away. If we missed it, we would be in "deep shit." We jogged up to the LZ and crouched down near the wire beside Mortarman and three or four other Marines.

Soon the Bru houseboy came by and told us that Captain Clarke was about to lead the local forces up Route 9 to the base and that we should di-di (hurry up) to Howard Johnson's where they were forming up. We didn't mention the inbound chopper, and he soon left. For a few minutes, we thought about joining the Bru. The Khe Sanh air team had radioed Tiddy nearly an hour earlier that the chopper was coming. What if it had been diverted elsewhere? I had burned the radios, so we had no way of knowing (my mind was slowly awakening to the stupidity of that act). How long should we wait?

Just then, we heard the throbbing of a propeller and saw an old, olive-colored CH-34 approaching from the east. The chopper hovered for a moment, then landed. We raced the ten meters across the LZ and dove headfirst through the door. An ARVN officer and his dog then clamored aboard. It appeared the officer had decided not to walk to the base with the other RFs. The engine roared and the chopper lurched forward. We struck the wall of the Special Forces compound, bounced backward and down. The two big doughnut-like front wheels barely avoided landing on the punji stakes. The load was too heavy. *Tries to get by chopper - load too heavy, but they get on anyway*

I watched the pilot turn around and look at the crew chief. He made animated hand and arm gestures. Despite the fact that they were conversing by intercom, the message was clear. Throw somebody out—and fast!

The engine noise inside the old chopper precluded any normal conversation. The crew chief turned to Tiddy and me, and gave a kind of butting motion with his head in the direction of the ARVN officer. Tiddy and I slid across the shiny, crenelated aluminum floor on our knees and, in a single motion, grabbed the guy and threw him off. His dog went to the edge of the doorway, stopped, and looked out—but did not want to follow. Its barking was soundless in the propeller noise. Tiddy tapped the animal on the rear with the toe of his boot, and it disappeared out the doorway. Though I never saw the man or his dog again, I assume they caught up with the other ARVNs walking to Khe Sanh Combat Base and made it there safely.

The crew chief signaled to the pilot and the engine roared overhead until the whole frame of the chopper shook. We pulled up, drifted backwards for several feet, then lurched forward, upward, and steeply up to the left, barely clearing the wall.

Sliding back over to the small open window on the port side next to the crew chief, who was now cocking the machine gun, I hooked one arm through the nylon webbing on the interior bulkhead to stabilize myself, then stuck the barrel of my M-16 out the window. As we rose and continued to bank, we were looking straight down. The machine gunner and I both saw an NVA soldier lying near the edge of the LZ. The gunner reacted instantly, firing a long burst at the man. I didn't shoot. It was obvious from the way he was laying on his side that he was dead, but the gunner continued to fire at the body until we passed over the treetops to the south. I was glad he stopped shooting because the hot brass casings from the machine gun were bouncing all over me, going into my pockets and down my shirt.

The flight back to Khe Sanh Combat Base, which was only about two miles away, seemed to take forever. From my window, I could see an endless line of people walking up Route 9 toward the base. At first, I thought they were NVA, but with a longer look, it became clear they were mostly civilians. I was glad the door gunner didn't open fire on them. We took a wide swing out to the east, then approached the base directly over the runway.

At first glance, the place appeared enshrouded in fog, yet it was a bright, clear day. What I was seeing was smoke and my mind was having trouble registering the extent of the devastation. From where I sat, it seemed as if half the base was missing. I had been equating it with safety for so long that I was stunned to see it looking in worse shape than the battle zone I had just left.

The morning before, several well-aimed enemy rockets struck the ammo dump at the east end of the base, where 11,000 artillery and mortar shells packed in wooden crates were stacked in a series of open pits. The eruption of our own ammunition supplies caused the subsequent destruction. The shells cooked off in a kind of chain reaction, raining down on the base, exploding or starting fires.

The area where my tent had been was now just a large scorched spot. I was immediately concerned about my buddies who had lived there with me. I was later relieved to find them uninjured because they had moved underground just days before the attack. The thought occurred to me that, between what smoldered below in the ashes of my tent and what I had thrown away less than an hour ago in the village, my total worldly possessions consisted of only the clothes I was wearing and my rifle. We landed near the helicopter revetments on the north side of the runway, thanking the crew with raised thumbs and big smiles. It was good to be away from the village.

After crossing the runway, we turned east toward the COC. Tiddy and I wore helmets; Mortarman had on only a soft cover. Walking on the road near the LSA we passed two Shore Patrol guards leading an NVA prisoner. The man had his hands tied behind him and a woven nylon sandbag over his head. As they came past us, Mortarman turned to the prisoner and spat, "Coc a dau, motherfucker!" (Roughly translated, "You had better talk, or else!") The guards did nothing, but there was an officer following along behind them.

When he overheard the remark, he confronted Mortarman. "Where's your helmet, Marine?" the officer asked. Mortarman replied with unconcealed mirth, "Back in the ville, Sir." The officer advised him that it was now required we wear helmets and flak jackets at all times; he then moved down the road to catch up with the prisoner. After the officer was out of earshot, Mortarman finished his sentence, ". . . and I'd be much obliged if you would get it for me." Our elation at being out of the village coupled with the ironic fact that Mortarman, like Balanco, refused to wear a helmet even during the most intense combat there, incited us to fits of hysterical laughter—the insane, uncontrollable, tranquilizing laughter of the spared.

The prisoner was a defector by the name of First Lieutenant Than Tonc. Three days earlier, Tonc had surrendered at the east end of the runway under a white flag. Disgruntled due to lack of promotion, he gave up an incredible amount of intelligence information about the upcoming attack on Khe Sanh, as well as the forthcoming Tet Offensive that would begin in about two weeks. Most thought Lieutenant Tonc was a spy, sent over in order to mislead us. Nevertheless, nearly everything he described either happened or was corroborated by other intelligence sources. The information he gave about the NVA battle plan for Khe Sanh probably saved hundreds of Marine lives—perhaps even the base itself. Yet this intelligence also led directly to the deaths of thousands of his fellow soldiers. I'm not sure if being passed over for a promotion would justify having to live with something like that on your conscience. I'm glad he defected, but a part of me also hopes that he was not too successful later in life.

Meanwhile, the Special Forces unit at FOB-3 that had been monitoring the enemy radio frequencies now had reason to believe that the NVA would not reenter Khe Sanh Village until after nightfall. Captain Clarke, who had just walked to the base with his ARVNs, immediately organized a patrol of the indigenous FOB troops to walk back down to the village. Their mission was to destroy over a ton of rice warehoused next to the district headquarters compound. Denying food to an enemy as mobile and active as the NVA was nearly as important as denying them ammunition. The patrol met no serious resistance and destroyed the rice, as well as the truck parked in front of the district headquarters building. They went into the comm bunker and found my two radios, undamaged, with green crud all over them. To my embarrassment, what I thought was a thermite grenade was actually a smoke grenade.

A few nights later, a Special Forces lieutenant who had accompanied Captain Clarke back to the village that day, came down to the COC looking for me. He found me on radio duty and began deriding me for leaving the radios behind and for my lame attempt to destroy them with a harmless smoke grenade. It was unusual for an officer to personalize, let alone publicly express, such loathing toward a subordinate. This was especially true of a lowly PFC like me who was, by my very lack of experience, generally considered an idiot anyway.

I was embarrassed, of course, yet still a bit euphoric at having gotten out of that place alive, so I let it go without comment. The lieutenant then continued talking about the unwillingness of the Marines to provide the village with necessary relief forces and support, and other issues over which I personally had no control. I would later wonder if Captain Clarke had sent this officer to the COC because he was still angry with Colonel Lownds for not sending reinforcements to the village. Lownds, who was within earshot of the lieutenant's lecture, may have been the actual addressee.

This episode did nothing to make me dislike Captain Clarke or his Special Forces people any less than I had at the village. Yet, I had to agree with him about the colonel's decision not to reinforce us. Over time though, I would reconsider things and eventually accept the colonel's choice as the correct one—despite the enormous peril in which it had left us. A week after the district headquarters fell to the enemy, an NVA deserter told our intelligence people that they were waiting to spring a sizable ambush on the Marine relief force as it entered the village. So, it is highly doubtful they would have made it to us anyway.

On their return to the village that day, Clarke's men captured an RPG-7. It was the first time one of these state-of-the-art grenade launchers had been captured. The rocket-powered grenade launched by an RPG-7 could punch through several feet of earthen defenses before detonating. I am still amazed the NVA were unable to capture the district headquarters that morning of the attack. They could have easily placed this powerful weapon within forty meters of the comm bunker, which was above ground and close to the perimeter. With all the comings and goings of the not-always-so-loyal indigenous forces, they must have known exactly where it was located. A single, well-placed RPG rocket in the first few minutes of the attack would have destroyed the comm bunker and prevented me from calling in the prearranged defensive artillery fire on the attackers. This would have probably insured them a quick victory.

The NVA were meticulous tactical planners, yet the assault failed. I would like to think that at the first sound of battle, PFC Whiting stepped out of his little cell and, heedless of the public relations problem he had caused two weeks before, fired yet another M-79 grenade on to the roof of the Buddhist shrine, killing an enemy RPG team and saving the CAC.

In the end, the NVA got what they wanted when we abandoned the Huong Hoa District Headquarters. This proved to be a significant propaganda coup because it was the first time a seat of governmental authority had been captured in South Vietnam. It also proved to be a tactical victory because it effectively cut off the Lang Vei Special Forces camp from the base, as well as any chance of overland relief to that outpost. But for this victory, the NVA paid a high price. Between Sergeant Balanco's body count on the west side of the district headquarters compound, the count given by the Special Forces later that morning, and estimates given by the air observers and other sources, it appears 200–300 NVA soldiers were killed, most in the initial attack. This figure was supported nine days later when a young North Vietnamese soldier surrendered just down the road at the Special Forces camp at Lang Vei. His unit had been among our attackers at Khe Sanh Village where, he claimed, the 66th Regiment lost over half its troops.

I was grateful to have survived the ordeal in the village and be back at the base. But I would soon find out I was no safer. Now, with over 30,000 of their troops assembling in the area, the NVA set their sights on an even greater propaganda victory—annihilating the U.S. Marines at Khe Sanh Combat Base.

* * * *

NVA not finished — want to finish marines off

The Worst Place on Earth

✶ ✶ ✶

Upon arriving back in the 26th Marine Headquarters Company area, I went to the regimental communications office to give Top Reyna, the company first sergeant, the COI (classified radio codebook) I had brought back from the village. On the way there, I found the company commander, a major, standing near the tent that served as an administrative office. He appeared to be in a trance. Shortly before I arrived, Howard "Howie" Johnson (not to be confused with the village brothel of a similar name) had been killed there.

Johnson had been sitting in the tent at a little portable field desk doing some paper work with Sergeants Wright and Meier when a 122mm rocket came chugging in from the west. The motors in those big Soviet-made rockets sounded like runaway locomotives, which often gave us a brief warning before their arrival. Meier and Wright dove straight to the ground. Johnson stood up to run somewhere—the first impulse of a new guy—and died instantly. Mickey Meier later told me that they could not even attempt to administer first aid to Johnson because the shrapnel had literally nailed his flak jacket to his body.

I got the whole story sometime later that day from PFC Morley Sweet IV. It appears that Johnson's demise started the night before, during a poker game. Poker was the number one recreational diversion at Khe Sanh, if you didn't count complaining about the Corps or spinning magnificent lies about one's sexual exploits back in the "World." On the evening after the initial attack, the poker game in the old mortar pit bunker lasted longer than usual. This was because no one knew what was going to happen next and, in the absence of facts, gossip was just as good.

Johnson, who was new to the unit, arriving just after I had left for the village, was in the game. Unfortunately, he was not paying sufficient attention to the pearls of wisdom coming from the more experienced Marines. At one point, Johnson was holding two pair—aces and eights. Morley Sweet, who was kibitzing, leaned over and suggested Johnson fold the hand because it was the "Dead Man's Hand" (the same hand Wild Bill Hickcock was said to have been holding when he was murdered). Johnson looked at the two dollar pot—a relatively large amount of money for enlisted men in 1968—and chose to ignore the advice. The next day he was killed. There was not a Marine there that night who later doubted his poker hand had as much to do with his death as the incoming rocket.

The major was staring at the bloody stains on the ground where Johnson's body, recently removed to Graves Registration, had been laying. I approached and told him I was back from the village and had the codebook. He finally came around, as if shaking off sleep, and asked where the radios were. I told him I had burned them (I did not yet know about the smoke grenade mix-up). That made him angry and he scolded me for several minutes about how the company now needed every radio it could get. We then stood in silence for a while. I was not sure what to do next, so I left.

I went down into the COC to look in on the other radio operators and thank them for their support. When I entered the main map room, I saw Lieutenant Stamper on the far side briefing Colonel Lownds and the other regimental officers. When Stamper saw me, he stopped talking to them and hurried over. He slapped my back and vigorously shook my hand, all the while telling me what a great job I had done. I was proud to hear that, but also slightly embarrassed by the fact that he was keeping the base commander waiting for a lowly enlisted man like me.

I then went to thank the artillery officers for the way their 13th Marine Battalion "cannon cockers" had stood out in their own explosions at the base, exposed to extreme danger, and fired to save us at the village. Overt sentimentality, like the type Stamper had just displayed, was not always suitable. Instead, Captain Steen, the Fire Support Coordinator, and I joked good-naturedly about the relative effectiveness of artillery support versus aerial bombing. "Why you couldn't even kill me," I chided him. "And I told you exactly where I was standing. An A-6 would have gotten the job done in no time." But Steen knew that his guys had saved my life, and I knew it too.

I received many more handshakes and backslaps and was treated defer-entially when I got back to the base, probably because I was the only voice they heard coming from the village. I reciprocated, particularly with the radio operators who had broken procedure throughout that night to whis-per words of encouragement to me when Staff Sergeant Allen wasn't nearby to supervise. Captain Donaghy, my Air Team Officer, had me go sleep in the officer's quarters in the COC. It was dark and quiet in this un-derground cell, and I finally got more than two hours of sleep for the first time in days. Early the next morning Staff Sergeant Allen, the radio pla-toon sergeant, briefed me on what had been happening at the base in my absence. Almost everyone had found living quarters underground, he said. The bulk of our platoon was currently living in an abandoned mortar pit across the road from the COC. He suggested that I should go and see if I could "squeeze in." I asked him where all the refugees streaming up the road from the village were being placed. He did not know, but passed on a rumor that the NVA had raped Suzie, the crippled magazine vendor, and that some villagers carried her to the base on a stretcher. The NVA were not averse to making examples out of civilians who befriended Americans. But then again, I was learning Allen's "scoops" were not always reliable.

The staff sergeant then advised me that since I had left my letters from home in the village, the NVA would probably use the addresses on them to harass my friends and family. It was a stupid concern, but I was young and still stunned from the events of the past few days. I had a list of mail-ing addresses in my wallet, so I immediately sent letters to everyone whose addresses I might have left in the village, warning them about receiving hate mail from Communists. I regretted having done this almost as soon as I mailed the letters. Fortunately, the recipients thought I was joking, as I did often in my letters home. It saved me from the embarrassment of later having to explain to them that I wasn't.

Despite my haste to get those letters to the base post office, mail had become a low priority item and none left Khe Sanh for over a week after the siege began. This was hard on worried family members back in the States who were getting daily news reports about the fighting. This was particularly difficult for my parents. They had taken a trip to Las Vegas and just before leaving home had received a letter from me describing my new duty station with the CAC in Khe Sanh Village. On the return trip home, they stopped for lunch in Barstow, California. As they were leaving the restaurant, my dad purchased a newspaper, then froze in his tracks. The large headline read, "Marine Base at Khe Sanh Attacked." Just below that, in slightly smaller font was, "Khe Sanh Village Overrun." They were stunned and drove the several hundred miles back to Oakland in silence.

Although I wrote them as soon as I returned from the village, to let them know I was alive, they did not get the letter for fourteen days. Each day they waited for the doorbell to ring with a Marine officer standing there with official condolences. It was very difficult for my mom. Of all the things I did in my youth to make her worry, I most regret having put her through those two weeks.

On the evening of January 23, the night after I returned from the village, Sergeant Balanco found me near the old mortar pit bunker. He and the other CAC survivors were living with Captain Clarke and his indigenous forces down by the main gate of the base in the FOB-3 compound. Balanco had come over to our area to be sure that Tiddy and I had gotten out of the village safely. He also wanted to thank me for the job I had done on the radio. I returned the gratitude, thanking him for keeping everyone's spirits up and constantly crisscrossing the compound, under continuous enemy fire to ensure there were no gaps in the line that could be exploited by our attackers. I saw that he was still wearing only a soft cover on his head and joked with him about his still refusing to wear a helmet. I suggested that if the Marine Corps couldn't provide one that fit, maybe he should have borrowed a pith helmet from one of the bodies he was out counting the previous morning. My comment reminded him that he had taken a couple of belts from the dead NVA; one, with a golden star on the buckle, was a style that was highly prized. He told me to come by his new digs at FOB because he wanted to give me one. It was good talking to him and seeing that his exuberance had not diminished; but as it turned out, I never made it over to FOB nor saw him again.

* * * *

I returned to regular radio duty with the air team, which was still located in the regimental Combat Operations Center on the base. Oz, my old mentor, seemed glad to see me. I may have even earned a bit of his respect because he now refrained from routinely calling me "Nicky New Guy." He filled me in on some of the changes that had occurred while I'd been gone. For one, those helicopters not destroyed on the ground by incoming had left Khe Sanh and relocated at Dong Ha. In addition, though we now had more aircraft flying around than ever before, they would no longer park at the base.

Our air team responsibilities had also changed. No longer able to keep track of all the aircraft, we stopped trying to warn them about where friendly artillery was being directed. Between all the out-going artillery and the enemy incoming, we decided to adopt the "Big Sky" approach. That is, the sky was big enough to accommodate everything. (As far as we know, none of the aircraft around Khe Sanh were ever knocked down by a bad luck collision with our artillery; although Lance Corporal Reath did get chewed out once by a livid helicopter pilot who had watched one of our outgoing artillery shells streak just a few feet past his cockpit windshield.) After the siege began in late-January, we air team radio operators spent

U.S fighter-bomber attacks an NVA trench line just outside our perimeter. Pig and Old Woman's bunker is located in the right forefront

much of our time coordinating medevacs and helicopter resupply to the hill outposts. By mid-February, this had become nasty business. Bad weather and intense enemy anti-aircraft fire often prevented the medical evacuation of the wounded from the hills—sometimes for more than a week. Occasionally, wounded men, who would normally have survived, died because they could not get to a hospital for days.

Once, on Hill 881S, Marines had to bury several dead comrades because of uncertainty as to how long it would be before the next chopper could land there. About ten days later, they disinterred the bodies and flew them out. When requesting a medevac, the radioman at the outposts would identify the relative urgency by identifying it in one of three categories: routine, priority, or emergency. Routine medevacs were typically non-life threatening situations. Before the siege began, they were often for dental, mental, or foot problems. A routine medevac was also for the removal of our dead. Priority medevacs were more serious—usually not immediately life threatening at the time of the call, but still urgent. These often involved shrapnel or bullet wounds where bleeding and vital signs had been stabilized. Emergency medevacs were situations where the injuries were so severe that the victim would likely lose a limb, or die, without immediate and more sophisticated medical treatment.

Often the fog was so thick that landing a helicopter on the hills was impossible. Yet, almost every pilot I spoke to was willing to try. Captain Donaghy, the senior TACP officer, was ultimately responsible for making these decisions.

The ghostly forms of destroyed structures loom in the evening fog   *Courtesy Cliff Braisted*

One day, a radio operator on Hill 881S, located about three miles from us, had reported the same priority medevac all day. Dense fog at the base and near zero visibility on the Hill prevented any effort to reach the wounded man. That evening he called to upgrade the medevac request to emergency status. The wounded man had taken a turn for the worse and the radioman's voice was now noticeably more emotional. Every half hour he would transmit again, each time a bit more frantic, each call imploring us to get a chopper there as fast as possible. Finally, his desperation gave way to anger. "Will you fucking people do something!" he shouted. Then a long period of silence followed.

Call in Medevacs

Throughout this time, Captain Donaghy was listening to all this on my radio's squawk-box speaker without saying a word. Several times, he went up to ground level to check the weather. The captain held to his decision not to risk the chopper crews on a mission with such a low probability of success. Finally, the radio operator said again in a terse monotone, "Intrigue, this is Dunbar County. Change that emergency medevac to routine." The man had died. The cold emptiness of that kid's voice brought everyone in the FSCC room to an abrupt silence. Captain Donaghy stood silently staring at the squawk box for several seconds; tears welled up in his eyes. We all looked away.

* * * *

Another of our duties as TACP radio operators was to monitor the results of the TPQ-10 radar-controlled bombing missions. The Air Support Radar Team (ASRAT), an Air Force detachment located out by the main gate of the base, was responsible for guiding the planes over the target. Typically, the Marine Target Information Officer in the COC would provide the map coordinates of a target, based on a number of intelligence resources—most often aerial reconnaissance photos, electronic sensors, and intercepted enemy communications. He would then give the coordinates to a member of the air team, who would telephone the information to ASRAT. Because the Pentagon gave the defense of Khe Sanh such a high priority, we had a constant stream of bombers on station waiting to deploy.

The ASRAT would direct the next available aircraft over the new target, telling it precisely when to "pickle" (the aviators' term for "release") its bomb load. The team always used the same precise and steady mantra, "Stand byyyy . . . Stand byyyy . . . Mark! Mark!"

The air team radio operators would monitor these sorties to assess bomb damage. After attacking the target but before returning to his base, the pilot would radio us if he observed any secondary explosions (more explosions than the number of bombs dropped). At first, it was exciting to hear how extensive the damage was that we were inflicting on the enemy from the air. But after listening to hundreds of these sorties, I became adept at knowing when some of the pilots were either wrong or embellishing the damage they had done. For example, if I knew the target was a platoon-size NVA unit on the move, rather than trucks or an enemy supply point (the pilots did not know the nature of the target), and they radioed back that there had subsequently been numerous, large secondary explosions, I usually treated that with some skepticism.

Weather permitting, an aerial inspection of the bombing site was attempted as soon as possible. The NVA, however, were meticulous in hiding their damage and dead. Eventually, we came to the conclusion that bomb damage assessment by the bomber pilots was less than scientific and as the sheer numbers of TPQ-10s increased, collecting such information became less important to us.

We often had so many aircraft circling above us that we had to send them back without dropping their bombs. This was usually due to fuel considerations. A heavy bomb-laden aircraft coming from Da Nang or Chu Lai would have only about twelve minutes on station over Khe Sanh before having to return to base. Since the planes could not, by regulation, land with bombs still attached, they were required to drop them in certain designated areas. If the planes were carrier-based or returning to airfields near the coast they usually dropped their unused bombs in the ocean. Bombers from Udorn, Thailand, and other bases in the interior, often used the A Shau Valley, twenty miles south of Khe Sanh, as their dumping ground when returning from Khe Sanh. The A Shau was so heavily occupied by the NVA it was felt that a bomb dropped there randomly had a good chance of hitting someone.

Because of this abundance of air power, the Target Information Office would occasionally give the air team radio operators some old information on enemy movements and let us plot their probable location for the next TPQ-10 bombing. This was heady stuff for a nineteen-year-old PFC. Of course we listened intently to these sorties on our PRC-41 radio and were much more likely to accept the pilot's estimate of secondary explosions without skepticism.

* * * *

On January 24, the NVA turned their big 152mm guns on Khe Sanh Combat Base for the first time. One of these shells killed several recon Marines while they were inside a bunker. After this, we never felt safe anymore, anywhere.

The artillery fire was coming from Co Roc Mountain in Laos, six miles from the Khe Sanh Combat Base. The mountain ranges of western South Vietnam and Laos formed about 360 million years ago when the South China tectonic plate collided with a vast granite extrusion called the Kontum Massif. In the area several miles west of present-day Khe Sanh, the ancient sea floor rose thousands of feet and formed a huge limestone cliff. Over the centuries, the leaching of water through this limestone formed numerous large caves. It was in these caves that the NVA installed their big guns.

The guns would roll out, fire, then quickly return to the safety of the caves. The largest artillery pieces the Marines had at Khe Sanh were 155mm Howitzer cannons. These were designed so that the shells would travel in a high arc, making them capable of reaching targets that were not in direct line of fire, such as reverse hillsides. Because of this design feature, the Marine cannons gave up distance. The NVA, however, had guns rather than cannons. The arc of the projectile was much flatter than a Howitzer's, so the range of the guns was much greater. In other words, they could hit us but we couldn't hit them.

The benefit of this longer range would not have made these NVA guns efficient for use against most targets at Khe Sanh Combat Base, such as berm-protected trenches and bunkers or other fortified sites, had it not been for a certain geographic circumstance favorable to the NVA. Because the Co Roc cliffs rose over 800 meters above sea level, 1,200 feet higher than the Khe Sanh base, the arc of the artillery projectile was exaggerated by the pull of the earth's gravity—the longer it was in the air, the greater was the increase to the arc. This, coupled with the fact that the NVA maximized the elevation of the gun barrel, caused the shell to "drop" down on to the base rather than arrive more horizontally. This is also the primary reason these guns were not used against our more elevated hilltop outposts. Of course, General Giap and his artillery experts had factored all this into the plan of attack, long before the siege commenced.

While our fortifications were more at risk because of the arc desired by the NVA, it actually proved to be beneficial to us in another way. A 152mm gun shot at its normal ballistic trajectory would provide us almost no time to find cover, if we were outside. This is because the shell is on a more direct path and, with a muzzle velocity of 655 meters-per-second, is traveling faster than the sound of the shot. With the increased arc, we had a few seconds to seek cover. To those of us who were about to be in the impact zone, the sound of those guns at Co Roc was quite distinctive from the sound of other enemy incoming. It had a faint, hollow rumble, like the murmuring of deep and distant voices. Some speculated that the "hollow" quality, which made the sound unique, was the result of a slight reverberation from the cave opening in which the gun sat. Even when we were underground, we could often hear (perhaps "feel" is a better word) the rumble of those distant guns.

An incident that would give the North Vietnamese this advantage in the range of their artillery occurred the prior summer. On July 19, 1967, a convoy transporting the U.S. Army's big mechanized 175mm guns (with a range capable of reaching Co Roc from Khe Sanh) was slowly traveling up Route 9 to the base. Five miles east of Khe Sanh, Marine patrols moving in advance of the convoy detected a large NVA ambush. The big guns returned to Camp Carroll, where they could still provide us with artillery fire around Khe Sanh—but not all the way to Co Roc.

Sending in troops to destroy the gun emplacements was also out of the question. The NVA had the Co Roc so well fortified that several Special Forces FOB patrols attempting to gather information in the area between 1965 and 1968 were annihilated. In April 1968, a FOB team inserted there was extracted after only eighteen hours due to the large number of NVA nearby searching for them. As a result, we had to rely on our aircraft to bomb these NVA gun sites.

Late one afternoon, I was speaking on the radio to an air observer. He had been circling over Co Roc most of the afternoon trying to find a particular gun that was pounding us at will. The NVA on the mountain would listen for the sound of the plane and pull the gun back into the cave when he got too close. The AO became quite frustrated as I told him we were, at that very moment, still taking incoming fire from Co Roc. He could not locate a muzzle flash or smoke. In desperation, he turned off the plane engine and began a glide. He then opened the door and stuck his head out of the plane. With the engine noise gone, the NVA thought that he was too, so they fired again. This time he heard the shot and found the gun. He closed the door, turned on the engine and fired some smoke rockets to mark the target. Within minutes, bombers were pounding the position with high explosives, resulting in several secondary explosions. I was never prouder to be on the air team than that day.

* * * *

Me at the entrance of my home, the old mortar pit bunker

After returning from the village, I took up residence in the old mortar pit bunker. The first Americans at Khe Sanh had built this concrete-lined, circular pit years before. But as the base expanded and mortars were placed out closer to the new perimeter, the pit was abandoned.

Panels of steel runway matting now roofed it, and several layers of sandbags covered the matting. It gave us protection from the shrapnel and may have withstood a 60mm mortar round landing on it, but certainly nothing larger. The pit was quite crowded those first few nights. Since it was a circular space, about twelve feet in diameter, we slept like spokes in a wheel with our feet at the hub.

Eventually some people moved out into new holes. Although we tried to avoid work details ordered by superiors, everyone pitched in when it came to digging a friend's hole. The ground at Khe Sanh was baked hard, even within a few days of rain, and we struck clay at only two or three feet. It was necessary to use the pick end of the entrenching tool to bust the ground into clods, which we then crumbled into granules for filling sandbags.

Often, more dirt came out of a hole than was needed to make sandbags that would later cover it. Loose dirt was highly prized, and so was given to your buddies first, before it could be stolen. It was not uncommon to stand armed guard over a pile of dirt, until your buddy could return with more empty sandbags. Loose dirt translated into sandbags made with relatively little effort and less time exposed to the incoming.

I decided to stay in the mortar pit because I managed to get one of the two little wooden bunks in a tiny cell located down a few steps from the rest of the main pit. This little concrete room, originally designed to house two mortar men, was a bit deeper in the earth and covered by a cap of reinforced concrete about two feet thick. I felt somewhat safer when I was in there.

Sergeant Harry Stroud had the other bunk. He was the company electrician, so we always had electrical power from one of the generators he maintained. Once the electricity was switched on, Harry hooked up his reel-to-reel tape recorder and played the same sixty-minute Elvis Presley tape every day, over and over, until he went home in March. This produced an effect on me not unlike that resulting from aversion therapy; and for several years thereafter, the very first note of an Elvis song made my neck descend imperceptibly into my shoulders in anticipation of an incoming round.

One evening during the first week after the initial rocket attack, I was sitting outside the bunker with Steve Orr and a few others. There had been a break in the monsoon clouds during that week. This was unfortunate for the enemy because they no longer had the bad weather to conceal their movements and artillery fire. In fact, we had received no incoming rounds for several hours. In this relaxed frame of mind, our conversation soon got around to how much we would like a beer.

Someone mentioned that the officer's club, which was only thirty feet from where we were sitting, had lots of beer. The club was partially subterranean, its corrugated metal roof peaking about five feet above the ground. Both the club and the mess hall located next to it had taken direct hits from rockets. The entrance to the club was down five or six steps and consisted of a half-inch thick steel door that was chained and padlocked.

"What if we get caught?" a voice whispered in the darkness. Orr replied quickly, trivializing the risks in what would become our favorite rhetorical question, "What are they going to do? Shave our heads and send us to 'Nam'?"

Our plan quickly unfolded. Sergeant Billy Hyde and I were selected for the mission because of our lean builds. Several of the more burly Marines jammed their hands into the doorframe and began pulling the bottom of the door back until it bent ten or twelve inches. Billy and I squeezed through the opening.

The rocket had really made a mess of things inside. The entry hole in the roof was already covered with plastic on the outside to keep out the rain. The explosion had knocked over chairs and tables. Chunks of concrete and other debris littered the floor. Shrapnel holes spattered the walls. With tiny votive candles, we searched the area until we found the back room where the cases of beer and soda pop were stacked. Billy and I each grabbed a case of beer and worked our way back to the door. It was eerie. Incoming was still so strange to us, its destructive power so new. We stopped a moment, raising our candles above our heads to light up more of the room and absorb as much damage information as we could.

At the door, eager hands reached through to take the beer. Hyde squeezed out ahead of me, seniority and rank prevailing. Most of the door-pullers departed up the stairs with Hyde and the beer, leaving me inside. Finally, appealing to their esprit d' corps—you never leave another Marine behind—a few of them reluctantly returned to pull the door open, allowing me to slither out. We made another run the following night, but that would be the last. In our stupidity, or I prefer to think our rebelliousness, we threw the empty beer cans out the bunker door and they soon littered the area. Once the officers noticed this, they removed the rest of the beer to a secret location. Interestingly, they never questioned where the empty cans had come from or investigated the break-in of their club.

* * * *

About a week after I had returned from the village to the base, several explosions occurred nearby, and soon gas began seeping into our bunker. Eyes started to burn, noses began to run. I could taste the distinct, astringent tang of tear gas. I was familiar with the odor from my gas mask training at Camp Pendleton. I was not comforted, however, by the fact that this might only be tear gas. There had been many rumors about gas: nerve gas, poison gas, opium gas, gas that would make you blind or cause you to vomit until you drowned in it. Everyone in the bunker immediately located their gas masks and put them on. Unfortunately, I had thrown mine away in the village.

Looking around the bunker, I became increasingly fearful. Familiar faces of friends were now housed behind those hideous, bug-eyed, black rubber masks. My eyes burned fiercely and my gag reflexes triggered. I panicked, grabbed my rifle, and started for the hatchway. "Where you going?" a muffled voice asked. "Calm down," said others. Easy for them to say, I thought, under the circumstances.

Orr then asked me what I was doing. I said that I was going to the company supply to get a mask. He advised me that the initial rocket attack had destroyed the supply tent. "Then," I said, "I'm going topside, find the first person I don't know, and take his gas mask—even if I have to kill him for it." I started up through the hatch. Tiddy grabbed me, pulled me back, and spun me around. Orr punched me on the jaw. When I went down, they threw an old wool blanket over me and as one held me down, the other poured water from a five-gallon can over the blanket. This acted as a protective filter from the gas—and it worked pretty well.

As it turned out, the gas was not nerve or poison gas. It was merely a diversion. The NVA immediately followed with a sustained rocket attack to catch those who fled from the gas out into the open.

Panic in combat is a product of surprise. This is why experienced veterans are less prone to it. From that night forward, I never again felt the undertow of hysteria tugging at my feet. It was not that I had lost my fear—I was just no longer a slave to it. There would be no more surprises for me at Khe Sanh. I had lived through this last one, thanks to Steve Orr's well-aimed right uppercut to my chin.

In addition to gas and the regular fragmentation and high explosive rounds, the NVA would also shoot propaganda leaflets at us. These would arrive in artillery shells and usually explode in airbursts, scattering over the area in the breeze. I have kept one all these years. On one side of the leaflet were arguments against U.S. involvement in the war, supported by quotes from the *New York Times*. On the reverse, was an offer for us to surrender, with a promise of humane treatment if we complied. Later, we would hear of GIs who had gone over to the other side and were leading VC and NVA troops against us. But to those of us hunkered down at Khe Sanh, that was inconceivable.

We also shot propaganda leaflets at the enemy. These leaflets pictured a B-52 bomber dropping its entire bomb load. Enemy defectors made clear that this was the weapon they most feared. On the reverse side of the leaflet was a photograph of a smiling, friendly ARVN pointing a seemingly bewildered but grateful VC soldier the way to the nearest POW camp. The picture was so far removed from the reality of things, a kind of Vietnamese Norman Rockwell portrait, that it often became the object of darkly humorous comments like, "I wonder if that Cong will still be smiling once they've attached the electrode to his balls?"

My feeling was that neither side's propaganda was effective. However, I was amused by the incongruity of these little "love notes" being delivered by such lethal means.

* * * *

On January 23, 1968, North Korean naval vessels and MIG jets attacked the USS *Pueblo*, as it gathered intelligence off the coast of North Korea. One man died and several were wounded. Eighty-two surviving crewmembers were captured. The Pueblo incident occurred almost simultaneously with the initial attacks on Khe Sanh, but I gave little thought to it—until January 31.

That day, the NVA and Viet Cong attacked every major city and military installation in South Vietnam. Because they took place on the first feast day of the Vietnamese New Year, or Tet, these attacks would come to be known as the Tet Offensive. Although the *Pueblo* incident occurred nearly two thousand miles away, it presented disturbing possibilities for those of us now trapped at Khe Sanh by an enemy force of vastly superior numbers. Some of us began to fear that U.S. aircraft and troops would be diverted from Southeast Asia to fight a new war in Korea. I wondered if the Pentagon might now deem us expendable in the wake of some newly devised national defense strategy. I didn't think this fear was necessarily overwrought. Only a week earlier, in Khe Sanh Village, I had felt the sting of being judged dispensable as a matter of tactical practicality.

Just four months earlier, in October 1967, Che Guevarra had been captured and executed in the mountains of southeast Bolivia. Guevarra had been a hero of the 1959 Cuban revolution. He had, however, looked far beyond Cuba, wanting to spawn "100 Vietnams." He was trying to organize a guerrilla army in Bolivia, when CIA-trained, local army commandos caught up with him. I already knew about Che from having spent time on Telegraph Avenue in Berkeley. The area near the University of California campus was a hotbed of antiwar and pro-Communist sympathy at that time. Che was already an idol to many.

With the capture of the *Pueblo*, I worried that Che's vision of "100 Vietnams" was being orchestrated by an international conspiracy of Communist nations. If all this was now coming true, the United States might not be powerful enough to take them all on at once; and I could not have picked a worse place to be.

* * * *

During the week of January 22–28, the last of our reinforcements flew into Khe Sanh. This would increase our total troop strength, including the hills, to about 6,000 men.

The 1st Battalion, 9th Marine Regiment took up positions on the southwest side of the base and in the rock quarry to the west. Although we were all pleased to have another Marine battalion to help us, we were a little concerned that it was this infamous battalion in particular. Since its arrival in Vietnam, this battalion had encountered so much combat that it seemed the NVA were picking on them in particular. Due to the inordinately high number of casualties they sustained, the battalion was soon nicknamed the "Walking Dead." Their arrival at Khe Sanh insured there was going to be plenty more trouble ahead.

In addition, during that same week the ARVN 37th Ranger Battalion arrived and took up positions on the southeast side of the defensive perimeter. The effectiveness of the Army of the Republic of Vietnam was continuously being undermined by the corruption and political manipulation of their military coup leaders. The best troops were kept close to Saigon, to discourage any new coups. Nepotism and jealousy weakened the officer ranks. In the mid-1970s, after the war finally ended, several high-ranking ARVN officers were discovered to have been working for the enemy and were decorated by the North Vietnamese for their contributions to the war effort. While the typical ARVN soldier often proved to be loyal and dedicated, and the ARVN Rangers had a reputation for toughness in combat, most Marines, as a rule, distrusted them. Once they settled in, the ARVN soldiers often wandered around the base looking for things to steal. Since many Marines did the same thing, this was not considered to be too out of line.

A few days after their arrival, I went to company sickbay with a touch of dysentery. While waiting for the corpsman to find a bottle of medicine for me, I noticed an ARVN Ranger sitting on an examination table nearby. His right boot was off and he had a clean round bullet entrance wound through the top of his foot. He did not seem to be in much pain. The corpsman was dabbing the wound with a long cotton swab. Before long, an ARVN officer came striding in. He was extremely clean and well groomed and wore an impeccably starched utility uniform with a yellow cravat. He got up in front of the man and started chastising him in Vietnamese. I don't understand the language, but I had a pretty good idea what he was saying. The soldier quickly jumped down off the table, picked up his boot, and hopped out the door. The "accidental" shooting had not gotten him out of the war and now he had to rely on one good foot to get him out of the way of the incoming.

Doc Topmiller was the corpsman who gave me the medicine. Doc loathed all Marines at the time, considering us all no better than imbeciles. Later we would become good friends.

Doc had already gotten a reputation for bravery on the very first morning of the attack. The exploding ammo dump had sent a white phosphorus round into a group of Marine artillerymen. One Marine struck by the searing phosphorus was in excruciating pain. Doc went to his aid, despite the extreme danger, and saved his life. In less dangerous situations, the traditional antagonism between Marines and sailors goes on as it has for centuries; but in war, there are few people held in higher regard by a Marine than his Navy Corpsman.

* * * *

In early February, the NVA artillery pounding of the base began in earnest. The small grave that had protected me on the day I was caught alone in the incoming was actually the beginning of a bunker later occupied by Pig and Old Woman. Pig earned his nickname more because he was a slob than because he was overweight. Pig arrived in December, shortly after Orr. He was loud and abrasive. He would say whatever he was thinking at any time, regardless of who was within earshot. This is never a good thing in a military environment.

Despite all of this, Pig was accepted and even liked by most of us. He recognized that he was different and attributed it to the fact that he had been hit in the head with a chain during a bar fight while stationed at Pensacola, Florida, a year earlier. He claimed to hear a constant buzzing sound in his head, and I do recall him, on more than one occasion, shaking his head and slapping one side of it with his open palm as if he were a swimmer trying to get water out of an ear.

Pig was one of the four air team radio operators. He worked the day shift with Lance Corporal Reath. Pig never considered himself a victim of fate or inevitability and was always prepared for the worst the NVA could field. He rarely went anywhere unless he was bristling with weapons. It was not unusual to see Pig carrying a rifle and a .45 pistol, several cloth bandoliers of M-16 magazines crisscrossing his chest, and a half-dozen assorted hand grenades dangling from his webbed suspenders. When he sensed the enemy to be unusually close, Pig would sling a couple of anti-tank rocket launcher tubes over his shoulder for good measure. Captain Harry Baig, the TIO, once commented that if Pig ever took a direct hit from enemy fire, the secondary explosions would go on for hours.

Because Pig was so gross in his personal hygiene habits, no one wanted to live with him. Even when we all still lived above ground in the tent, there were always vacant cots on either side of his. When we moved underground after the siege began, he found it nearly impossible to find a bunker mate.

Old Woman could not have been less like Pig. He was tall, thin, neat, and soft spoken. Old Woman received his nickname because he constantly whined about everything in a high-pitched nasally voice. When he was whining, his posture would collapse forward into a kind of dowager's hump. No one wanted to live with him either.

The first week in February, Old Woman and Pig began digging their hole. Many of us helped them for a while, hacking at the hard clay. The style of bunker was intended to be standard, that is, with a hole being dug three to five feet deep. Usually half the bunker was underground with the upper half constructed of sandbag walls. The roof was made of metal runway matting on which more sandbags were stacked. Roof designs varied from hole to hole. Often an air space was left between layers of sandbags to allow the incoming to "predetonate." None of these designs was based on scientific evidence. I think we all discussed them in a serious way to convince ourselves that we could be safe from the incoming. We soon learned that almost all direct hits on a bunker resulted in the death of the occupants.

On February 2, incoming rounds struck the U.S. Army Signal Battalion bunker, killing all four occupants. The location of this bunker had been easily discernible to us, and probably the enemy too, by the large twin lollipop-shaped antenna nearby. Still early in the siege, it was one of the first bunkers directly struck. We were all interested in what the effect had been. A Marine who helped remove the bodies later told me that although the rocket had partially penetrated the bunker, two of the dead men did not have a scratch on them. This phenomenon has been recognized since at least World War I, when soldiers were found dead near an explosion despite having no external injuries. The actual cause of death is still a subject for debate. One recent study attributed such deaths to "the sharp instantaneous rise in ambient atmospheric pressure resulting from explosive detonation or firing of weapons."[13] The immense pressure of the blast on the chest ruptures delicate lung tissue, admitting air bubbles into the arteries that travel to the heart, brain, and other organs causing sudden death.

At Khe Sanh in 1968, we knew nothing about "ambient atmospheric pressure." The story the Marine told me was that the two men suffered from a "concussion" that "rattled their brains until they died." The story was believable and therefore believed. The only bunker on the base capable of withstanding a direct hit from the NVA guns was the Seabees (Naval Construction Battalion) bunker. It was deep, thanks to their access to earthmoving equipment, and covered with many layers of earth and steel matting supported by huge timbers. Rumor had it that inside the bunker the Seabees had a modern kitchen, beds with sheets, and stockpiles of real food and liquor. Surprisingly, we did not begrudge them these luxuries because they had the dangerous job of going out onto the runway during incoming barrages to fix the damaged matting. There was no place to hide on the runway and the Seabees suffered a number of casualties.

At the other end of the bunker-spectrum from the Seabee's comfortable subterranean dwelling was the one built by Pig and Old Woman. Their hole was only about two-feet deep with sandbag walls rising another four feet above the ground. This design evolved because they were essentially lazy, and it was much less difficult for them to go out and steal dirt for their sandbags than to dig a deeper hole in the ground. In addition to sandbags, they piled an incredible amount of garbage and debris on top of the roof.

The rat problem was already bad in the Headquarters Company area, but with the construction of Pig's bunker, it seemed to get worse. The bunker was located directly across the road from the enlisted men's crapper. One night while I was walking on the road, a herd of six to eight rats scurried from the crapper, passed in front of me, and disappeared down the hatch into Pig's bunker. The rats plunged down the bunker hatchway with such confidence that I had the impression they made this trip frequently. We later joked that the rats were probably confused as to which place actually was the crapper.

Pig and Old Woman initially had difficulty sleeping because of the sheer number of rats shuttling in and out of their bunker. Pig, who among his many talents was an accomplished thief, returned to the bunker one day with a hammock, which he hung several feet above the floor. Canvass and mosquito netting completely enclosed the hammock and it could be zipped closed from the inside. After that, he slept like a baby, fully insulated from the rats on the floor.

This drove Old Woman crazy. He could not find anything like what Pig had, and his complaining became constant and more irritating than before. One morning he went out and scavenged some plywood and wire mesh screen. He began to assemble a sleeping box in front of his bunker. He worked all day, sawing and hammering, stopping only long enough to dive for cover from the incoming. By late afternoon, he had created a large box with a hinged door that he could lock from the inside. He was proud of his accomplishment until he dragged it to the entrance of the bunker only to find it was far too large for the opening.

Pig (with C-ration pineapple slice in his mouth) and Old Woman in the vermin-infested trash heap they called "home"   *Courtesy Raul Orozco*

I will never forget how high-pitched his voice became as he wailed those obscenities. He began pounding the box with his hammer, smashing off great chunks of plywood, then halting every few minutes to push his eyeglasses back up on his nose with a forefinger. This went on until the sweat poured off him and he fell to his knees exhausted. The remnants of the sleeping box soon joined the other trash on top of their bunker.

Old Woman now resigned himself to sleeping back on the floor of the bunker. He never complained about this again, although his personality became noticeably more subdued and distant. Eventually, rats bit several members of our company causing them to undergo painful rabies treatments; but they never bit Old Woman. By the time we left Khe Sanh, Old Woman's face seemed to have become narrower, his nose a little more pointed; his blond mustache frayed at the ends like long, fine whiskers. The magnification caused by his eyeglasses confirmed our worst fears—his eyes had gotten tinier and pink around the edges. It was as if he had become one of them.

As if having to worry about rabies wasn't bad enough, there was also the Bubonic Plague. Many of the rats would range outside our defensive perimeter and feed on the carnage. There they came in contact with plague-infected fleas, which they carried back to the base. That meant inoculations for everyone.

In addition to being plague-ridden, the Khe Sanh rats were downright aggressive. A radio relay operator named Weaver, who slept on the floor of the mortar pit bunker, awoke one night to find a huge rat standing on his chest and chewing on his lower lip. Wolverton, the radioman at the CAC, told me that once, several months before I had arrived, he had been sitting in the comm bunker one night with his right hand dangling down between his knees. Feeling something, he looked down to see a large rat chewing on his finger. These rats apparently were not dining on the men's flesh as much as on the unwashed food residue on their lips and fingers. Both men had to undergo several weeks of painful injections to avoid contracting rabies. Peter Brush, author of *The Vietnam Generation* and a Khe Sanh veteran, tried to get a sense of just how many rats there may have been at Khe Sanh during the siege:

Even though the Marines never attempted a census, estimates using certain assumptions can be made. The lesser bandicoot (*bandicota bengalensis*) is one species of rat common to southern Asia. Each female can produce a litter per month, with seven pups per litter, for a daily rate of increase of over eleven percent.

The rats at Khe Sanh may or may not have been reproducing at their biological maximum (i.e., rats were being killed by Marines, but it is also likely they were being driven into the base from without by aerial bombardment). There are approximately as many rats in the world as people, unevenly distributed. If the rat population equaled the human population at Khe Sanh, and assuming the above optimum rate of increase, theoretically there could have been one hundred thousand rats by day 27 of the siege, one-half million rats on day 43, and over one million by day 50.[14]

In the mortar pit bunker, particularly down in the cell where I slept, when it was very quiet I could hear rats constantly burrowing in the ground around me, chewing and gnawing through the earth and concrete. This was quite disconcerting, particularly during the times when we believed the enemy was tunneling under the base. I often slept with my M-16 next to me, just in case the dusty head of an NVA miner should suddenly poke through the wall.

We had a particularly large rat that invaded the mortar pit at night, and we became obsessed with defending ourselves against it. During our spare time, we would make special bullets. The idea was to develop something that would injure the rat, but, if we missed, not kill a human occupant of the bunker. I made a full twenty-round magazine of rat bullets for my rifle. Using pliers, I pulled the lead bullet out of the brass, emptied about half the gunpowder, and then pressed the open end of the brass cartridge into a bar of soap. I then pushed tiny pieces of metal solder into the soap bullet, a sort of "rat shrapnel." I even taped a flashlight to the barrel of my M-16. But the big rat had the instincts of an NVA sapper and consistently evaded our efforts to catch it.

We finally procured a big rat trap, about a foot-and-a-half long. It took the strength of two men to set it. That night we baited it with the tastiest treat in our C-rations (three-flavored cheese) and slid it carefully behind some gear stacked up against the wall. The next morning we pulled the packs away and there, glaring up at us with the big trap clamped to the back of its neck, as if it were only a minor nuisance, was the largest and most pissed-off rat I had ever seen. Its rubbery tail, nearly as long again as its sleek, black body, lashed about defiantly. Its eyes glowed, its fanged jaws snapped convulsively. The rat's total absence of fear amazed me.

Weaver, who had already been bitten by a rat and had endured the painful rabies inoculation series, was given the honor of disposing of it. The animal's high-pitched squeal began when Weaver carefully picked the trap up with a large pair of pliers. Outside, he doused the snarling creature with lighter fluid, ignited it with his Zippo, opened the trap, and dropped the rat onto the ground. Engulfed in a shroud of pale blue flame, the burning rat ran zigzag down the road, its shrill screams soon fading away. Never having considered myself a cruel person, I was surprised at the pleasure that its suffering gave me at that moment. There was nothing we loathed more than those rats—not even the NVA.

When we weren't waiting in ambush for rats, playing poker, or tediously narrating our pre-Khe Sanh lives, we often passed the time in our bunkers making up inane games. Private First Class Borgardis was a master of these. Of less than average height, with a curly blond topnotch and a perpetual smirk transfixed to the corner of his mouth, Bogardis probably had the highest IQ of anyone at Khe Sanh. Officially, he was our radio repair technician. But because he had such a broad understanding of electronics and could read complex wiring schematics with ease, he was sought out to look at almost every malfunctioning electrical device on the base.

He lived in the mortar pit bunker for a time but moved frequently because he did not get along well with others. Bogardis particularly disdained staff NCOs and officers and took every opportunity to anger and humiliate them. I suspected this was one of the reasons he never rose above the rank of PFC, despite the fact that he had been in the Marines Corps nearly three years. He often complained that someone had rigged his orders to Khe Sanh in order to punish him for his bad attitude.

Once, I saw him in the alcove at the north end of the COC corridor, playing simultaneous games of chess with Gunny Rich and Captain Fitzsimmons (a newly arrived Regimental Air Officer). Bogardis had his back to both boards, and had admonished his opponents to tell him "only once" where they had moved their pieces. He beat them both and walked away arrogantly shaking his head in a gesture of mock sympathy. The blood glowed on the back of the gunny's neck as he sat there in silent, homicidal rage.

Some days, when the incoming pinned us down in our bunker, Bogardis and I would play quiz games. One simple game, which went on intermittently for a few weeks, involved one of us saying the name of a country, state, or city. The other would have to use the last letter of that name as the first letter of another place. Once a name was used, it could not be repeated. The game took our minds off our immediate predicament and forced us to think of places other than Khe Sanh. I held my own for a while: from Uruguay to Yemen, Natchez to Zurich, Houston to Nairobi. Finally, I was out of names; but Bogardis played on from Indio to Oberammergau to Ursk. His knowledge seemed limitless.

Many of us thought Bogardis' antagonism toward his superiors was brave and rebellious, in a James Dean kind of way. Yet I also wondered what someone with his deep resentment of authority was doing in the Marines Corps, and why a person with his incredible intellect felt compelled to demonstrate it so often to those he held in such contempt. Because he moved from bunker to bunker so frequently, it was a long time before most of us realized he had left Khe Sanh and gone home.

That fact illustrated a facet of life under siege that was like no other in the military. Because our platoon never assembled aboveground in typical military formations but remained in a number of small bunkers scattered in the general area of the COC, we often didn't know other people in our unit. With varying shifts and duties, a person could go for months at Khe Sanh Combat Base and never even see someone living ten feet away. There were just so few places to congregate. One of our favorites, however, was the "porch" in front of Orr's bunker.

Orr and Tiddy finished their hole about the same time as Pig. But, unlike Pig and Old Woman's wretched hovel, their bunker was state-of-the-art Khe Sanh living. It had clean, elevated sleeping recesses, *Playboy* centerfold wallpaper, and a wooden floor constructed of cargo pallets. The front porch, constructed of discarded plywood, boasted several wooden chairs that Orr and Tiddy had "borrowed" from the nearby officer's club. The porch was a good place to visit, and between barrages of incoming shells, it became a meeting place for many of us.

Over time, incoming blew apart the chairs on the porch, and it became an ongoing project to rebuild them when we met and talked. We used nails, glue, and electrical tape; but eventually only one chair remained intact—a small symbol of our defiance. Until the day we left Khe Sanh, there was always a functional chair occupying Orr's front porch.

Despite Orr and Tiddy's efforts to better the neighborhood, the base had become an absolute mess. The commander of the 1st Air Cavalry Division, General Tolson, was horrified when he first flew in to the base to

discuss the upcoming relief operation. "It was the most depressing, demoralizing place I ever visited," he said. "It was a very distressing sight, completely unpoliced, strewn with rubble, dud rounds, and damaged equipment, and with the troops living a life more similar to rats than human beings."[15]

Me, sitting amid the ruins in the only chair left

In late February, the title of a news magazine article dubbed Khe Sanh Combat Base "The Worst

Place on Earth." Most of us did not need convincing on that point. I did overhear, however, a Marine from Detroit wondering what improvements his hometown had made since he left to cause it to lose that title.

We occasionally made efforts to remove the trash that was strewn everywhere. One such clean-up campaign occurred early March. For several days, one NCO or another ordered us to police the area. Yet they would never stay to supervise us; and as soon as they departed, so did we. One morning Staff Sergeant Allen, still smarting from a recent ass chewing by the company commander over the rubbish issue, came down into the mortar pit bunker and found me sleeping in my little chamber. He angrily ordered me topside to clean up the area. If it was not done within two hours, he barked, I would be held personally responsible.

I had just come off my usual twelve-hour radio shift and had to get my sleep during the day. Tired of being awakened every morning for this duty, I decided to end the problem once and for all. I collected all the combustible trash—wood from cargo pallets and blown-up buildings, discarded C-ration cartons, fragments of tent canvas, and so forth—into a large pile between the mortar pit bunker and Orr and Tiddy's hole. I then took one of the five-gallon gasoline cans that Harry Stroud used to keep his generators going, and poured half the contents on the pile. I doused a piece of cardboard with the gasoline, ignited it with my Zippo, and tossed it on the stack. The gasoline exploded with a great sucking sound, burned furiously for several minutes, and was soon a smoldering heap of crackling plywood and glowing corrugated paper.

Still muttering angrily about my interrupted sleep, I patrolled the area in wider and wider circles looking for more fuel for the fire. As I passed near the gutted mess hall building, I saw a cardboard box. When I tried to lift it, I realized it was full. Inside were twelve, sixteen-ounce cans of B-ration salmon, intentionally passed over by the countless Marine scavengers who had otherwise stripped the mess hall of anything useful for improving their diet or the ambiance of their holes. I hoisted the box to my shoulder, walked to the edge of the fire and, in an act entirely devoid of reason or common sense, committed it to the flames.

Then I went back down into my bunker for sleep, satisfied that this was the last I would ever hear of this particular problem. Shortly after I drifted off to sleep, the first can of fish exploded.

By late afternoon, nuggets of reeking salmon, like little pink shards of shrapnel, covered an extensive area. A thick cloud of flies descended, sticking aggressively to anyone who walked by, buzzing into open mouths and eyes, and coming down into bunkers to annoy slumbering Marines. Rumor

The regimental mess hall after a 122mm rocket plowed through the corrugated metal roof and exploded. Hills 950 (left), and 1015 (right), can be seen in the distance

quickly spread that the flies had come up from the ravines where they had been dining on the bodies of the "dead dinks." This added a certain insult-to-injury aspect to their annoyance. Later that night, droves of rats invaded the area, slithering like snakes in the cinders among the scorched and burst cans. My popularity was soon at an all-time low.

Just before concluding my radio watch at 0600 the following morning, Oz warned me that the entire company was so angry with me, I might be shot on sight if I returned to the mortar pit bunker. I hid out for a couple of days in a small abandoned bunker I found behind the officers quarters. It was an odd place, long and narrow with one side completely open, and covered in chicken wire. It provided great ventilation, but not very good protection. Consequently, I didn't get much sleep and was happy when the great plague of vermin, which I had brought down upon the men of Headquarters Company, finally subsided, and I was able to return.

* * * *

The enlisted men's crapper, across from Pig's hole, was a six-hole outhouse surrounded by several 55-gallon drums filled with dirt in order to protect the occupants from shrapnel. Before the siege, burning the "honey buckets" was a job done by the Bru. After the initial attack on the base, this duty went unassigned. The buckets soon foamed over with throbbing masses of maggots, so full that they dropped in large dun-colored clumps down the side. As a lowly PFC, I was very likely to be stuck with the incredibly disgusting task of burning those seething pots. I was careful to avoid certain NCOs and officers, consequently managing to evade that particularly distasteful duty.

Everything at Khe Sanh had some risk attached to it. The best you could do was to minimize that risk. Even simple things like going to the head, things you had never given thought to before, now required planning and proper timing. Many days, when the fog hugged the ground, and the incoming was relatively light, it was not so much of a problem. But as the monsoon waned and the fog diminished, the incoming increased and was constant most of the day.

I developed a routine for these times. While still in my bunker, I would loosen my belt and pants and hold them up with my left hand. In my right hand, I'd hold the toilet paper squares, which came in the C-ration package. Then I would listen for the pattern of incoming for a few minutes. If it was the big artillery from Co Roc, the sequence of fire was generally uniform, that is, the NVA would fire a barrage for a few minutes, then pull the guns into the safety of the caves for a while. Rockets from Hill 881N had a similar timing. This was always an opportune time to head for the crapper. If the enemy was instead firing mortars or recoilless rifles, the pattern was more sporadic and unpredictable. Then I had to rely more on my intuition. When I felt that the time was just right, I would race across the road into the little building, do my business, and be back in my bunker within five minutes. No one wanted to die in the crapper. I don't know exactly why; it just seemed to matter.

There were some who tried to avoid complying with these basic sanitation practices, as in the case of the Teletype Sergeant. The teletype operators communicated on a highly secure network with the outside world. The bunker where they worked was one of the newer ones built at Khe Sanh. Constructed of three interconnected metal cargo boxes sunk into a large hole, the bunker was covered with many layers of sandbags. Because it was almost entirely metal on the inside, it was clean and relatively dust free.

Morley Sweet, who lived in the mortar pit bunker with us, worked in the teletype bunker and despised the sergeant. Sweet told us how the sergeant, who both lived and worked in the teletype bunker, was too afraid of the incoming to even step outside, so was crapping in empty C-ration cartons and throwing them out the door. This behavior, particularly from "a lifer," disgusted Sweet. He began writing the sergeant's name on pieces of masking tape and sticking them to .45-caliber bullets, leaving them for the sergeant to find. But the Teletype Sergeant didn't get the message and continued his poor hygiene habits. One day, Sweet took a hand grenade, unscrewed the firing mechanism, and exploded the blasting cap (like a large firecracker) in an empty metal ammo box. He then screwed the mechanism back on and reinserted the safety pin.

That night, Sweet began screaming insanely that he was going to kill the Teletype Sergeant if he did not stop crapping in cardboard boxes. Suddenly, Sweet produced the dud grenade and pulled the pin. The sergeant ran around a security partition used to block the view of the teletype machines from the rest of the bunker. Sweet rolled the grenade under the partition, where it came to rest next to the sergeant's boot. He just froze. Unbelievably, he never reported Sweet for doing this.

Sweet's tossing that grenade convinced the Teletype Sergeant to start using the crapper the next day. On that morning, Oz and I happened to be on a work detail, adding more sandbags to the roof of the bunker that served as the regimental communications office. The bunker, which was about ten feet above the ground and taller than the other structures around it, provided us with an excellent view of the rest of the base, including the runway about 150 meters to the north. We saw the sergeant poke his head timidly from the door of the teletype bunker and for several minutes stand there motionless, listening for incoming. Sensing it was safe, he began a careful, crouching trudge toward the crapper.

He did not see us up on the roof as he walked by. We knew what to do. Oz nodded to me and I made a high-pitched whistling sound like a recoilless rifle round coming in. Oz then tossed a heavy sandbag, which landed with a great thud just behind the man. The sergeant froze for what seemed like ten seconds, then turned and loped back to the safety of the teletype bunker. It appeared from his gait that he might have taken care of his business without even the benefit of a cardboard box. Oz and I laughed so hard we nearly rolled off the roof. When we told Sweet about it later, he was not amused because he worried that all his efforts may have gone for naught, and the sergeant would now revert to his old habits. The teletype sergeant, however, did not resume his "reuse" of the C-ration boxes, and life in the teletype bunker returned to normal—well, as normal as it could be with a guy like Morley Sweet working there.

Sometimes it seemed as though Sweet considered the siege to be one long high school prank, so when you were around him, even for a few minutes, the situation always seemed a little less serious. He had a somewhat enigmatic personality and was always doing things that made us laugh, despite the fact that he had no apparent sense of humor himself. At age seventeen (he had lied about his age and enlisted when he was sixteen), he was the youngest man in our company. Yet, he often seemed like the oldest because of the seriousness with which he said and did everything.

In February, Sweet received a large pair of women's red panties in the mail. The arrival of these panties began to worry some of us. Had the stress of daily life at Khe Sanh produced a fetish, or worse, in Sweet's young psyche?

The next day we discovered the reason he had requested the underwear from home. Just after several incoming rounds exploded nearby, a broom handle with the red panties attached to one end popped out of the hatch of Sweet's bunker and waved back and forth. This, as every Marine knows, is called "Maggie's Drawers." For decades, Marine rifle ranges had used a red flag (later a red disk) to indicate when the shooter completely missed a target. Maggie's Drawers were waved back and forth for each missed shot. Sweet was using the panties to taunt the NVA gunners, and he was not joking.

Throughout February, the NVA laid siege to Khe Sanh. They first dug a trench line completely around the base, paralleling our own trench lines. From there, they began to dig trenches toward our lines. Like at the siege of Dien Bien Phu, they intended to eventually launch a general attack, emerging from the protection of these trenches close to our defensive perimeter. They dug at night or during the dense morning fog that at times prevented us from seeing something more than a few meters away.

Sweet was determined to use the NVA tactics against them. So most mornings after his watch ended, he would take his C-rations and his rifle, and go over to the base perimeter. Sitting in a trench line, he would chew his food while intently staring down the barrel of his rifle into the fog. As the sun began to rise, a slight breeze would often stir the fog, shredding it just enough to catch a glimpse of some spectral figure busily hacking at the ground with a pick. Sweet would stop chewing and squeeze off several rounds. He never admitted to any actual kills, but told us it did wonders for his digestion.

Marines on the Khe Sanh perimeter wait in the dense fog for the enemy to come

Courtesy of David Douglas Duncan

One morning, a Marine sniper asked him to stop doing this. Snipers were well trained for this job and had special rifles with telescopic sights. The sniper explained that he didn't want Sweet alerting the diggers to the fact that they were now visible because the fog was lifting. It ruined the sniper's chances for a confirmed kill, which was how they measured their job performance. Sweet, who was often belligerent when ordered to do something, readily agreed to this. He later told me that the sniper had a strange look in his eyes when he spoke and that scrawled on the back of his flak jacket was this brief self-assessment: "The Only Thing I Feel When I Kill is Recoil." Sweet believed it.

Despite Sweet's best attempts and the Marine snipers' ability to pick off the enemy during breaks in the weather, the NVA noose continued to tighten around the base. At the same time, the enemy was well aware that the fog and monsoon cloud cover would not last forever and that, to have a reasonable chance of destroying the Khe Sanh Combat Base and its outposts, they would have to act soon. Unfortunately, we knew it too.

* * * *

Incoming and Outgoing

★ ★ ★

Captain Mirzah "Harry" Baig, the most interesting person I have ever known, arrived at Khe Sanh on January 23. Baig was a peculiar Marine—born in India and educated in England, he spoke with a distinct British accent. Baig had a refined, almost priggish manner. His utility uniform, including the semitar he wore in his belt, were always immaculate. He and his assistant, Staff Sergeant Bolsey, were veterans of Con Thien during the months of intense NVA artillery pounding of that Marine outpost the year before. It was clear they had been in this situation before. They were very professional, very cool. I was interested in learning more about that now famous place.

Captain Baig was a Target Information Officer (TIO). It was his job to quickly synthesize intelligence information, determine the enemy's whereabouts and intentions, and destroy them. His TIO map was just six feet from our TACP map so, because he preferred the night shift, I was able to work alongside him twelve hours a day for the next three months. Baig, like everyone else at Khe Sanh, had no training on how to interpret the electronic sensor information, called SPOTLIGHT reports. The "signature" data in the Infiltration Surveillance Center computers in Thailand, used to analyze new transmissions to determine what caused the sensor to activate, was not always accurate. Passing animals, or even our own artillery and bomb explosions at some distance from the sensor, would sometimes be incorrectly identified as enemy vehicles or NVA troops on the move.

The hundreds of electronic sensors now positioned around Khe Sanh Combat Base, which had cost the U.S. government about a billion dollars to develop,[16] may have proven to be worthless if it were not for Captain Baig. Utilizing the sensor data in conjunction with other sources of intelligence information, his understanding of terrain conditions, and most importantly, his seemingly telepathic familiarity with the tactics of the extremely mobile NVA—Harry Baig could see targets where others could not.

The first time I saw Captain Baig was outside the COC on his first day at Khe Sanh. A recoilless rifle round had whizzed in and exploded, leaving a small crater. Baig strolled out of the south entrance of the COC, where he'd been standing, and took a tape measure out of his pocket. He measured the length, width, and depth of the little hole. He walked around the immediate area until he found a thumb-size piece of shrapnel, still so hot he had to bounce it in his palm, and examined the little piece of metal for a moment then went back into the COC. There he looked at his map for a few minutes and then ordered artillery fire onto a particular coordinate south of the base where he reckoned the enemy gun was located. I was amused at the time by this odd little man, thinking he was quite eccentric. However, after seeing the results of his later work, I have no doubt that he knocked out an NVA recoilless rifle team that day. Just four days after Baig's arrival, he'd identified an NVA artillery headquarters between Khe Sanh Village and the base. The air strike he ordered resulted in over thirty secondary explosions.

By January 30, he had identified a target in eastern Laos from radio transmissions, spies, and aerial photos. He believed this to be the headquarters for the entire NVA operation against Khe Sanh. There was even some hope that General Giap, the highest-ranking soldier in North Vietnam and architect of the French defeat at Dien Bien Phu, might be there. During the 1930s, the French colonial government held Giap as a political prisoner in nearby Lao Bao prison, so he had an intimate familiarity with the Khe Sanh area.

I saw the aerial photo prior to our strike. The target looked like only a few thatched huts on a rise above the bend of a wide river. The headquarters was deep beneath in a tunnel complex. That day, Baig diverted every available B-52 in the country to this target, resulting in the largest bomber strike of the war. Observers counted at least eighty-five secondary explosions after the bombing had ceased. No radio transmissions were ever heard from the site again. A few days later, we were all disappointed to discover that General Giap was not among those in the collapsed tunnel system. He was photographed in Hanoi, attending a parade.

Two weeks later, while reviewing an aerial reconnaissance photograph, Baig thought he recognized truck tire tracks converging on a certain location just southeast of Hill 471. I was looking over his shoulder at the photo and couldn't see anything. But by now, I'd become a believer in Baig's power of intuition. As the bomber approached the target that night, which was about two miles away, I went outside to watch. The little hill erupted in tremendous secondary explosions. It continued to burn and explode for the rest of the night. In less than three weeks, Baig had found a major enemy ammunition dump, that had probably taken the NVA years to stock.

I believe it was these early, crippling strikes against enemy supply and command centers that disrupted the NVA plan for a major assault on the base. I think they would have had greater success had they attacked before February. Captain Baig's "guesses" saved hundreds, maybe thousands, of Marine lives.

The NVA were not the only people outside the base who were paying a price. In the last week of January, about two thousand Laotian civilians and six thousand Bru tribesmen appeared at the main gate of the base hoping for protection from the ever-increasing hostile fire. Colonel Lownds evacuated a few hundred before turning the rest away. Because he was concerned that NVA infiltrators might be among them, the colonel personally assured the civilians that the village would be safe from further air and artillery strikes. In quieter times, Lownds would visit the village, attending the weddings of prominent villagers and taking meals with the Bru elders who generally trusted and respected him.

Therefore, with the colonel's promise and no real alternative, the civilians at the gate turned around and walked back down to the village. Lownds ordered Captain Baig not to bomb, or otherwise fire upon, the village. Baig drew a circle in grease pencil on his acetate-covered TIO map, and put a cluster of little X marks in the middle of the circle to show it was a fire-free zone. The enemy, however, figured this out quickly. They soon hid their tanks and trucks in the larger buildings and placed anti-aircraft artillery and mortars inside the dwellings, tearing holes in the roofs through which to shoot. This became a continuous source of irritation to Baig, and he was quite vocal about it.

On February 27, as the enemy massed their troops and tanks to make one last big push to take the base, Baig erased the grease pencil circle on his map with a small piece of cheesecloth and ordered a B-52 strike on the village. While that bombing mission undoubtedly preempted the NVA plan for a massive attack on our southern perimeter, it was later estimated that over a thousand civilians were killed that afternoon.

I was sitting right there when Colonel Lownds stormed into the FSCC room that evening. I had never seen him so angry. "Harry," he shouted, "I understand that you just bombed the ville?" Baig courteously replied,

"Yes, Sir." Lownds reminded him that he had strictly forbidden it. Baig calmly explained the necessity of having to do it—the tanks, assault troops, and anti-aircraft guns—and then stood there, silent. I will never forget the look on the colonel's face. It was part anger at the insubordination and part resignation to the fact that it was done and there was nothing he could now do about it. He stared silently at Baig for several moments and then said with sincerity, "Harry, I wouldn't want to be you when the war crimes trials start." The colonel turned and left the room.

The whole episode again made me suspect that Captain Baig was accountable to a superior officer higher up the chain of command than Colonel Lownds—and I think Lownds knew it, too.

The enlisted men soon dubbed the captain "Butcher Baig." Though this new moniker spread quickly among the troops, I do not recall it ever used in his presence. Even Pig, who occasionally incurred Baig's wrath with comments about the captain's heritage or by doing crude impersonations of his British accent, never referred to him directly by that name.

On March 7, the surviving Bru civilians came to the front gate again; there were only 1,247 left. Lownds let them in this time and had them flown out to safety over the next three days. A few weeks later, somebody passed a copy of *The Berkeley Barb*, a radical left-wing newspaper, around the COC. In it was an article about how we had turned the Bru away to certain death. I was familiar with the *Barb* from having gone to high school in Berkeley and was surprised how accurately they had reported the event. I presumed that one of the many reporters for the major news services, who now seemed to be everywhere at Khe Sanh, also doubled as a *Barb* reporter.

Since the *Barb* represented the anti-war sentiment in the U.S., we were all angry about their scoop. I remember feeling a twinge of guilt though, even then. The Bru had fought hard at the village a few weeks before. I was probably alive because of their courage. Although there was nothing I could have done to help them, I did not even care about their fate. Some of the guilt I experienced in the years after I left Vietnam had to do with my recognition that these primitive people may have had more honor and loyalty than I did.

Between January and March 1968, nearly 10,000 civilians perished, predominately Bru, most as a result of artillery fire and bombing by U.S. forces. They were sacrificed for the security of Khe Sanh Combat Base. The Bru tribe suffered more and deserved it less than any populace in the war. They were devoted and trusting. Tragically, they were also in the way.

* * * *

A B-52 bombing mission, code named "Arc Light," was the most powerful weapon we had and was the centerpiece of General Westmoreland's strategy at Khe Sanh. Westmoreland had been planning this battle for some time. He had intentionally put us out as bait, to draw the NVA into attempting another Dien Bien Phu—a single dramatic victory that would turn the war in their favor. Westmoreland wanted to lure thousands of enemy soldiers to this place and annihilate them with this awesome firepower. He labeled his plan "Operation Niagara." Baig's job was to implement the operation to drown the NVA, as it were, in a Niagara Falls of bombs.

The concentration of firepower each Arc Light supplied was overwhelming. North Vietnamese Army POWs and deserters who had survived these attacks told chilling stories of entire companies of troops reduced to body parts no larger than a leg, of deafness and blindness, and of terror and madness.

A typical mission consisted of two sets (called "sticks") of three bombers, ten minutes apart, passing over a target area approximately one-mile long by one-half-mile wide. Each plane dropped one hundred and eight, 500-pound high explosive bombs. The whole mission delivered a total of 160 tons of explosives from an altitude of over 30,000 feet. Because of the incredible destructive power of these missions, special permission was required to have them bomb closer than 3,000 meters from friendly ground troops. At Khe Sanh, Baig had that permission.

The enemy, who was aware of the 3,000-meter restriction, moved troops close to the base, seeking protection from the B-52s. On February 26, as an NVA battalion assembled nearby for an attack, Baig called for an Arc Light within 750 meters of us. It was late afternoon, still daylight, and I went up to watch. The bombs struck just beyond the northeast corner of the runway. They did not make the high whistling sound I was used to hearing in war movies. Instead, just before impact, the air filled with what I can only describe as a loud, collective, honking noise.

The hillside bloomed in hundreds of brown smoky puffs, running from west to east for about a mile. Not since our ammo dump had exploded in January had the base rocked like that. My gaze turned down to the road leading off in the direction of the explosions, and I could see it undulating in the throes of a powerful earth tremor. A few seconds later, the wave passed beneath me so strongly that it nearly knocked me off my feet. I was back underground when the second flight of bombers delivered their payload. The bunker roof beams groaned and dust sifted down onto us.

Baig had several acetate overlays on his TIO map. He used four of them to plot Arc Lights. They covered the map in rectangular grids, two kilometers long by one kilometer wide. One overlay had the rectangles running diagonally from upper right to lower left. The next diagonally from upper left to lower right. The other two laid out the rectangles laterally from east to west, and north to south. Each rectangular grid had an identification number. A potential Arc Light mission covered every part of the map.

One night I commented to Captain Baig that our COC was located in the center of one of those grids. "That is correct, Bru (my nickname by then)," he replied. "We are targeted too, just in case this place should abruptly change ownership." Then, greatly amused at his dark little joke, Baig chuckled in short bursts for several seconds. It occurred to me that this particular grid was not unlike my plan in the village to hold a grenade to my head if the comm bunker fell to the enemy—only this was a 160-ton grenade!

Captain Baig would develop, or help perfect, a number of creative ways to deliver firepower to meet the unique challenges presented by the enemy. With his time-on-target (TOT) mission called a "Micro-Arc Light," he could quickly have artillery and 4.2-inch mortars shells from Khe Sanh Combat Base and big 175mm rounds from Camp Carroll arriving over a target at exactly the same moment, saturating an area 500 meters square with devastating effects on enemy troops caught out in the open. His "Mini-Arc Light," which took a little longer to prepare, covered a somewhat larger area and was often coordinated with a TPQ-10 bombing. This ingenious duet of air and artillery power resulted in stunning destruction.

When helicopters resupplying our hill outposts could no longer safely run the gauntlet of enemy anti-aircraft fire, Baig helped develop the "Super Gaggle." This complicated, precisely timed combination of smoke obfuscation and deadly curtains of suppressive artillery and aircraft fire created a narrow corridor allowing the choppers to get in to the hill and out again safely.

* * * *

Miraculously, the Combat Operations Center bunker never sustained a direct hit from any big enemy artillery. But it was not for want of trying. The area around the COC took an inordinately large number of incoming artillery and rocket rounds during the siege. I know this because I lived just across the road. Colonel Lownd's hut, which sat at a road intersection next to the COC, was hit several times early in the siege. The 3rd Reconnaissance Battalion area, which was across the road to the north of the COC, was hit often—with much loss of life. It was hit so often, in fact, that we wondered if the enemy believed the recon bunker was actually the

Combat Operations Center. Later, the 1st Battalion, 26th Marines command bunker at the east end of the base was struck by incoming, killing both officers and enlisted men.

Yet the enemy had been observing the buildup at Khe Sanh from nearby since the first Americans had arrived six years earlier. It was clear that not all the Vietnamese and Bru, who had been free to walk around the base right up until January, were on our side. It is impossible for me to believe that the enemy did not know exactly where the COC was. A direct hit over the big map room, with a large, delay-fused artillery round, would probably have killed most of the regimental command officers and interrupted the coordinated defense of the base and outposts for quite some time. It was hard to understand why the NVA did not exploit this knowledge. Their fathers seem to have been better organized against the French. But then again, their fathers didn't have Arc Light missions disrupting their plans day and night.

As if the enemy needed more help figuring out where the COC was located, a twenty-foot high observation tower stood next to the south entrance to the bunker. It was easily one of the highest structures on the base and could be seen from miles away. In early February, a large artillery shell from Co Roc barely missed the COC but jolted the place so violently that cement dust knocked down from the ceiling filled the FSCC room, as if with smoke. Webbed gear was shaken loose from pegs on the wall and coffee cups danced off desktops. The next day the tower was removed.

Colonel Lownds understood that the enemy knew exactly where the COC was located and from the beginning ordered a new regimental COC constructed out near the runway, west of the LSA. This bunker was touted as being much more artillery resistant than the current command bunker. However, we all dreaded moving there because not only did we feel lucky in our current position, but we also had a natural reluctance to move any closer to the airstrip that had been dubbed the "Mortar Magnet."

One day in early March, we were packing in preparation for moving that evening, under cover of darkness, to the new COC. Then, incredibly, the landline telephone rang bringing word that a 152mm enemy artillery shell had just punched through a wall of the new COC bunker and destroyed it. Consequently, we unpacked and stayed in the old bunker until the day our regiment left, never sustaining a direct hit. Many of us wondered if the NVA had somehow found out about the move and just fired a day too early. Anything was possible.

In fact, we learned of enemy spies on several occasions during the battle for Khe Sanh. One afternoon in mid-February, several of us were sitting

The Regimental Commander's hut was struck by enemy rockets early in the initial attack on Khe Sanh Combat Base

out on Orr's front porch enjoying a brief respite from the incoming when someone in our group silently signaled for us to look across the road. There, an ARVN soldier, who had evidently come up from the 37th Ranger lines, strode suspiciously along the road past the COC. The more we looked at him, the more we realized that he was not just walking but was actually pacing off the length of the command bunker—first on the west side and then along the north. Then, as if he had lost his concentration, he started doing it a second time. We could not believe it! He was so obvious that even his lips were moving as he counted the steps. We immediately grabbed him and took him to the Shore Patrol; they took him back to the ARVN line. I don't know if they stood him before a firing squad, but they should have.

Undoubtedly, a few of the Montagnards, who before the siege were trucked from the base on a daily basis to do menial tasks, were not trustworthy and were sources of information for the enemy. From what I had seen, they were not very closely supervised. The fact that one of the first enemy rockets fired on the morning of January 20, 1968 struck a direct hit on the base commander's hut, also lends some support to this theory.

Also remarkable was information provided by NVA Lieutenant Le Than Dong. Dong surrendered in mid-March after losing his entire platoon.

Baig and Major Hudson had located Dong's bunker complex by analyzing aerial reconnaissance photos. Getting a bit creative, we on the air team ordered a single, 2,000-pound bomb with a "C" (chemical) fuse set for a twelve-hour delay. The following day, an aircraft locked into a precise, ground radar controlled bombing run with ASRAT and dropped the big bomb squarely in the center of the enemy bunker complex. The NVA spent several hours digging up the bomb, which they thought to be a dud, and many were standing nearby when it finally detonated. Lieutenant Dong, who had been some distance away at the time, survived. Fearing punishment from his superiors for losing most of the platoon, he surrendered under a white flag.

During his interrogation, Dong told our intelligence people that the NVA received frequent warnings about the location of B-52 strikes, often up to twenty-four hours in advance. He claimed to know the time of the strikes, as well as the alternate targets. He credited the information to secret agents. Numerous other NVA defectors told similar stories during the war. They claimed this information on the direction of B-52 flights came not just from Russian electronic spying equipment on board trawlers off the coast, but also from high-level spies within the U.S. military.

Despite these inside sources of information and their own systematic observation of the base over the years, the North Vietnamese still failed to capitalize on the few battlefield advantages the information provided. The NVA could appear so imaginative and resourceful at certain times, yet so inept at others.

As an example, they never interrupted our water supply. Fresh water was, of course, critical to our ability to withstand a long siege, and it was questionable whether enough water could have been flown in to sustain us. At the very least, it would have created the need to reprioritize the delivery of other essential resources. The hill outposts had no natural source of water and, as such, limited amounts had to be containerized and flown to them periodically by helicopter. Cumulatively, there were far fewer troops on these hills than at the combat base. So, the difficulty of keeping them supplied with water demonstrated the enormous task of keeping all 6,000 of us supplied.

The main base at Khe Sanh relied on a single pipe, through which water was pumped ninety vertical feet up from a man-made reservoir that had been blasted into the bed of the Rao Quan River in October 1967. The reservoir was over 150 meters outside the base perimeter. The little dam of metal runway matting and earth that formed it was easily visible to anyone walking along the riverbank. Military historians still debate why the NVA did not simply cap the pipe. Some have speculated the NVA did not know where the water pipe was located, but I believe that was highly unlikely since they clearly observed the reservoir being built. Others have marveled that the enemy did not poison the water supply at the source.

One morning, while filling my water can, I spoke to one of the engineers at the water purification site. I asked him why the NVA hadn't poisoned us. He said the enemy was contaminating the water, that he had tested the water recently and found microbes from what appeared to be human feces and decomposing animal carcasses. He told me there had been a case of cholera reported among the indigenous troops at FOB-3. We Marines had all received cholera vaccinations, and they appeared to be working. The engineers also used large quantities of chlorine to kill these microbes. Consequently, the water always smelled and tasted like liquid laundry bleach.

Ironically, it was not until the siege lifted that we got sick from the water. The contaminant turned out to be soap used by U.S. Air Cavalry troops who were bathing in the river near the intake pipe. The soapy water went undetected by the engineers and eventually gave several hundred of us diarrhea.

Incoming often hit the big rubber water storage bladders. Sometimes we would be without water for two or three days. Our standard ration was two canteens per man, per day. Because of the rationing, the Marines at Khe Sanh base exhibited varying degrees of cleanliness. Typically, we washed ourselves with a damp rag, one part of the body each day over a two-to-three-day cycle, shaving every third day, or so. We almost never removed our boots, except to wash our feet. When our combat utility uniforms became so filthy or smelly or tattered that we could no longer stand being in them, which was usually about every three weeks, we would walk over to Charlie Med, the main medical facility at Khe Sanh. There was always a pile of used clothing out in front, taken from those treated for wounds or illnesses, or those who would no longer be needing clothes. Though a morbid task, it always made me feel slightly lucky when I found both trousers and a utility shirt that were not too badly stained with body fluids.

Some, like Pig, abstained from ever changing their clothes. Eventually, the combination of stains from sweat, mud, and coffee and food spills from hastily consumed C-rations, created a kind of camouflaged effect, that was in an odd way, almost stylish.

A few Marines managed to maintain a normal level of hygiene, as in the case of a fellow radio operator, PFC Rodriguez. Rodriguez was from Puerto

Rico and been living the last few years in Neptune, New Jersey. He was the kind of Marine often referred to as "squared away." Rodriguez was married with a son, and always seemed more highly principled and mature than the rest of us. We gave him the nickname "Savage," because of his curious habit of biting people when he became overly enthused about something. While others might demonstrate their excitement with a slap

The "Savage" at his clothesline

on the back, a punch on the arm, or crushing bear hug, Savage would bite a nearby arm or shoulder. He was a stickler for cleanliness, however, and did not let the fact that he was forced to live in a hole in the ground, with only two quarts of water per day, change that.

Shortly after the siege began, Savage dug a bunker of his own, and moved out of the old mortar pit. During this time, he evidently developed a supplemental source of water, because soon, a clothesline fashioned from two discarded fence posts and some telephone wire was standing atop the roof of his bunker. Every few days Savage would hand wash a second set of combat utilities, and hang them out on his clothesline to dry. In the foggy climate of Khe Sanh, it would often take several days for the garments to dry, during which time shrapnel from incoming shells would repeatedly pierce them. By March, it was hard not to notice the clumsy needlework repairs to numerous ragged shrapnel nicks on Savage's otherwise spotless uniforms.

Unlike our precarious water source, the food supply at the base was sufficient for several months: C-rations, or MCI (Meal/Combat/Individual), were all we had to eat. I generally only ate two meals each day because the C-rations were quite filling. Each case contained twelve smaller cartons of meals, each of which, in turn, contained cans of various foods. Most of the MCI we had at Khe Sanh was packaged in the mid-to-late

1950s and some meals were more popular than others. The ham and lima beans, for example, was not popular. My favorite was Beans and Weenies—a twelve-ounce can of baked beans with chunks of hot dog floating in it. I had a special recipe for preparing them. Once bubbling, I would insert a large round dry cracker into the can to absorb the rainbow of grease forming on the top. Later, I'd toss the cracker. Then at just the right moment, I'd open a small tin of hickory-flavored cheese and melt the contents on top. I never got tired of this.

The blandness of the C-rations, however, did get monotonous after a while. In every letter home, I asked my mom to mail an onion. One day a package arrived from her. The box had evidently been in route for a long time and at some point was crushed under a heavier object. I knew what it contained, even before I opened it, because the green tentacle of a living onion had crept through an opening in the broken box and was curling up along its side.

The arrival of the onion made me very popular. I honed the blade of my KA-Bar (fighting knife) into a razor and, for those I liked, I sliced away a disk of onion so thin you could nearly read newsprint through it. Even then, it was all gone within a week. Boy, did I miss that onion.

Orr and I met for breakfast each morning about 0630. We made little heat tab stoves out of discarded cans and cooked our breakfast, eating right out of the cans. We would make instant coffee and drink it out of an empty can. For dessert, there was a small four-ounce can of pecan roll that was good even fifteen years out of the oven. Orr didn't smoke, so he gave me his little four-pack of cigarettes. Each of us carried a tiny P-38 can opener, known simply as a "John Wayne." Many Marines attached their John Waynes to the dog tag chain around their necks. Because I preferred not to wear dog tags around my neck, attaching them instead to the laces of my boots, I kept my John Wayne in my pocket, along with my lucky fifty-cent piece. I never went anywhere without those two items.

Orr and I kept to our breakfast routine as a way to insure, at least once a day, that the other was still alive. We always started out the morning with a little game of trying to be the first one to utter the phrase, "Tonight's the night." This was a reference to the big attack we expected from the thousands of NVA massing just a few hundred meters outside our perimeter. The joke was in the absurdity that one of us was going to be correct eventually and, probably, not live to gloat about it the following morning.

I had reason to be concerned about Orr's day-to-day existence because he had very little patience with the incoming. While many of us would wander off toward our bunkers whenever the incoming resumed, Orr—

who always seemed irritated by the interruption—would defiantly stay seated in his chair for a while. Once, I looked out from the hatchway of my bunker and saw him still sitting on his porch as the enemy mortar fire began to bracket our area. Orr was not playing a game of chicken with the enemy; he was just being obstinate.

In addition to worrying about Orr's stubborn streak and the constant mortar and artillery pounding of our area of the base, sniper fire was also a problem. In the area where I resided, the sniper fire came from the north or south. On the north side of the base, holed up in a small cave and shooting a .50-caliber machine gun—in single shots—was an enemy sniper we called "Luke the Gook." Luke worked hard each day to kill us. He may have succeeded, but if he did, I never heard about it. If you took a walk at midday, after the fog burned away, you would often hear the zeep-zeep of Luke's bullets traveling south about three feet above your head. He always seemed to be shooting too high, at times so high that I wondered if he might accidentally hit one of his own guys on the south side of our defenses.

As many Khe Sanh Marines will attest, we began to develop a certain affinity for Luke. He was dependable. Not everyone shared that feeling, however, and soon a 106mm recoilless rifle was ordered to take him out. After a dozen shells slammed into the mountainside, Luke came out of his hole and fired off a shot.

The Air Officer ordered napalm to be dropped on the poor underachiever. We somewhat reluctantly targeted him for the strike, then went outside to watch and pay our last respects. A Phantom F-4 fighter-bomber rolled in and dispensed two napalm canisters right on him. The orange flame rolled, billowed, and vanished, leaving an oily black haze over Luke's hole, which must have been deeper than we realized, because several shots soon came from the direction of the scorched hillside. A few Marines even cheered. Luke was still there and would become forever a part of Khe Sanh lore.

On the south side, the enemy snipers were closer, often within 100 meters, so had a better chance of hitting us. The closest I came to being shot by a sniper on the south side was when I volunteered to help Sergeant Meier repair a telephone landline behind the trenches occupied by Bravo Company, 1st Battalion, 26th Marines. Mickey Meier was an unassuming leader, whom I respected immensely. He had been at Khe Sanh for eleven months and, even before the siege began, opted to sleep each night in an underground bunker while the rest of us slept in tents. Unlike most of us in Headquarters Company, Meier knew well the sound of incoming from

Napalm bomb strikes an enemy position near the Khe Sanh Combat Base front gate

Courtesy of Steve Orr

the days of the Hill Fights in May and June of 1967. He always knew it would happen again someday.

Either an incoming round or gnawing rats had severed the telephone line and we were tracking it west. Meier was proud to be from Wisconsin and was wearing a bright red University of Wisconsin Badgers sweatshirt. We were walking along concentrating on finding the break in the wire. It was late afternoon and the mist was beginning to rise out of the ravines below. At first we did not distinctly hear the pop of the rifle, but sensed something was wrong. I looked over to the grunts in the trench line who were busy aiming and pointing at something outside the barbed wire.

Then it became apparent. A bullet whizzed by my head and a second, right on its tail, slapped into a pile of sandbags behind us. Meier froze upright and then slowly lowered his chin toward his bright red sweatshirt. His eyes widened as he realized he was probably visible all the way to Hanoi. Without saying a word, we both simultaneously began running away from the perimeter, doing little zigzag moves and laughing so hard at Meier's crimson sweatshirt that we were soon gasping for breath. Just then, a grunt fired a burst of M-60 machine gun fire at something down the gully, but we didn't look back.

Back in my bunker, we sat to catch our breath and wipe the tears away. Meier got me laughing again, when he said, with mock seriousness, "He must be a Minnesota fan." However, not getting the telephone line repaired, because of the sniper shooting at Mickey Meier's red sweatshirt, caused me some anxiety later that night.

After arriving on duty, I was told that the Air Support Radar Team (ASRAT), the local Air Force detachment responsible for guiding our radar controlled bombing sorties, did not have the night's bombing target coordinates because the telephone line was still severed. We did not have secure radio communications, so someone would have to walk the list of bombing targets to them.

Still the "new guy" on the air team, I got the task. This filled me with dread; the ASRAT was way down by the main gate. I had never been there and had no idea even what I would be looking for. It was dark, so I could not take a flashlight because of enemy snipers and artillery spotters. To make matters worse, rumors of the NVA tunneling under us were now at their peak. Reports of NVA soldiers sighted here or there within the base had everyone's nerves on edge. One of the grunts guarding the COC claimed to have seen an infiltrator the night before on the roof of the mess hall just across the road. I didn't believe him at the time, but now I could not get his claim out of my mind.

I first tried going back down to the trench line where Meier and I had been earlier but was soon lost in a maze of wires going in all directions. I fell several times in the darkness, once into a large shell crater, and became disoriented. Finally, I worked my way back to the COC and then proceeded down the road past Charlie Med in the general direction of the main gate. Fortunately, it was a clear, starry night and the enemy incoming was light. I would have liked a little moonlight, but it never came over the horizon.

I decided it was best to make noise to warn others of my approach. I figured that my odds of being shot by a frightened Marine sentry were higher than being shot by an enemy infiltrator. I had to stop at several bunkers along the way to ask for directions.

Somehow, I found the ASRAT. It was a spacious bunker, though entirely above ground. Against the far wall was an elevated platform behind which was a large, active radar screen. A single radar operator sat at the controls in front of it, wearing a radio headset and speaking directly to the aircraft. The bunker was less than fifty meters from the perimeter. I wondered why it was way out here instead of in the middle of the base. The enemy would likely have overrun it early in an attack. I left the written bombing coordinates with the radar man and backtracked to the COC.

The next day, they fixed the telephone line. I wanted it fixed so badly I almost volunteered for that work detail—almost. Despite my growing reluctance to volunteer for anything, there was the occasional exception.

One such exception was the task given to a TACP radio operator to go up on the road at sunrise and retrieve the aerial reconnaissance photos from the prior day. The operator would mark the site with a smoke grenade and the pilot of a low-flying single-engine Cessna would drop a canvas sack out the window as close as he could to the smoke. I liked doing this because they always included some goodies for me in the bag: a can of soda pop, candy bars, or a copy of Playboy. Pig was originally assigned to this task because of his relative seniority, but was relieved after

The first week in February 1968 was a desperate time at Khe Sanh. As outposts fell to massive enemy assaults, every decision became critical. Officers pore over Harry Baig's Target Information map, trying to devise a way to slow the onslaught. Left to right: Major Hudson, Lieutenant Colonel Hennely, Captain Steen, Colonel Lownds, Captain Baig, and Captain Fitzsimmons   *Courtesy of David Douglas Duncan*

nearly setting a hut on fire while (intentionally) marking the drop site with a deadly white phosphorous grenade instead of signal smoke.

I would often kibitz when Major Hudson and Captain Baig looked at the reconnaissance photos. Of all the pictures I managed to glimpse, two still haunt me. One was of Lang Vei the morning after it fell. On February 7, a large enemy force supported by ten Soviet-made PT-76 tanks overran the seemingly impregnable Lang Vei Special Forces Camp. This was the first use of tanks in battle by the NVA in South Vietnam.

The night of the attack, I listened on the base defense network as the Special Forces radio operator (call sign "Spunky Hansen") pled for help. I had been in a somewhat similar situation two weeks before at Khe Sanh Village, which was located just four miles from Lang Vei, so I knew what that kid was going through. The 26th Marines had responsibility for providing Lang Vei with reinforcements in case of an attack. Two months earlier, during quieter times, Colonel Lownds had rehearsed the plan, sending a company of Marines overland to Lang Vei by a route other than Route 9—it took them nineteen hours to get there. Now with the real thing happening, Colonel Lownds refused to dispatch a relief force. Although he was criticized by some for this decision, what most of us didn't know at the time was that an NVA defector, Master Sergeant Du, had told interrogators that the enemy planned to ambush and annihilate any relief force that came overland from the base or attempted a helicopter insertion near the Lang Vei camp.

An NVA tank was soon sitting atop the Lang Vei communications bunker, knocking down antennae and rocking back and forth to try to cave in the structure. Spunky Hansen soon fell silent on our network. About noon the next day, I picked up some aerial reconnaissance photos dropped into us and brought them to Major Hudson. Among them was one of a destroyed enemy tank. The ground all around it was scorched and its turret was blown off, landing several meters away. What appeared to be the body of a soldier was lying in the doorway of a nearby bunker. I wondered if it was the radioman. We would never know. When the fighting at Lang Vei ended, over 300 indigenous defenders were dead. Twenty-one of the twenty-four Americans there were killed, wounded, or missing. Like Khe Sanh Village two weeks before, Lang Vei had fallen to the enemy.

The other photo I will never forget is one dropped into us on February 26, the day after a platoon from Bravo Company, 1st Battalion, 26th Marines, known ever after as the "Ghost Patrol," was ambushed just 500 meters outside our perimeter. Two survivors made it back to our lines; a third was taken prisoner and not released until 1973. The photo showed twenty-three Marine bodies in line, forming a kind of L-shape. They appeared to have been stripped of their uniforms. The resolution of the photo was not clear enough to identify them individually or determine whether they were mutilated.

Most often the photos dropped in to us showed the daily progress of the enemy trench lines as they crept toward the base. Sometimes they would reveal the occasional bunker complex the enemy had failed to conceal properly. The NVA moved most often at night, so it was seldom that living enemy soldiers would appear in these reconnaissance photos. We had attempted using infrared technology one night early in the siege, when "Super Spooky," a Gatling-gun laden C-47 equipped with infrared sights, appeared in the dark skies above Khe Sanh. Our regimental Air Officer gave it a target area to strafe to the southwest of us, around Hill 689, where enemy bunker complexes and troop staging areas were known to exist. I was excited about the prospect of us finally being able to "see" the enemy at night coupled with such immediate and overwhelming firepower. But the infrared equipment failed to work properly, so Super Spooky departed after only an hour and never returned.

By mid-March, Pig had inveigled his way back into the good graces of Staff Sergeant Allen, bumping me from the morning photo retrieval duty.

* * * *

The fall of the Special Forces camp at Lang Vei was only one in a series of ferocious and bloody battles during the first week of February 1968. A large NVA force overran the Marine position held by Echo Company, 2nd Battalion, 26th Marines on Hill 861A, a fortified knoll adjacent to Hill 861. The enemy attackers swarmed among the defenders, often engaging in hand-to-hand fighting. Some Marines survived by employing a remarkable blend of ingenuity and sheer guts: rolling hand grenades a few feet into the advancing enemy, then curling up into a tight, fetal ball with their backs to the explosion. While all suffered wounds to some degree, their helmets and flak jackets absorbed most of the deadly shrapnel. At dawn, the surviving Marines pushed the attackers off Hill 861A.

Later, an Echo Company radio operator told me an interesting story. After the fighting ended, a Marine went into his bunker and found an enemy soldier, lying on his cot, eating his C-rations and leafing through a Playboy magazine. The Marine shot and killed the intruder. Evidently, the NVA soldier had gotten as far as this bunker during the battle and decided to let his buddies do the rest of the fighting.

The NVA had intended the attack on Hill 861A to be coordinated with a similar sized assault against the Marines on Hill 881S, about a mile from Hill 861A. Captain Baig had already received intelligence information from ground sensors telling him large numbers of NVA were on the move. Baig guessed the enemy plan was to launch a single, massive assault against Hill 881S just before dawn. He correctly pinpointed their avenue of assault and as they began their attack, enveloped the enemy in a murderous box of intense artillery fire. Audio sensors near the point of attack clearly recorded the anguished cries of the NVA soldiers retreating in terror from the wall of exploding shells. Hill 881S was spared.

But what Captain Baig had not guessed was that part of the advancing NVA force would also move against Hill 861A, so he did not prepare a plan for using artillery fire to close on the enemy approaches to that hill. Consequently, once the enemy had gotten too close to the Marines to make artillery support an option, the men of Echo Company had to repel them unassisted. Captain Baig, ever the perfectionist, would never forgive himself for allowing the enemy to deceive him that morning.

The overall situation continued to deteriorate when, just three days after the battle on Hill 861A, a platoon of Alpha Company, 1st Battalion, 9th Marines, was overrun near the rock quarry, just a few hundred yards west of the base. Later that morning, a relief force fought its way through to the survivors. Twenty-four Marines lay dead, and another twenty-nine were seriously wounded. As a sad and troubling footnote to this bloody engagement, many Marines were lost because their M-16 rifles malfunctioned. Some bodies were found still holding cleaning rods jammed into the barrels of their weapons.

These were desperate days for us. With the fall of Lang Vei and ferocious attacks on nearby hills, now it seemed that the enemy might take Khe Sanh Combat Base. Perhaps the momentum generated by these two NVA divisions with their tanks and artillery might not be stopped. I recognized the feeling of hopelessness taking hold of me again. It was that cold sense of abandonment I had experienced two weeks earlier in the village. Soon a subtle, but unmistakable, sense of doom was evident on the faces and in the conversations of everyone. By the end of that first week in February, it was like the cold, gloomy Khe Sanh fog had crept down into the corridors of the COC and hung over all our heads.

This gloom permeated all the way to Washington, D.C. President Johnson was anxious that Khe Sanh might fall ("I don't want any damned Din-Bin-Foo!"). He had a sand model of the Khe Sanh area constructed in the situation room of the White House. Often in the middle of the night, he could be found in his pajamas and robe staring at the mockup. So concerned was he about the ability of the Khe Sanh defenders to hold, he ordered the unprecedented step of asking every member of the Joint Chiefs of Staff to sign a document swearing that "the Marines will prevail at Khe Sanh."

The generals, in turn, immediately began to consider a plan, code named "Fracture Jaw," for the use of tactical nuclear weapons to save the base. By the second week of February, rumors circulated among enlisted men at the base that special gun sights had arrived for the purpose of firing nuclear artillery shells. This turned out to be incorrect. But on February 10, the NVA withdrew five regiments from the Khe Sanh battlefield. Intelligence sources considered this to be largely due to a Washington press release that nuclear weapons were being considered for use in the Khe Sanh area. This still left about 25,000 NVA troops in our immediate vicinity.

During the 1954 siege of Dien Bien Phu, the head of the U.S. Joint Chiefs of Staff had recommended to President Eisenhower a proposed military operation code-named "Vulture." Operation Vulture called for an intense U.S. bombing campaign around the besieged French fortress, which was to include the use of three small nuclear weapons. The French government gratefully agreed knowing it was the only way to save its trapped forces. The Democrats in Congress fought successfully against this intervention. Ironically, as Senate minority leader, Lyndon Johnson was at the forefront of the fight to stop this action. It was Johnson, as president fourteen years later, who would face a similar situation at Khe Sanh (even

facing the same North Vietnamese general) and have to consider the use
of tactical nuclear weapons to save his fortress.

The similarities between Khe Sanh and Dien Bien Phu were obvious,
but not exact. Bruno Piccinini, a French survivor of that 1954 battle and
the subsequent horrors of POW life under the Viet Minh, was so moved
by what was occurring at Khe Sanh, that he sent his identification bracelet
and military ID card to Colonel Lownds, via the U.S. Defense attaché in
Paris. Piccinini wrote that despite his government's official attitude of un-
friendliness toward U.S. efforts in Vietnam, "there are many Frenchmen
who understand and sympathize with what you are trying to do." He went
on to say that as a former radioman at Dien Bien Phu, he hoped his gift
would go to a radioman at Khe Sanh. It was presented to Steve Orr.

Monsieur Piccinini's sense of déja vu was not imagined. The North
Vietnamese were in fact following the same battle plan as they had in
1954. By mid-February 1968, their concealed artillery was pounding us at
will. In addition, the Khe Sanh Combat Base was now completely encircled by enemy trench lines. Each morning, when the fog lifted, we could
clearly see more and more zigzag trenches branching off, creeping toward
our positions. We knew they would soon be coming for the base, the only
question now was how many would be coming.

* * * *

We Gotta Get Out of this Place

★ ★ ★

On February 29, 1968, the NVA sent a large probe of about 100 men against the ARVN 37th Ranger line, along the southeast perimeter of Khe Sanh base. This was followed by NVA attacks against the base on March 1 and again on March 8. The enemy force was estimated to be from 700 to 1,000 troops in strength. Electronic sensors picked up their movement. By the time they grouped nearby for the assault, our bombs were raining down on them.

Several enemy tanks were involved in the March 1 attack. Seismic sensors located these tanks moving to within a mile of the base, yet mysteriously not one made it into our wire. An after action report written by FOB-3 may explain what happened. Forward Operating Base 3, that ménage of Asian mercenaries and U.S. Special Forces advisors who were protecting part of our southern perimeter, routinely monitored the radio frequencies of nearby enemy units. Like us, NVA radiomen often passed classified information unencrypted over the radio for the sake of expediency. By this means, just hours before the March 1 attack on Khe Sanh Combat Base, FOB-3 radio operators determined the colors and sequence of flares the enemy intended to use, including those that would signal a retreat. According to the report, as the NVA attack got underway, FOB-3 troops sent up those particular signal flares that turned the tanks around.[17]

During the following week, enemy anti-aircraft gunners around the airstrip were enjoying their greatest success. I watched one morning from the edge of the airstrip as a C-130 cargo plane was approaching us from the east. I could hear the thumping of the enemy's .50-caliber machine gun positioned just a hundred yards off the end of the runway. The plane passed directly over it. Just as the plane touched the runway, mortar explosions erupted behind both wings. As it raced down the runway, the mortars chased it along, rounds exploding just behind the tail. The enemy mortar men's timing was off just by a split second, but I was quite impressed by their dead reckoning skills. The plane quickly off-loaded its cargo and sped back down the runway. While no mortars chased it this time, the same enemy machine gun worked the plane over as it lifted off. Miraculously, the C-130 made it back to Da Nang. The next day, employing the same type of fire, the enemy downed a C-130 as it was about to land. Six people died in the crash.

On March 6, an Air Force C-123, carrying five crewmen and forty-four passengers, many of them Marines returning from prior medevacs, approached the runway from the east. A small aircraft piloted by an ARVN, which had not obtained clearance from the tower, suddenly tried to land ahead of it. The Air Force plane was forced to abort the landing and make a hard turn in order to avoid a collision. As it circled back around to attempt another landing, enemy anti-aircraft fire tore through its belly. Despite a heroic effort by the pilot, the plane crashed into a hillside about four miles east of the base. There were no survivors. It would take nine months to recover the remains of the crash victims. Immediately following

NVA artillery damage to the protective blast wall of earth-filled drums just outside the mortar pit bunker

All that remained of a C-123 shot down trying to land at Khe Sanh Combat Base

that crash, the Khe Sanh Combat Base airstrip was closed to all fixed-wing aircraft and would remain so until the middle of April. The bulk of our supplies would now be dropped in to us by parachute, while smaller loads, mail, and personnel were brought in by helicopter.

Steve Orr knew the dangers of flying in and out of Khe Sanh. In February, he had flown down to Da Nang to train on a new type of antenna we were going to use. On the way out of Khe Sanh, Steve had helped carry several body bags onto the CH-46 helicopter he was about to board. As it climbed off the end of the airstrip, enemy .50-caliber machine gun fire ripped through the floor of the chopper. Orr said he would never forget the sickening sight of Marine corpses "dancing around" in the body bags as the bullets ripped through the floor of the chopper, punching them in the back.

After the failure of the March attacks on the base, the digging of trenches and tunneling toward our lines seemed to slow. The enemy remained close by, though, and did try one more time, sending approximately 600 troops against the ARVN 37th Ranger position. As the enemy moved into the ARVN defensive outer wire, we directed a radar-controlled bomber over them. The bombs, which were supposed to hit a safe distance away, exploded right in front of the ARVN defensive lines. One actually fell behind the

After intense enemy gunfire closed the Khe Sanh airstrip, supplies were parachuted in   *USMC*

defenders. The American liaison officer attached to the Rangers later reported that the bombs had so accurately targeted the attacking enemy force that body parts were raining down on the defenders. Rather than lodge a complaint about the bomb that struck inside their defensive position, the officer praised the mission. He informed us that the ARVN troops had asked if we could prearrange the same bomb pattern before the next enemy assault against them. It was the only time I can recall when the air team was ever thanked for accidentally bombing our own forces.

The enemy had chosen to attack the Khe Sanh base through the ARVN line several times during the siege. I wondered if it was because they had less respect for the Rangers ability (or will) to resist. Or, perhaps it was a punitive measure against fellow Vietnamese who sided with the Americans. More likely, given the NVA penchant for logical and systematic planning, it was a tactical decision based on the fact that the ARVN fortifications were about 100 meters farther out than the Marine trench line, and thus was a much closer objective.

Although the ground attacks lessened, the incoming did not; it actually seemed to increase. On the afternoon and evening of March 22, more than 1,300 rounds of enemy artillery pounded the base. It was probably twice that number, but 1,300 was as high as the Counter Mortar Radar (CMR), a device we used to estimate the number of projectiles inbound to the base, could count in a day.

This was the most intense day of incoming I recall. For hours the enemy gunners walked the artillery rounds the length of the base from west to east. A few minutes would pass; then it would start all over again. Each time the shelling turned back towards us, the suspense became maddening. We began to recognize a pattern developing. Soon, we were able to count the number of rounds coming toward us and predict which one in the sequence was going to be the closest. When we knew that shell was on its way, we would all clench our teeth and stick fingers in our ears. It would seem like forever before it landed. Finally it would come crashing in, barely missing us. Spared for a few more minutes.

After numerous salvos, each noticeably closer to our hole than the previous one, we were sure the next one would be it. I remember looking around in the dim light of the bunker. Everyone was tense. Some had that far-away look of deep concentration. On some, lips moved fitfully in silent prayer. Some, like me, searched the faces of the others for answers. There were none. We were in some serious shit this time.

Then it struck. It wasn't quite a direct hit because the roof didn't collapse, but it couldn't have been closer. There was absolutely no sound. We were inside the explosion. Instantly, a vacuum occurred within the bunker, violently sucking dust, paper, and other light objects out the hatchway. A painful pressure pressed on my eardrums. Then, as swiftly as it happened, it was over. The legendary concussion hadn't killed us after all.

The subsequent incoming rounds seemed to drift farther toward the center of the base and away from us. I learned something that afternoon: if it merely were a few rounds you had just survived, you would immediately check to make sure all your body parts were still attached and then make sure your buddies were okay. If, however, it were a couple of thousand artillery rounds you'd just survived, you would forget—for a few moments—such mundane things as body parts and buddies. Instead, you would inhale the sweet breath of life and sit there for a while smiling like Ghandi.

Or you went crazy. On that afternoon, Bill the Mess Sergeant went over the edge. Alone in his bunker, Bill took an E-tool and dug a foxhole into the dirt floor. Then he crawled down into it with his M-16 rifle and several bandoleers of ammunition and began shooting at anyone who approached the doorway. As a Marine who witnessed the event later told me, Bill was convinced that the base had fallen and that everyone outside his bunker was the enemy. His friends called down to him to come out; but he believed the enemy was coercing them. After a standoff of many hours, they finally talked Bill into coming out of the hole.

The Shore Patrol took him to Charlie Med, and he was medevaced out. This event was of concern to us all. Bill was not only a nice, friendly, "normal" guy, he was a genuine war hero. Of all the men in Headquarters Company, Bill had been battle tested the most severely. He had survived the incredible ordeal on Hill 950 the previous June, rallying a handful of Marines who eventually prevailed. He was the last person we thought would crack under the strain. If it could happen to Bill, it could happen to anybody.

Others had suffered breakdowns from the stress of the constant incoming, but these incidents did not have the same impact on us as Bill's undoing. In late January, during the second week of the siege, the Shore Patrol took a Headquarters Company staff sergeant into protective custody because he was chasing incoming rounds—in order to get wounded! I had known the man because, in addition to his other duties, he acted as our company barber, from which he earned a few extra dollars each month. The staff sergeant was in his early thirties, medium build with thinning, dark, close-cropped hair. He was mild mannered, particularly for a career-oriented, noncommissioned officer, and nice to everyone; but he had a certain nervousness about him and a strange stare. Due to rotate back home in February, he evidently wanted to qualify for a Purple Heart before leaving.

Witnesses described the bizarre sight, which one said was somewhat reminiscent of a scene from a Buster Keaton silent movie. There was the staff sergeant running up and down the road. If an incoming shell exploded by the airfield logistical supply area, he would run up that way, hoping to catch the next one. But the next incoming round would explode back down the road by the recon area, so he would make a quick turn and trot off in that direction. Paradoxically, because he did not want to break a single military regulation, he always wore his helmet and flak jacket, which limited the likelihood of being wounded. The staff sergeant never was hit, not even a scratch. He was grinning, as he always seemed to be, the last time I saw him.

Weeks later, we found an unopened letter addressed to him. It had arrived the day he was medevaced out for his own safety. Since many of us had received no mail of our own for couple of weeks, we decided to read his; it was from his wife in Victorville, California. Three pages of complaining and nagging: how the van had broken down, how the kid was doing badly in school, and how his relatives were annoying her. She wanted to know why he wasn't doing more to help and being a better husband and father. I felt sorry for him after that. Here he was risking death in order to impress a woman who would write a letter like that. It was pathetic. After that letter, I quit chuckling when I thought of him chasing the incoming.

The regimental communications company commander was also the apparent victim of a mental collapse. Taciturn and humorless, the major always seemed to be squinting at something in the distance—even when indoors. Because he liked things to be tidy, the major often ordered us to pick up all the old shrapnel lying around on the ground. His theory was that the next incoming round would send this shrapnel litter flying about, possibly injuring someone. The problem with the major's directive, at least from the enlisted man's point of view, was that in order to get rid of the old stuff, we had to go out and expose ourselves to the newly arriving shrapnel. To many of us, the major's command was comparable to when, after colliding with an iceberg, the captain of *Titanic* ordered his crew to sweep the ice off the deck so no one would slip and fall. Most of us ignored the major's orders, but some did not. One obedient corporal caught a splinter of shrapnel on his upper arm from an incoming shell while performing this duty.

By February, as the enemy noose around Khe Sanh drew tighter and it was apparent that a large ground attack was imminent, the major decided to have an escape tunnel dug from the bunker that served as his office to the outside. Despite the fact that his aboveground bunker was heavily fortified with sandbags and already had exits on two sides, the major did not want to take any chances. He ordered us to carry out his plan in our off hours. We dug a shaft eight feet deep, down through the hard clay then tunneled east until we were on the other side of the bunker wall. Where the shaft was to come up, the major had us build a sandbag parapet facing south. This is where he planned to make his "last stand." Ludicrously, he had a difficult time deciding how it should end, that is, whether he should be shooting from the hip, at eye level, or somewhere in between; so we enlisted men spent the next half-hour adding and removing sandbags from the little wall, while the major struck various poses with a .45 pistol in his hand.

We thought this was all quite comical—until the tunnel collapsed on Tiddy. Digging swiftly, we dragged him out by his feet unharmed. Things now changed. It was clear that the major had become dangerously delusional. Word reached his superiors in the COC, and he was ordered to stop construction of his escape tunnel. Yet, the major kept his command and, despite his eccentric, almost Queeg-like persona, survived Khe Sanh and returned to the United States unharmed.

* * * *

"Operation Scotland," the code name for our defense of the Khe Sanh Combat Base, ended on March 31, 1968. The following day, "Operation Pegasus" commenced. Designed by General Westmoreland's staff to break the siege of Khe Sanh, Pegasus was a joint operation involving elements of the U.S. Army 1st Air Cavalry Division as well as several Marine and ARVN units. By April 8, the lead Air Cavalry unit reached Khe Sanh. Although it made for great news coverage ("beleaguered survivors welcome their saviors"), we were not thrilled that it was the U.S. Army being portrayed as our rescuers.

With their arrival, the sky around Khe Sanh was filled with an incredible number of helicopters, like endless flights of geese migrating in every direction. It was not just their sheer numbers that astounded me; I saw aircraft that I did not even know existed. The giant wasp-like Sikorsky Skycrane and the Huey Cobra, bristling with guns and rocket pods, seemed to me like something from the future, especially compared to what the Marine Corps had. The Army had so many Cobras they often attacked together in deadly tandem, the pilots naming themselves after legendary

World War I German swarms, like the Blue Max and the Flying Circus. It seemed to me there were more helicopters in the sky that one afternoon than the Marine Corps had in the whole world. I got a sick feeling in my stomach thinking how often Marines died because our medevac capability had proved insufficient. I stared upwards at them until the back of my neck began to ache and then uttered aloud, "Where in the hell have all these guys been for the last three months?"

Late that afternoon, Steve Orr, Morley Sweet, and I stood in our south trench line and watched a platoon of Air Cavalry troops land about fifty meters in front of us. As soon as the helicopters that brought them had departed, another chopper came in and landed. Large aluminum canisters of hot food were unloaded and the soldiers took mess kits from their packs, lined up, and were served hot, freshly cooked food. A tub filled with ice and individual-size cartons of milk was located at the end of their chow line.

The three of us had not tasted milk, or for that matter a meal other than C-rations, in nearly three months. Sweet immediately chambered a round in his rifle and sighted-in on a milk carton held by one of the men. He mumbled something to the effect that there would be no picnicking on his lawn. We reminded him of his previously poor performance as a sniper, adding that whether he hit the carton or the man, it was still going to be an inexcusable waste of milk. Morley finally agreed not to take the shot. Later that night, however, at the east end of the runway there was an exchange of gunfire between the Marines and Army soldiers. I'm pretty sure it was about milk.

Several of the Marine units who had endured the long siege, and were anxious to get out and fight the enemy, were finally turned loose. On March 30, 1968, Bravo Company, 1st Battalion, 26th Marines went out to recover the twenty-three bodies of the doomed "Ghost Patrol," who had, about a month before, been ambushed just 500 meters outside our perimeter. These were fellow Bravo Company Marines, their friends, and they had a score to settle. The combat was furious, often hand-to-hand. If there had been any thought that the enemy had backed away from Khe Sanh Combat Base, it was now certainly dispelled.

I watched from the Bravo Company trench line at the base, where machine guns, mortars, and 106mm recoilless rifles fired in support of the Marines. Enemy artillery, firing in support of their own troops, tried to suppress this fire by raining shells on our trench lines. Despite all the supporting fire for Bravo Company, the close air support bombing being directed from above them by an airborne forward air controller, and the fact that the bodies they had set out to recover were only a few hundred meters from us, the recovery effort was unsuccessful. The Marines of Bravo Company were in the fight of their lives against a regimental-size enemy force. In the end, they suffered nine dead, three missing, and nearly 100 wounded.[18] Due to the stiff NVA resistance, Bravo Company was only able to recover two bodies from the original patrol. The others would not be retrieved for another week, when the NVA regiment would be outflanked and forced to retreat.

On April 4, 1968, the 1st Battalion, 9th Marines, pushed out from the base to attack the enemy on Hill 471 about a mile south of us. Later that evening I was on the radio with the new Alpha Company Tactical Air Control Party radioman. We conversed in a combination of military jargon and radioman slang. This allowed us to obtain information from each other without compromising our radio security and procedure too much. He told me about Captain Jones, the company Air Officer who had been killed by mortar fire during the assault on Hill 471 that morning. Jones, a Marine pilot doing his ground duty, was supposed to have rotated back to the States the next day. His replacement had not arrived and, like most Marines who had hunkered down at the base for months enduring the relentless artillery pounding, he was anxious to be part of the breakout. He had volunteered for this one last mission.

In the early hours of April 5, a battalion of NVA tried to retake Hill 471. During the fighting, I recall the radioman rather calmly saying, "Intrigue, hold one moment, over." He was off the air for about thirty seconds. When he came back, he told me that he had just shot an NVA soldier who had been moving up the hill toward him. Then he said, in a kind of surprised voice, "Wow! This thing (a .45-caliber pistol) is way more accurate than I thought."

I had to laugh. The M-1911, .45-caliber pistol was standard issue for Marine Corps radiomen. Logic dictated that since we had one hand occupied with the radio handset, we would need a handgun for the other one. The problem was that this particular pistol had a reputation for being highly inaccurate. This belief was so strong and so ingrained in us since Radio School, that almost every radio operator obtained an M-16 rifle in addition to his pistol. It struck me as highly amusing that the weapon's dismal reputation was so bad that this radio operator—in the midst of fighting for his life against hundreds of charging NVA—actually stopped in mid-battle to reflect aloud what an unusual feat it was to have hit something with it. The fight ended at dawn with 170 enemy dead. The radio operator survived the night.

Hill 471 had long been the closest NVA observation position to the base. We bombed it routinely, and it was a regular target on our ASRAT bombing list. Unfortunately, someone forgot to take it off the list.

About noon the following day, I was walking on the road between my bunker and the COC. It was a warm, clear day and I could, by squinting just a bit, see the troops moving around on top of Hill 471. Off in the distance, I heard the familiar sound of an A-6 Intruder at about 15,000 feet (the usual bombing altitude for radar-controlled flights). The A-6 was one of our favorite close-air support bombers. A real workhorse, it carried twenty-eight, 500-pound bombs. I heard the groaning of bombs as they descended on the target. Then, in utter disbelief, I watched as puffs of bomb impacts walked across the top of the hill.

I raced down into the COC and found Captain Donaghy standing in front of the TACP map. "Captain," I said, as calmly I could, "we just bombed the Marines on Hill 471." I could tell by the look on his face that Donaghy could instantly visualize the ASRAT target list in his mind's eye. He was positive that he had directed ASRAT to remove Hill 471 from the target list, but bombs had just fallen. His apprehension at that moment was palpable. (A later investigation determined that our air team was not at fault in the mishap.)

Lance Corporal Reath immediately began calling the Alpha Company air team radio operator, but without success. The fact that no one was answering began to worry us. Soon, an officer stuck his head through the opening from the Big Map room to say the commanding officer of the 1st Battalion, 9th Marines, was calling in and angrily complaining that we had just dropped a bunch of dud bombs on Alpha Company.

Duds? As incredible as it still seems to me to this day, the pilot of that A-6 forgot to flick the switch electronically arming the bombs as he approached the target. This mistake happened perhaps once in 100 sorties. He just forgot. The puffs I witnessed on the hill were plumes of dust from the bomb impacts, not explosions. That bombing mission was truly a miracle of inefficiency.

My few months in Vietnam had already left me with the impression that large numbers of Americans had been injured, or killed, by our own weapons—a phenomenon ironically referred to as "friendly fire." The only good thing about being besieged at Khe Sanh, was that it was evident to everyone where our own troops were located. Clearly, Alpha Company no longer held that advantage.

The rest of 1st Battalion, 9th Marines, however, was not so lucky. On April 16, they assaulted and took the enemy stronghold on Hill 689, about one-and-one-half mile west of Hill 471. A surprise counterattack by the NVA on a weakly guarded flank resulted in over seventy Marine casualties, including forty killed. Most of the dead were not recovered for over a week due to the continuing presence of a large enemy force in the area. Once again, the "Walking Dead" had, in a sad turn of the phrase, lived up to their reputation.

In conjunction with the Marine breakout from Khe Sanh base, after blasting a series of helicopter landing zones, the U.S. Army and ARVN units quickly leap-frogged down Route 9 hoping to entrap the NVA 304th Division. Fierce fighting took place at the old French fort, where a battalion of NVA held on most of the day. After the battle ended and the enemy driven off, a search of the area was conducted for the bodies of those who, in the previous January, died trying to reach us in the village. Among the remains were those of Colonel Seymoe, the officer who had commanded the original rescue operation, still pinned under his crashed helicopter.

Khe Sanh Village, less than a mile down the road, was so badly destroyed by our artillery and bombing that there was not much left to fight over. Three weeks later, PFC Albert Taylor, a Marine who would be dead by May, wrote this description to his mother in California:

> Mom, a couple of days ago, while I was up on Hill 471, I took my platoon down to Khe Sanh Village. Boy, it was really bombed out. There was [sic] bodies all over, cars, motor scooters, trucks, and toys.[19]

Not far from the village, American forces discovered a large, abandoned North Vietnamese Army bunker complex. It contained a spacious command post, mess hall, and kitchen capable of catering to several hundred troops. Some of the seventy-five subterranean dwellings had running water and bathtubs. A few included sun decks with thatched roofs and porches with furniture on them. The latter feature was strangely reminiscent of the porch adjacent to Steve Orr's bunker at the base—less than three miles away! The American troops were amazed at the level of comfort the NVA provided themselves so close to the Khe Sanh base.

However, times had changed for the enemy, and American and ARVN soldiers were soon discovering gruesome evidence of how badly the North Vietnamese had suffered. Hundreds of NVA bodies were found in hurriedly dug shallow graves; hundreds more, in varying degrees of decomposition, lay strewn about where they had fallen. By the time they had reached the destroyed Special Forces camp at Lang Vei, allied forces found and destroyed nearly 800 weapons ranging from rifles to crew-served arms such as anti-aircraft guns. In addition, they captured numerous vehicles, including a PT-76 tank, trucks, and motor bikes. The enemy, in their haste to get back across the Xe Pon River to the safety of neutral Laos, left behind tons of ammunition, food, and other equipment—including radios. That latter bit of news gave me a somewhat perverse feeling that a score had been settled; since I, too, had hastily abandoned my radios on that very same stretch of road three months earlier.

On April 14, 1968, Easter Sunday morning, the men of 3rd Battalion, 26th Marines, moved off Hill 881S to attack Hill 881N about one mile away. Though briefly captured by Marines in fierce combat a year earlier in April 1967, Hill 881N had been securely in the hands of the enemy ever since. Honeycombed with tunnels, which protected the enemy troops from our artillery and air strikes, they had used Hill 881N to launch hundreds of rockets at the base during the siege.

Fighting up the slopes of the hill, the Marines were surprised to discover how atrophied their muscles had become from months of inactivity in the trenches. At days end, six Marines were killed and nineteen were wounded; 106 enemy lay dead. By late afternoon the "Stars and Stripes" were raised on a burned tree limb atop the hill. The victorious Marines arrived back to the safety of Hill 881S by dark. The next morning the flag was gone.

* * * *

April 18, 1968, was the day we never thought would come; the day our platoon was to leave Khe Sanh. The night before, in the mortar pit bunker, we listened to Eric Burdon and The Animals on Armed Forces radio and raucously howled along: "We gotta get out of this place/If it's the last thing we ever do." We scrawled messages on the concrete walls with paint and colored marking pens in the traditional "Kilroy-was-here" style. But, later that night I could not sleep. Laying on my back, staring blindly into the pitch darkness of my little cell, a profound sadness engulfed me.

The morning of our departure, Staff Sergeant Allen ordered us to assemble at 0800 in the 3rd Reconnaissance Battalion area. We immediately thought it was a bad choice because it had been the target of so much incoming over the last few months. We all arrived early though and stood in front of the recon bunker, making subdued conversation. Suddenly we heard the muted bump-bump sound of artillery coming from Co Roc. It surprised me because the big guns had been quiet for several days. Oz and I looked at each other with the same question: Are we going to get it now, when we are so close to getting away?

We scurried into the bunker just as the first of several large shells slammed in all around us. In the dim light of the bunker, I could clearly see the anxiety locked on the faces of everyone, even the longtime veterans of this place. No one tried to joke away his fear, not on this day, not on this "last" day.

It was different now. Throughout the siege, it seemed as if we had been performers in a kind of dark comedy. But at this moment, in the murkiness of the recon bunker, that show had ended. I knew it was because we now had hope of getting out of that place, of surviving all this—something we had not seriously contemplated before.

The incoming finally stopped, and we went outside. A Marine was lying on the road in front of the COC. Voices shouted for a corpsman. We stayed low because it was apparent that an enemy artillery spotter had seen us grouping. The truck finally arrived and we scrambled aboard for the bumpy ride to the LZ. I was standing up, facing forward, holding onto the roof of the truck's cab. The roar of the truck engine was deafening and made me nervous because I could not hear the incoming shells.

Troops from the 1st Battalion, 1st Marines, trudged in single file along both sides of the road. This was Tom Mahoney's unit, and they were taking operational control of Khe Sanh Combat Base that very day. Enemy mortar fire began exploding on the road ahead of us. It was dreamlike to see the dark plumes of gunpowder and dust, but not hear the explosion over the howling truck motor. A half-minute later, we were going by the point of impact. A Marine was laying face down on the side of the road. He was not moving; no one had gotten to him yet. I'm not sure why, but I stared hard at him to see if it might be Mahoney, but I was unable to tell. It struck me as strange that I was suddenly so concerned for Tom's safety. He had already been through some of the worst fighting of the war at Hue city in February of 1968; but I had this gut feeling that Khe Sanh would grind down whoever came to take our place. There were far too many "bad guys" here, and they just wouldn't go away.

Our helicopter landing zone was located at the west end of the Khe Sanh airfield. It was a large, uncomfortably flat space with little cover. Thankfully, the incoming had abated. About 100 meters away, the carcass of a C-130 Hercules cargo plane, which had been shot down a month earlier, tilted drunkenly to the left, its wingtip touching the ground as if for support. A small, smoky fire burned within its interior. A Marine, who had been nearby when we arrived, told us that the plane had been struck by incoming mortars minutes earlier. It seemed odd that the enemy would shoot at a plane they had already knocked down. It gave me some concern that they may just be passing time until a more opportune target appeared—like the choppers inbound to pick us up.

Upon arriving at the LZ, we instinctively fanned out over the area, individually or in twos, in order to make smaller targets. The west end of the Khe Sanh Combat Base airstrip served as kind of a graveyard for ruined aircraft. I walked over to the crumpled hulk of a nearby CH-34 helicopter, the oxidized lime-green paint of its bulkhead spattered with shrapnel holes. Sunlight was beginning to break through the morning cloud cover as I peered into its interior, wondering if this might have been the same chopper that rescued me from the village months before. Months before. The phrase sounded almost meaningless for a moment. I had long ago stopped thinking about ever leaving Khe Sanh; in a strange way, I didn't want to leave. For many of us, the routine of daily life, as dangerous as it was, had made Khe Sanh our home and aroused our territorial instincts. As long as we remained here, prepared to fight, the enemy would never prevail. To us, Khe Sanh was not just a cluster of colored pins on General Westmoreland's map, it was a tangible thing, now made priceless with the blood of our friends.

If a Marine was nearing the end of his tour of duty and facing imminent return to the "World," a future began to shimmer once again on his horizon. But, for most of us, life consisted only of our memories and Khe Sanh. Time now seemed cyclical, where a single day repeated itself endlessly and gratefully. As I stared into the shattered hulk of the chopper, it occurred to me that I had arrived at this airstrip on a cool rainy afternoon in late autumn; I was now leaving on a warm spring morning. Living in the belly of Khe Sanh, seasons had become irrelevant.

During the last eleven weeks, tens of thousands of incoming shells had slammed into our base. Yet, here I was about to leave. Unfamiliar feelings began to stir within me and new questions crossed my mind. What would it be like to live above ground once again, to no longer walk in the Khe Sanh "crouch," or be unceasingly attentive to the murmurs of those distant guns? What would it be like without the constant and undeniable possibility that every moment might be my last? I was suddenly anxious to find out.

Soon the husky pop, pop, pop, of the approaching CH-46 helicopter propellers drew us back toward the place where we had stacked our gear. I slung my M-16 over one shoulder and hoisted my sea bag onto the other. A few minutes later, the first chopper touched down, lowered the rear ramp, and I raced aboard with a dozen others. The chopper spiraled up to about 1,000 feet over the base and went into a holding pattern to await another helicopter.

As we circled, I had an opportunity to view the countryside. It was difficult to believe it was the same place I had flown into just five months earlier. No longer verdant jungle and grassy hills, it was now a moonscape of interlocking craters. In every direction, as far as I could see, the devastation was astonishing. I could not easily find where the village had been, but eventually located it: a large, chalky smudge between the river and Route 9. Part of the old French fort seemed to be intact, but nothing of the District Headquarters building or the Buddhist shrine was recognizable to me.

My eyes tried following the course of Route 9 to the west. The devastation was so complete, I had to look nearly into Laos to see forest canopy. There, off to the west, I could finally see the Co Roc Massif where, less than an hour earlier, the big guns it concealed had tried to kill us one last time. It looked just as I'd imagined it would from the topographical map: an immense escarpment rising up from the Xe Pon River, topped by a broad, flat, nearly unbroken plateau running west across Laos into the mist. I tried to burn these images into my mind, not because I knew I'd never return to this place but because I instinctively knew that someday I'd need to assure myself it had all been real.

I was glad the other chopper pilot was taking his time below, but by the time he finally did get airborne, I had seen enough. I was happy to be heading east and away from there.

* * * *

An omen that the days of a Western presence at Khe Sanh might be numbered occurred just five days earlier on April 13, 1968. That morning a Marine C-130 cargo plane crashed as it was landing on the Khe Sanh airstrip. The fuel tanks ruptured and the plane burst into flames. Everyone

This C-130, which had been shot down a month before at Khe Sanh Combat Base, is inexplicably struck again by enemy mortar shells

on board escaped unharmed, except the one civilian passenger—Felix Poilane, the plantation owner.

Felix and his family fled Khe Sanh in late January. In February, we bombed the old Poilane house to rubble after spotting an NVA soldier standing in an upper-floor bedroom window spying on the base with binoculars. Rumor had it that while in Da Nang, Poilane had hired an attorney to file a lawsuit against the U.S. government for the loss of his buildings and orchards. Because of that story, we were not particularly saddened to hear of his death.

Like his father, Eugene, an early colonial settler in the valley and the victim of a Viet Cong ambush less than a mile away, Felix Poilane's life also ended violently at Khe Sanh. Only the coffee trees, some of which survived the devastation of war and once again flourish in the Khe Sanh valley, remain as evidence that the Poilane's were ever there.

* * * *

Tom Mahoney and I had exchanged several letters while we were in Vietnam. To mail another Marine within the country, a letter had to go all the way to Fleet Post Office in San Francisco, then back to Vietnam. Despite the fact that Mahoney and I were never more than forty miles from each other, our mail would have to travel nearly 12,000 miles. This often took several weeks, so limited the number of times we corresponded.

Generally, Mahoney sounded to be in better spirits than when I last saw him at the diner in Oceanside the previous November. He had developed a taste for the action and the military life, and in one letter surprised me by writing that he was considering making it a career. He and his platoon commander, Lieutenant Frank Ahearn, even discussed the possibility of Mahoney getting accepted to Officer's Candidate School. As Ahearn later described:

> [Lance Corporal] T.P. Mahoney was a good Marine. Sandy hair and a good build. Like all Marines from California, he was cocky, well trained, and quite a bit up on the issues involved with the Vietnamese war. He showed me a picture of his girl back home and she was a beautiful young lady. Blond hair, blue eyes, and that look of high expectations that so marked young ladies from that age. He was a little rambunctious and very experimental.
>
> He wasn't ever afraid of anything. He was a good point man and I could count on him to man his watch. I told his squad leader, Corporal "Snake" Fernandez, that if he [Mahoney] kept up his good record in battle, he could become a candidate in OCS (Officer's Candidate

School) for he reminded me a great deal of Ray Smith who was a former enlisted Marine and fine lieutenant in combat [Smith ended his career as a highly-decorated Marine Corps Major General]. That made Cpl. Fernandez mad because it set Mahoney off, and he became even more rambunctious and experimental. All in all, I thought that he was going to come thru Viet Nam just fine. I was wrong.[20]

* * * *

Mahoney arrived at the Khe Sanh Combat Base on April 19 and, as he mentioned in a subsequent letter, looked for me only to discover that we had missed seeing each other by less than twenty-four hours. He felt that we might still hook up while in Vietnam, but at the very least would have a great time the following New Years Eve when we would both be home.

Along with the rest of Bravo Company, Mahoney had been trucked up Route 9 from Ca Lu, just five miles east of Khe Sanh. Despite the relatively short distance, this narrow, winding, mountainous stretch of the highway had been closed since early 1967 due to enemy landmines and ambushes. Surprisingly, the Marine convoy encountered no resistance.

Bravo Company was soon patrolling the hills surrounding the Khe Sanh base in order to protect it from further attacks by enemy troops, mortars, and rockets. Occasionally they made contact with sizeable enemy forces. By late June, it was no longer the enemy causing all the explosions at the base. Marine engineers were now systematically dismantling and destroying the place.

On July 1, 1968, Captain Robert Black, the commanding officer of Bravo Company now atop Hill 881S, received official confirmation that Khe Sanh was being abandoned. He was ordered by the 1st Battalion commander to collapse the bunkers, cave in all the trenches, and destroy everything that could not be carried out on their backs.

Back in May of 1967, just a week before Mahoney and I left for boot camp, I had an unusually vivid dream that he was killed on Hill 881S. At the time I dreamt this, Marines had just fought a well-publicized battle there, that I followed with great interest in the newspapers and on television. Befitting the often theatric nature of a typical adolescent's imagination, I saw myself in the dream, kneeling beside Mahoney's lifeless body, weeping and wallowing in self-pity. Mulling it over afterwards, I rationalized the dream resulted from a combination of news stories and my anxiety over our impending departure. I did not consider it to have any significance. Like most dreams, it would not come true. But at Khe Sanh, the unimaginable was a common occurrence.

By July 6, 1968, there were no more explosions reverberating up the ravines and valleys from the base. The destruction of Khe Sanh Combat Base was officially completed. The men of Bravo Company had already dismantled the fortifications on Hill 881S and were waiting anxiously in their exposed positions for helicopters to evacuate them. To make the situation even more dangerous, the company had not received adequate troop replacements for some time. At that point they were operating at about half strength, living literally out in the open, and being told each day by radio from Battalion Headquarters that evacuation aircraft would arrive at any time; therefore, the men of Bravo Company stopped patrolling around the hilltop for signs of the enemy. Day after day, they could see Marine helicopters making frequent visits to other hills around Khe Sanh, but each evening they were still there. Some in Bravo Company were becoming increasingly apprehensive about remaining for so long in such a vulnerable situation. Finally, word came that helicopters would be there within the hour to extricate them.

Captain Black chose the westernmost of the hill's four landing zones for the evacuation, because it had taken the least amount of mortar fire during Bravo Company's occupation. He would have preferred that the helicopters arrive during the early morning, when a light fog always shrouded the hilltop. He knew the NVA were reluctant to waste their mortar ammunition on targets they could not see, so this would have provided a little more safety.

* * * *

Private First Class Bruce Bird, a friend of Tom Mahoney's, was becoming increasingly concerned about something else besides Bravo Company's vulnerability to enemy attack. Mahoney had recently received a "Dear John" letter from his girlfriend, and he was miserable. Linda was breaking up with him and not in a nice way. At about 1400 that day, Mahoney told Bird he was going to go outside of the defensive wire to take a crap. He did not have a rifle with him. Bird, like the others, was engaged in last minute preparations for departure, so understandably did not give this seemingly trivial matter much attention. A short time later, a Marine near the west gate into the Hill 881S fortification, heard a familiar voice coming from a short distance down the hill. It was Tom Mahoney shouting, "Help me!" A burst of enemy AK-47 rifle fire silenced him.

Immediately, Corporal Fernandez advised Lieutenant Frank Ahearn who was sitting in a large bomb crater waiting for the helicopter with some other Marines. Ahearn jumped up and headed toward the gate path through which Mahoney had exited the Marine's fortification. Just then,

The Marine outpost on Hill 881S in September 1967, a few months before the siege began. Khe Sanh Combat Base is approximately 3 miles away in the direction of the tall mountains in upper right. Tom Mahoney's body was finally abandoned after a fierce firefight at the south-western edge of the fortifications, located at the lower left of the photo   *Courtesy of Ray W. Stubbe*

an enemy mortar shell fell on the group wounding about a dozen men. Lieutenant Ahearn quickly returned to assist the wounded and soon noticed that the mortar shell had struck the very sandbag on which he had been sitting. He had avoided certain death by seconds. Ahearn ordered an immediate search of the hilltop to confirm that Mahoney had actually left the perimeter. Once it was evident that he was gone, the lieutenant and several volunteers set out through the gate. They soon spotted blood on the trail and found the motionless Mahoney laying on the ground about ten meters farther down the hill. As PFC Richard Delucie approached, he was wounded by automatic weapons fire and hand grenades erupting from concealed enemy positions just beyond where Mahoney was. Several other Marines, including PFC Bird, were also wounded in the rescue attempt. The NVA knew Marines always made an effort to recover their dead and were confident this day would be no exception. They had dragged Mahoney's body to a spot just in front of their small "spider hole" fortification and waited for the Marines to come.

The LZ that was to be used to extract the company remained under sporadic enemy 82mm mortar fire. Captain Black noticed that the area Ahearn and his men were trying to reach was also coming under mortar fire. After radioing for artillery fire to suppress the mortar, Black quickly began organizing his men, including the wounded in another LZ on the east side of the hill. Meanwhile, Lieutenant Ahearn and his men, still unable to recover Mahoney due to heavy enemy fire, tried distracting the enemy by using tear gas projectiles fired from an EE8 CS launcher. However, the enemy gunfire continued unchecked, and now their mortar shells were falling near these Marines with greater frequency. Soon, U.S. close air support bombers arrived in the sky over Hill 881S. Ahearn and his men backed off to let them try to knock out the enemy positions. When the smoke cleared, the enemy was still firing and shrapnel from the bombs had severely damaged Mahoney's upper torso. By this time, elements of Bravo Company were being lifted off the hill.

Captain Black, after first guessing that Tom Mahoney had sustained a fatal chest wound, now learned of the damage done by the bombs. There was no doubt Tom Mahoney was dead. With darkness setting in and enemy fire increasing, he ordered a halt to further attempts to recover the body. Despite a request by Lieutenant Ahearn and some of the 1st Platoon Marines that they be allowed to remain behind to try and reach Mahoney, Captain Black wisely ordered them to the east LZ for immediate evacuation. As dusk descended, the pilot of a Marine UH-1B helicopter gunship strafing the ambush site later confirmed that all he could see were "the bare legs of a Caucasian body."[21] An appalling end for such a fine young man.

The legendary Marine outpost on Hill 881S—wrested from the NVA in a bloody four-day battle in April 1967 and later held at great additional cost of life—was finally abandoned. The last Marine off the hill was Captain Robert Black, standing in the darkness with enemy mortar shells falling around him, directing his rescue chopper in with a pen light.

The evacuation choppers flew those in Bravo Company who were not wounded to nearby Hill 689, where they joined what remained of Alpha and Charlie companies. The following night, a numerically superior enemy force repeatedly attacked these depleted Marine units. After hours of vicious combat, the enemy finally retreated. Despite all that was going on, Captain Black immediately pressed his superiors for action to recover Mahoney's remains. Several days later, an intelligence officer at First Battalion Headquarters reported to Black that a Marine 1st Force Reconnaissance team had made a clandestine visit to the site on Hill 881S and recovered Tom's body. Neither Captain Black nor Lieutenant Ahearn would find out for another thirty-five years that this report had been incorrect.

The NVA troops who killed Tom were not in that particular location by accident. They had carefully chosen the site because it put them under the path of helicopters approaching and departing the westernmost of the four landing zones on Hill 881S—an LZ they anticipated the Marines would use to evacuate the hill. Many in Bravo Company, including Lieutenant Ahearn, have no doubt that had it not been for Tom Mahoney's inexplicable behavior, that inadvertently tipped them off to the presence of the NVA troops waiting nearby and the enemy mortar already sighted in on that LZ, their evacuation aircraft would have been shot down. Perhaps, as some later observed, an entire platoon or more would have been lost.

This conclusion appears to be supported by an NVA after action report discovered in August 2003 by MIA investigators while researching military records in Hanoi. Mahoney clearly spoiled the enemy plan to ambush the departing Americans when he, quite literally, came face-to-face with them.

> The five-person team [members of the NVA 246th Regiment] secretly crawled by seven barbed wire fences that evening [July 5, 1968]. They stopped and dug fortified positions at the eighth fence. Finally they arrived at the main entrance of the outpost [Hill 881S]. While sitting in the fortified positions they could clearly hear the voices of the Americans and smell cigarette smoke from the bunkers. They waited for the enemy all night long.

> At 1400 on the following day [July 6, 1968], we saw one American walking outside the entrance to the outpost. His face was red and his eyes were blue like a mean animal. He was looking toward Mr. Luong's team. The sounds of AK weapons roared immediately, and the American fell. Mr. Luong and Mr. Long jumped out of their positions and dragged the American's body down. They placed the body in front of them to create an ambush for the other Americans coming out of their bunkers. Ten aircraft of all types circled and bombed the area about five minutes later. The artillery from Hill A [unknown] and Ta Con [Khe Sanh Combat Base] fired at this location. However, the team was safe because they were very close to the enemy's location and could calmly observe their movements.[22]

I learned of Tom Mahoney's death about two weeks after it happened, while reading U.S. casualty reports in *Stars & Stripes*. His name was then listed under the heading "Missing in Action." A month later, I would see his name there again. This time he had moved down the column to a category titled "Missing to Dead." Before I left Vietnam, his name would appear one last time, in the column "Dead."

When I first read about it, my unit was located near Phu Bai, about forty miles west of Khe Sanh. On a hunch, I hitchhiked over to the hospital to see if any men from Bravo Company had been medevaced there. I found one wounded man who, I now believe, was PFC Bird. He told me that Tom had been acting "differently" in the days leading up to his getting killed. Saddened and bewildered by this bizarre story, I turned to leave. Bird, seeming to sense my pain, called me back and said, "For what it's worth, if Mahoney hadn't done what he did, the whole platoon would have been lost, shot down with the chopper on the way out."

A few days after talking to Bird, I received a letter from Mahoney. It was dated July 4, 1968, two days before his death. No longer the cheery, upbeat, and optimistic guy of his previous letters to me, his tone was now gloomy, almost despondent. He had gotten a letter from Linda, and the news wasn't good. He didn't elaborate but now sounded angry about the war, the Corps, and seemingly the world in general. Ominously, there was no more talk of our New Years Eve bash. Subsequently I lost all my correspondence before leaving Vietnam, but you never forget a letter from a dead man.

The question always lingered as to why Mahoney left the hill that afternoon. If in fact it was merely to defecate and get some privacy, then why didn't he use one of the many ruined trenches or bunkers within the defensive perimeter? Still more puzzling was how a seasoned combat veteran like Tom would venture into enemy territory without a weapon. All these factors led PFC Bird to comment later to another Marine that Mahoney may have been "inviting suicide."[23]

Never careless about such things before, Mahoney by all accounts was not thinking properly at the time. Others in his squad felt the "Dear John" letter had impaired his judgment. I would read that letter months later during a visit with his mother. It was among his personal affects mailed to her by Captain Black. I anticipated the letter would be hard to read, but I wasn't prepared for the level of animosity. Filled with the angry antiwar epithets, the letter ended with the words that must have hurt my friend the most. "I can't believe I ever cared for you," Linda wrote. "I never want to see you again."

Lieutenant Ahearn later told me he felt that while Mahoney could stoically endure the "pain of war" he was also a sentimental type, and perhaps that was his Achilles heel. An otherwise savvy, courageous, battle-hardened Marine, Tom Mahoney was undone by a broken heart. With his spirit crushed by a high school sweetheart and his dreams of future happiness now hopelessly lost, he stopped caring for a just a few moments—at Khe Sanh that was long enough to cost you your life.

* * * *

On May 23, 1968, during a White House ceremony, Colonel Lownds received the Presidential Unit Citation on behalf of the 26th Marine

Regiment. In addition, President Johnson awarded Lownds the Navy Cross, the second highest medal a Marine can receive.

I certainly didn't begrudge the colonel this medal. In his youth, he had fought on the bloody sands of Iwo Jima, the costliest battle in Marine Corps history. Later, as an officer, he looked out for his troops, doing the best he could with what he had to keep us alive at Khe Sanh. In a letter I sent my folks from Khe Sanh, I wrote:

> He's an OK guy. He covers up his silver birds and goes down on the perimeter to eat chow with the troops. They don't know who he is, so they just kick back and bitch about everything. After he comes back, he gets on somebody's back about why the troops on the line are not getting what they need. I can't complain about our colonel, he's a crazy old guy. But we couldn't have gotten a better one.

Despite the incessant anti-aircraft fire coming from the hills around Khe Sanh, Lownds flew to every hilltop outpost in the area to check on the condition of his troops. I received this information from Steve Orr who was Colonel Lownds' radio operator in those dangerous first weeks of February 1968.

Once back in the United States, Lownds would become somewhat of a celebrity for a while. He appeared on TV and radio talk shows and spoke to organizations. He once told an audience of West Point cadets, "You gentlemen take care of these enlisted people; they're going to determine whether you live or die."[24]

I believe the White House ceremony for Colonel Lownds was intentionally timed to obfuscate a Pentagon decision to abandon the Khe Sanh Combat Base. However, it seemed only to magnify the issue. If Khe Sanh had been so vital to the defense of South Vietnam, justifying such enormous bloodshed, why wasn't it still? Ceremoniously praising the great sacrifices made at Khe Sanh while at the same time surrendering it to the enemy was a contradiction many of us found difficult to accept.

General Westmorland's strategy of luring the enemy into catastrophic losses had not worked, because the enemy was willing to pay the price. In June 1968, General Creighton Abrams who, under orders from the Pentagon set in motion a plan to abandon Khe Sanh base, replaced Westmorland as commander of all U.S. forces in Vietnam. Among the official reasons for the decision was that a more mobile strategy was being introduced, which relied less on fixed fortifications. Khe Sanh's proximity to unabated enemy artillery fire from Laos had been a continuing problem; yet, none of the other U.S. bases along the DMZ were scheduled for abandonment, even though they regularly received artillery fire from inside North Vietnam.

National Security Adviser Walt W. Rostow noted, "I believe we have a serious problem—perhaps of substance, certainly of public relations." Rostow pointed out that intelligence estimates on the enemy order of battle still placed about 40,000 NVA troops in the DMZ area. "If it was good to pin down two divisions with 6,000 men, then why not now?" he asked. The Pentagon acknowledged the base closing announcement caused a "difficult public relations task."[25]

Throughout July 1968, Marines were still engaged in desperate fighting on Hill 689, within view of the now abandoned combat base. On August 1, 1968, the last Marine combat unit left the Khe Sanh area.

"Operation Charlie," the official military designation for the mission to destroy and abandon the Khe Sanh Combat Base, commenced on June 17, 1968 and ended nineteen days later on July 6, the day Tom Mahoney died. I was struck at the time by the irony of the name "Charlie" being our commonly used term for the Viet Cong, whose flag was spotted waving over the forsaken base the following morning by Marine aircraft. Bitter from the dual blow of the abandonment of Khe Sanh base to the enemy and the loss of my good friend, I was now fighting for no cause other than getting home alive.

On July 24, 1968, I wrote a letter to my parents:

Dear Mom & Dad,

Hi. How was your vacation? Hope you had a good time. We're here at Phu Bai, finally. It's not a bad place. Rains a lot here, I think the monsoon is going to come early.

I haven't been getting much mail lately. I guess I know why. I read about Tom, we get weekly casualty reports. I'm really going to miss him. He was about the best friend I ever had, I guess. I hope his mom will be able to take it.

As for me, I just don't know. I'm sick of it all, this lousy country and this war. A few more months and I'll be leaving and somebody else will take my place. One big waste. That's all it is.

Well I'd better go. Take care. I'm O.K. And I'll write again soon.

* * * *

During the early 1990s, in cooperation with the Socialist Republic of Vietnam, the United States set out to account for all servicemen who had not returned from Vietnam. In July 1993, a four-man team of Missing in Action (MIA) researchers armed with a copy of Tom Mahoney's dental records, went to the site of his death to investigate. Their usual technique would have included talking to civilians who lived nearby or, if possible, to any surviving veterans of the enemy unit that was involved in the action.

Unfortunately, there were no longer any civilians in the area at the time of his death and the enemy unit would not be identified for another ten years. Captain Robert Black later speculated that given the "consistent, logical manner with which the NVA carried out a mission," it was unlikely they dug a grave for Mahoney. If anything, they may have simply pulled his body into one of the little fortified positions they had dug for themselves the night before.[26] The MIA investigation team searched the area for bones, dog tags, and remnants of equipment. But, twenty-five years had passed and they found nothing.

Tom Mahoney was memorialized on the reverse side of his father's white marble headstone, which stands beneath a wind bent cypress on a hillside by the bay in the National Cemetery at San Francisco. Two terse epitaphs etched into a single stone; two generations of Mahoney men taken by war, lamented by a distant foghorn. It still breaks my heart.

* * * *

Over 1,000 Americans died fighting for Khe Sanh in 1968, and another 4,500 were wounded. The exact numbers are difficult to determine because of the unusual magnitude of the action, the chaotic battle-field conditions, and the variety of medevac desti-nations used. South Viet-namese military losses were in the range of 750 dead and 500 wounded. The North Vietnamese Army suffered nearly 12,000 dead with probably twice that many wounded.

Marines killed in action lie on the Khe Sanh airstrip awaiting a helicopter to begin the long ride home
Courtesy of David Douglas Duncan

Of the 20,000 civilians known to inhabit the Huong Hoa District at the time the fighting began, 10,000 disappeared and are presumed dead.[27] The bloody six-month battle for Khe Sanh ended on August 1, 1968, leaving nearly 50,000 casualties in its wake.

* * * *

After flying out of the Khe Sanh Combat Base on the morning of April 18, 1968, we landed at the Quang Tri airfield about forty minutes later. We were treated a bit like celebrities. Someone told me later that a band was there, playing the "Marine Corps Hymn" for us as we galloped off the choppers, but I don't recall hearing it. The sense of relief was unexpectedly elating. Here the sun was shining and people sauntered leisurely from place to place with uncrouched postures. No one wore flak jackets and helmets but us. Skin tones of rosy hues or dark healthy-looking tans stood in stark contrast to our own pale, milky pelts.

By order of the commanding general of the 3rd Marine Division, we were trucked to a safe area where tents and cots were already set up and waiting for us. They provided us with warm showers—my first in five months—and the clean, clear water turned to a gritty maroon puddle around my feet. We were then issued new clothes and boots, led to a mess hall, and given our first freshly cooked meal since January. The commanding general had ordered thick beefsteaks be served, but we found ourselves instead crowding around the dairy dispensers, chugging down glasses of the cold stuff. Then, as if on cue, we all ran out the back door of the mess hall and began vomiting. Soon the slight incline behind the building flowed with regurgitated milk. It was not that the milk had gone sour, but rather our digestive systems could no longer tolerate such rich food after months of eating bland C-rations. Eventually, we adjusted to the chow.

Although our hosts provided everything they could think of to make us comfortable, many of us took out our E-tools and dug fox holes just outside the tent from where we were about to lay down on soft, canvass cots for the night.

Within a week, I departed for five days of R&R. During the fighting at the village the prior January, I had kept Wolverton's mind off the pain of his wounded hand by talking about pleasant things. He had recently returned from leave in Singapore and insisted I go. I made one of those inane little contracts with fate, which we sometimes do in hopes of changing our luck, swearing to him with great resolve that if I survived Khe Sanh I would go on R&R there too.

Singapore had a positive post-Khe Sanh rehabilitative effect on me. It was a safe, cosmopolitan city, whose business district reminded me a little of Montgomery Street in San Francisco. I immediately purchased civilian clothes. My hotel room was clean, with all the modern conveniences. I slept under sheets for the first time in months and took hot showers whenever I felt like it. I called my family on the telephone and talked to each of them. When the time came to return to Vietnam, I was ready to face the next eight months I had left on my tour.

After leaving our long-time quarters at Khe Sanh Combat Base, we became gypsies or, as we described ourselves, "homeless bastards," packing up and moving nearly every four weeks until December when I rotated home. We came under much less enemy fire than we had before, because the regimental air team's main duty now was coordinating close air support bombers, medevac, and resupply choppers to Marine battalions out in the "bush"—most often the 1st Battalion, 26th Marines.

The 1st Battalion fought costly battles against the NVA in May 1968 around Dong Ha, near the DMZ in the north-east corner of the country, and again near An Hoa, about twenty miles southwest of Da Nang, in the summer of that year. As the monsoon season approached, large-scale contacts with the enemy tapered off, much like the year before just prior to the Tet offensive.

During the summer months, our air team was investigated on three separate occasions for possible negligence in the bombing deaths of friendly troops. In each case, the investigators determined that the deaths were due either to pilot error or the victim's belief that they were at another map coordinate location when, in fact, they were at the target area. In July 1968, during the last investigation, a Marine major questioned us radio operators collectively and individually for two days at Hill 55 west of Da Nang. With each of these investigations, I became slightly more paranoid and, by the second day, was sure I was going to the brig as a scapegoat, possibly to spare some culpable party the inconvenience. My fears proved to be unwarranted, however, as it was eventually ruled another case of "victim's error."

Throughout 1968, as we moved from place to place throughout South Vietnam's I Corps, our distrust of the general population increased. Wherever we went, the same pattern seemed evident: they were our friends by day and enemies by night. Each morning, roads would have to be cleared of mines and barbed wire defenses checked for cuts. Rarely a week went by that an attack on some American or ARVN encampment in Vietnam was not assisted, in some way, by insider intelligence or sabotage. It mattered little to us that we knew much of the civilian population was constantly involved in a deadly balancing act between pressure from the South Vietnamese and American forces on one hand and the Viet Cong and North Vietnamese on the other. After time, we cared more and more about making it home and less about the problems of the Vietnamese.

Between our growing distrust of the Vietnamese and the stream of bad news arriving from home, morale began to deteriorate. In an effort to keep troop spirits high, the *Stars & Stripes* and radio sources attempted to soften the bad news with carefully chosen stories and photos. But we did have access to news magazines such as *Time* and *Newsweek*, though they always seemed to be a week or two out of date by the time they got to us.

Even before we departed Khe Sanh, President Johnson announced that he was not going to seek another term, evidently acquiescing to antiwar pressure. Four days later, Martin Luther King Jr. was murdered. Images of the Washington Monument, standing against the backdrop of smoke from our riot-torn and burning national capital, was indeed discouraging. A month later, in May 1968, talks between representatives of the United States and North Vietnam began in Paris. A month later, an assassin took the life of Robert Kennedy. Throughout the summer months, there was rioting and large-scale antiwar protests not only in the United States, but around the world.

In October 1968, two black American athletes with heads bent in shame held raised fists during an Olympic medal ceremony in Mexico City, while the U.S. national anthem was being played. Most of us had a hard time fully comprehending some of the things happening in our country, but we could not mistake this intentional disrespect of our national anthem in front of the world. This image, seared into our memories, left us seething with anger. Our reaction was not entirely a result of patriotic feelings. We had seen firsthand the extremes of poverty and oppression in Asia; by that standard, the United States was a utopia. Most of us considered these protesters uninformed and ungrateful.

In November of that year, days before the presidential election, President Johnson ordered an end to the bombing of North Vietnam. Those of us engaged in endless interdiction of enemy supplies coming into South Vietnam from the North were not pleased with that news. A few days later, Richard Nixon, who promised to bring order to an internally battered United States and a "peace with honor" to Vietnam, won the election.

As 1968 ended, new people began to populate the ranks of Headquarters Company, 26th Marines. Often bored and with little respect for just how dangerous an enemy we faced, many turned to chronic drug use and became serious threats to our safety. Steve Orr, Savage, and I were anxious to get out of there and gratefully received our orders home on December 17, 1968.

That morning we boarded a truck to the Da Nang airbase, where we received medical tests for infectious diseases. This was always a nervous time for troops leaving Vietnam. Rumors prevailed about incurable diseases for which a luckless soldier could be detained indefinitely in Vietnam or in a "special" hospital in Japan. My chest X-ray for tuberculosis was negative as were all the tests for other diseases. While waiting in front of the medical building for the test results, I remembered the Kennedy half dollar that I had been carrying for good luck the last eleven months, since finding it on the mud floor of the comm bunker in Khe Sanh Village. I always kept the coin safe in a trouser pocket that I used infrequently. Though I really didn't believe the coin had charms, I was still afraid to part with it. During my last month in Vietnam, I had begun to fret over what I would do with it. I wanted to leave it there because I was afraid that if I did not, I would develop a neurotic attachment to it for the rest of my life. Yet, I felt unsafe without it. I finally decided to hold on to the coin until I was about to board the airplane the next day, then throw it as far down the runway as I could. I believed this plan would be acceptable to all the powers of the universe who might consider possession of the coin synonymous with my survival.

Having thus decided on a solution, I reached into my pocket to touch the coin once more for luck—but it was not there. It had disappeared. This gave me a strange, dreamlike sensation at that moment. To this day, I cannot explain it. I hope if someone else found the coin, it worked as well for him as it did for me.

Later that evening, we found cots in a transient barracks near the airfield. A nearby siren later awakened us, indicating the airfield was receiving incoming rockets (a nightly occurrence from what I later learned). We followed the others to a low-roofed bunker and crawled in. Despite the fact that the Da Nang air base was a vast complex and that we had not heard any explosions in our vicinity, we were not taking any chances on our last night. Already inside the bunker was a young enlisted man, about eighteen years old, who had evidently just arrived in country. He was on his knees rocking back and forth, weeping. All I could do was stare mutely at him. I wanted to feel sympathy, but nothing happened. I waited a bit longer to see if I would feel like mocking or encouraging him or telling him to get a grip on himself. There was nothing there. I could not even wish him luck when the all-clear signal sounded and we went back to the barracks.

The next day out on the airfield, I watched silently as Marines who had just disembarked from the airplane walked past those of us waiting to take their seats. Some in our group sang out "You'll be sor-r-r-e-e-e," the same serenade I had received a year before. My indifference surprised me. I fleetingly wondered to what degree I had changed in the last year. Just then, our line began to shuffle forward toward the plane. My heart was pounding with excitement. In a few minutes, I would be out of Vietnam. Nothing could wreck this long-awaited moment. However, as luck would have it, PFC "Savage" Rodriguez was behind me as we climbed the stairway onto the airplane. Unable to contain his joy, he suddenly bit me on my back with such enthusiasm he drew blood. I had the scar for months.

* * * *

On December 22, 1968, I sat down to dinner at home with my mother, father, and younger brothers and sister. I had just arrived back in the United States that morning, for twenty days of leave before reporting to my next duty station at Camp Pendleton. Mom was visibly relieved and could not stop grinning. Two of the last three years she had endured sons away at war. I could tell everyone else felt uneasy about my presence there, not quite knowing what to expect. I think my little brothers, subjected to a constant stream of horrific war atrocities reported in the news, were expecting me to produce a necklace of human ears before dessert. Dad mostly just repeated the phrase, "Geez its good to have you back," occasionally asking me several carefully-worded questions about the flight home and the weather in Vietnam. I answered in short replies, my conversation skills rusty and inhibited by my reluctance to use expletives in the presence of Mom and the little kids.

Mom had prepared a beef dish for dinner, which included a large bowl of steamed white rice on the side. Suddenly, I pulled the rice bowl to me, turned my spoon and fork around so the handles formed makeshift chopsticks, and began shoveling clumps of the stuff into my mouth, Asian style. Then, I turned to Mom and in pidgin blurted out, "Mama-san this rice numbah one. Make G.I. plenty *dinky-dau* [crazy]." No one knew what to do. I smiled and playfully admonished them saying, "Hey, it's just me." We all laughed—the long, breathless, teary-eyed laughter of relief. The ice had been broken. Maybe it was going to be okay after all.

* * * *

Mike

Homecoming

★ ★ ★

On December 23, 1968, the day after I arrived back in the United States, I went to visit Tom Mahoney's family. I stopped at the Seifert Floral Company to buy a flowering plant to take with me. Before my enlistment, I had driven a delivery truck for the company and it was good seeing Mr. Seifert and the others.

Seifert's eighteen-year-old son was visiting the shop that day; and as I chatted with the man, his son approached, interrupting us to rebuke me. "How can you justify what you've done?" he asked. "How can you live with yourself?" He demanded answers with such self-righteous conviction that I was momentarily at a loss for words. It was the first, but not the last, time I would be scolded for my participation in the war. I would be more prepared next time.

Mr. Seifert, who was a World War II Navy veteran and had seen his share of kamikazes during the invasion of Okinawa, told the young man he was out of line. He then apologized to me for his son's rudeness. Yet none of this affected me deeply, because I was preoccupied with—and dreading—the unpleasant task at hand.

I took the plant and drove over to the house on Fairmont Avenue where Tom's mother, grandmother, and sister still lived. I knocked on the door, and his grandmother answered. She stared at me for a moment with a look that clearly said, why are you alive instead of my Tommy? She never spoke, but wearily turned and walked back into the house leaving the door half-open. I waited on the porch for a while longer, then Tom's sister,

Claudia, came out. She was a classmate and a friend of my sister, Suzie. She hugged me, invited me in, and apologized for her grandmother's behavior. I sat down in the living room.

Soon Tom's mother came into the room. I didn't know what to expect after the grandmother's reception, but thankfully she was warm and friendly. On the piano was a frame that contained a picture of Tom in his dress blues, the citation for his Purple Heart, and the medal itself. His mother picked it up and handed it to me. We both started to cry.

We didn't speak for several minutes. The silence was finally broken by a question I hoped she wouldn't ask. "Do you think Tommy is still alive?" I said that "anything was possible," but I was not being honest with her. I knew Tom was dead. Although she had received a letter directly from Captain Black, Tom's company commander, stating that he was dead, she could not fully accept that as the truth. And I could not, either out of sympathy or timidity, bring myself to extinguish her last flicker of hope. I would later wonder whether my little lie helped her or merely prolonged her pain.

At that moment, though, she seemed buoyed by the prospect that Tom might eventually come home. She got up and left the room, returning shortly with a small cardboard box containing some letters. These were among his personal belongings, she explained, sent to her from Vietnam by Tom's company commander. One was a letter I had sent just before his death, reminding him of the great time we were going to have partying on New Years Eve.

The second letter was from Tom's former girlfriend. As she handed it to me, I asked Mrs. Mahoney if she ever saw Linda. She said that the girl had come by once, several weeks after the first news of Tom's disappearance. Linda had gone into the living room and sat silently on the floor by the piano for about an hour, then departed. Tom's mother thought it was "all very strange" and had not heard from her since.

As I began to read, I immediately realized it was the "Dear John" letter. When I had finished it, I was speechless, filled with resentment and anger. I could not imagine that in her long months of grief and pain, in her search for answers, Mrs. Mahoney had missed the possible role this letter played in the loss of her son. However, she made no comment. I handed her back the letter, which she carefully tucked into its envelope and returned to the little box. We sat silently for several more minutes, then I excused myself and left.

* * * *

In January 1969, I reported to 5th Communications Company, Camp Pendleton, California, then was transferred to Marine Corps Air Station, Kaneohe Bay, Oahu, Hawaii, in September of that year. There I served as a radio operator with First Air and Naval Gunfire Liaison Company (ANGLICO). The Marine Corps had begun downsizing its forces and my occupational specialty qualified me for early separation from active duty. In February 1970, four months earlier than my enlistment required, I was sent to the Treasure Island Naval Facility in San Francisco for my transfer to civilian life.

While there, I saw PFC Brown, the Marine who had jumped on the last truck out of Khe Sanh Village. We were being separated from active duty at the same time. I don't know if he recognized me. Although I never harbored strong feelings of resentment against him for what he did that afternoon in the village, I also had no desire to talk to him—and didn't.

On a foggy late-February morning in 1970, upon the small parade ground next to the barracks at the Treasure Island Naval Facility, I stood in formation with about twelve other Marines. The chilly dampness in the middle of San Francisco Bay had me shivering beneath my green, winter service gabardine uniform. This was our final formation. Once the staff sergeant ordered us dismissed, we followed tradition by pulling the garrison covers from our heads and throwing them into the air in celebration. As I leaned over to pick mine back up off the asphalt, I saw Steve Orr in a nearby parking lot, wearing civilian clothes and leaning against his brand new MG sports car.

After Vietnam, Steve had been stationed at the Marine Corps Air Station in Yuma, Arizona. Since I was getting an "early-out" and had not written to tell him, I fully expected him to be still on active duty. I relished the thought and believed I would have the last word in our ongoing game of one-upmanship. But, as luck would have it, he received an earlier "early-out" than I had. He was there to give me a ride home and, of course, remind me that, while he may have been a "boot to the bush," that is arriving at Khe Sanh after me, now I was and would forever be a "lifer" for having been on active duty a whopping three days longer than he. Steve Orr has remained my closest friend throughout the years. Such a thing occurred rarely among Vietnam veterans who often did not wish to reacquaint themselves with their buddies for decades. I have long since stopped wondering why this happened. I just consider myself lucky.

* * * *

Occasionally word arrived about others with whom I had served; my suspicions about the danger of complacency and the increasing drug use in Headquarters Company 26th Marines proved tragically correct. In February

1969, two months after I left Vietnam, they sustained heavy casualties when attacked and overrun by the enemy near Dai La Pass, west of Da Nang. This was part of a series of NVA and VC attacks around the country, which were later termed the Tet Offensive of 1969. I received a letter from PFC Joe Wojcinowicz, a fellow radioman we had nicknamed "Alphabet" because we could not pronounce his name. Alphabet came to our unit in late April 1968, just a week after we left Khe Sanh. He was a likeable, conscientious kid from Milford, Connecticut, who stayed out of trouble. In his letter, Joe described the events of that awful morning, as recalled or pieced together later from fellow survivors. The enemy caught them completely by surprise just before dawn, blowing up several huts filled with sleeping Marines. Before Alphabet could enter the fight, the attackers shot him three times in the back; he was also blinded in one eye by grenade fragments.

He told of how one of the dead Viet Cong had been our barber. This man was allowed access to our camp every day for months to give us haircuts. I remember him always chattering in pidgin in the most ingratiating and fawning way. I imagine he could listen as well and picked up a lot of information from the chitchat of Marines awaiting their turns in the chair.

Yet, even more shameful was that the two Marines responsible for watching the road on which the enemy soldiers approached that morning, had smoked dope in the guardhouse and fallen asleep. They were later found dead, exactly where they had lain down to nap—their throats slashed by the VC.

Morley Sweet, whose unusual antics during the siege at Khe Sanh had made life a little more interesting, voluntarily extended his tour of duty in Vietnam in the fall of 1968. During the attack on 26th Marines headquarters at Dai La Pass, Sweet was seriously wounded by an enemy grenade, permanently losing the use of his left arm.

News of others I had known at Khe Sanh trickled in from time to time. Pig survived the war but was killed less than a year later when, in April 1969, his frenetic nature finally got the best of him, and he crashed his car just outside the main gate of the Twenty-Nine Palms Marine base in southern California. He was doing well over 100 miles an hour.

The two remaining radio operators on the Khe Sanh air team, Raul "Oz" Orozco and Mike Reath, both survived. Decades later, I would happily discover that they had retained the same irreverent sense of humor that helped us all through the long months of siege.

After being his radio operator at the battle for Khe Sanh village, I lost touch with Lieutenant Stamper for twenty years. Eventually, I located him and wrote a letter in 1988, reminding him jokingly of his promise to buy me an entire bottle of scotch if we survived that night in the village. By then he was sick with cancer, but sent a nice reply vowing to make good on his promise someday. He died a few months later.

Although I never saw Captain Harry Baig again, I did hear from a former Marine officer and acquaintance of Baig's that three years after leaving Khe Sanh, on April 20, 1971, he died along with his wife and daughter in their room at the Imperial Hotel in Bangkok. A fire had been deliberately set and the fire escape on Baig's floor was suspiciously chained shut from the outside. Baig was in Thailand visiting with his family after spending time working secretly in Laos on a mission related to the negotiations with the North Vietnamese to end the U.S. involvement in Vietnam. Dark, diminutive, and fluent in French, Baig would not have drawn much attention to himself in that part of the world. The circumstances of his death remain suspicious but point to an assassination.[28] Even at Khe Sanh, most of us believed Captain Baig was answerable to a different authority than the Marine Corps chain of command; some speculated he was an agent of the CIA.

Tiddy, Savage, Old Woman, and the rest, whose well-being had once been as important to me as my own, faded out of my life almost as though they had never existed. Unlike past wars, most veterans of Vietnam did not perceive it as a shared effort in the common cause of victory. It seemed that each man's tour there was an individual war of its own.

Although American troops fought in Vietnam for another five years, I would rarely pay attention to reports of the war in newspapers or on television. The news on TV was not about my war. My war was over.

There was, I think, another reason I lost interest in the war once I was home. My experiences in South Vietnam, as much as I disliked thinking about it, had convinced me that both time and history were on the side of the enemy. However optimistic the daily Pentagon news briefing may have sounded, it was not going to change the outcome of things. Five hundred years before the first Westerners arrived in Southeast Asia, the Vietnamese General Tran Hung Dao defeated the vastly superior Mongol invasion force of Kublai Khan by employing a strategy of not defending prestige positions. The General later wrote: "When the enemy is away from home for a long time and produces no victories, and families learn of their dead, then the enemy population becomes dissatisfied . . . Time is always in our favor. Our climate, our mountains and jungles, discourage the enemy . . .."[29] It sometimes seemed to me that the only way to avoid defeat in Vietnam was to fight on forever.

The transition from Vietnam back to the United States was difficult. Although I had been exposed to anti-war demonstrations and protests in

San Francisco and Berkeley before departing for boot camp in early 1967, and had read about the escalating violence occurring in American cities throughout 1968, I was not prepared for the level of hostility I met upon my return.

I had lost touch with nearly all of my friends from home. Jack Mooseau was the exception. Also a good friend of Tom Mahoney, he was saddened and troubled by Tom's death. I had known Jack since we were both nine years old, but while I was away in Vietnam, he had come to view the war as wrong, even criminal. He attended San Francisco State University and supported the student strike that shut down the campus in protest of United States policy in South Vietnam. Mooseau wrote me regularly while I was in Vietnam, though never using his letters as a platform to lecture me about the war. I appreciated that and knew Jack to be a sincere person who cared about his country. I had difficulty equating him with the image I had of other war protesters whom I considered to be at best rabidly intolerant of opposing opinions and at worst, as in the case of Tom Mahoney's girl-friend, lethally judgmental. I believed a person's principles had only as much value as the degree of sacrifice they were willing to make for them. It did not occur to me that those who opposed the war and the draft did so as a matter of conscience. It just seemed too convenient, too self-serving.

I did not enlist in the Marines out of patriotism, nor was I really concerned about the welfare of the South Vietnamese. I was going for the adventure, to prove myself. Yet, the USMC taught me about the need to protect South Vietnam from the North's aggression. A Communist regime would stifle all political opposition, seize all private property, and persecute religion—rights Americans held dear. If allowed to go unchecked in South Vietnam, Soviet-sponsored Communist uprisings would spread in Asia, then Africa, and soon, like Cuba, be at our very doorstep again. It made sense to me, and I believed in the cause on the day I arrived in Vietnam. There I came to know the unconscionable brutality of North Vietnam's terror apparatus, most horribly in the mass graves we unearthed during "Operation Rice" south of Hue city in May 1968, where we found the remains of hundreds of defenseless civilians rounded up and executed by the enemy.

By the time I had returned to civilian life, my frustration was intense. In college, I would occasionally argue that the North Vietnamese and Viet Cong were thugs and cold-blooded killers who intimidated, robbed, and often murdered the civilian population. But their image on American campuses, as long-suffering champions of the peasant, was now so thoroughly accepted that I was pitied as an imbecile for having made such remarks. If I did find a person who was objective enough to at least consider my point of view, their reply was often, "It's a Vietnamese war. If they want to do

that to each other, let them. It's not our problem." I soon stopped argu-
ing, convinced that those who had not shared my experiences had nothing
of value to offer. But Jack continued to write, as if in a strange extension of
our wartime correspondence. Through his letters I was able to again visit
the warm, untroubled summers of our childhood and laugh aloud at tales
of our charming stupidity. Before long, we were celebrating the births of
our children and regaling each other with accounts of their innocent antics. Jack Mooseau kept me connected with a part of myself that lay buried
beneath the trauma and despair of war. For that, I am ever grateful.

Returning to the Oakland-Berkeley area added an almost surreal aspect
to my growing sense of alienation. As an example, U.S. Postal Service
mail-drop receptacles were painted red on the top, blue on the bottom. I
found that many of these mailboxes now had large yellow stars stenciled
on them, right where the two colors met. The addition of this star made
the sides of the mailboxes resemble the Viet Cong flag. During my first
week back from Vietnam, a swift, uncomfortable sensation of delirium
gripped me each time I came upon one of these mailboxes.

While I was away, Berkeley changed the name of Willard Park, where I
used to play two-hand touch football as a kid, to "Ho Chi Minh Park."
Actually, the rhetoric of the time was that "the people" had "liberated" the
park. It was not unusual to hear an acquaintance casually say something
like, "I've got a softball game at Ho Chi Minh today, but I can meet you
after." I wondered how many years in a labor camp old Uncle Ho would
have expected of such undisciplined disciples before allowing them "to
share the fruits" of his revolution.

Here was the place I had longed to be more than any other; the land of
my dreams that was the endless topic of conversation with Vietnam buddies. It was the "Big PX," the "World." And when you had only a few
numbers left showing on your short-timer's calendar, it became a word
spoken in sappy and sentimental murmurs that made your insides go light
with excitement. "Home." However, it turned out be none of those
things. The author Gertrude Stein, also an Oakland native, once returned
for a visit only to find her childhood home destroyed by fire. She subsequently penned the oft-quoted phrase, "There is no there, there." It was
the only thing she ever wrote that I understood, but I understood it pro-
foundly. I moved away from the Bay Area as soon as I could and never returned except for an occasional visit.

My anger and frustration were sometimes overwhelming. I did not
know who to hold responsible for the way I was feeling. Oddly, I no
longer felt any animosity toward my father or the North Vietnamese, but
I blamed nearly everyone else. I blamed the South Vietnamese Army for

not fighting hard enough. I blamed the hippies and antiwar protesters for taking the easy way out and for their naively romanticized image of Ho Chi Minh. I blamed American politicians for vacillating in their resolve and the military for providing dishonest assessments of the situation. I began to feel that I had been used or abused by each of them. I felt stupid because I had not figured all this out earlier. Above all, I could not let Tom Mahoney's death and the deaths of tens of thousands of other men like him to have been for nothing. This bitterness smoldered within me for nearly twenty years before it eventually, mercifully, sputtered out.

Yet, there were times during those years when I could close my eyes and see the insolent young faces of my buddies, the fine red dust of Khe Sanh etched into their every pore. The ease, humor, and courage with which they endured such relentless peril would sometimes seem to me like a dream. In those moments, it did not matter how I felt about the war, the nation that wished to forget, or myself. It mattered only that I was proud to have stood with them and defended a little patch of ground.

* * * *

Private First Class Michael John Archer, 1968
Courtesy of Raul Orozco

Notes

* * *

1. Pisor, Robert, *The End of the Line: The Siege of Khe Sanh*, N.Y.: Ballantine Books, 1982, p. 126.
2. 26th Marine Regiment After Action Report, USMC Historical Center, Washington DC, quoted from Hammel, Eric, *Khe Sanh, Siege in the Clouds*, Crown Publishers, 1989, p. 7.
3. Pisor, *End of the Line*, p. 76.
4. Ibid., p. 86.
5. Ibid., p. 87.
6. Lanning, Michael and Dan Cragg, *Inside the VC and NVA: The Story of North Vietnams' Armed Forces*, Fawcett Columbine, p. 39.
7. Ibid., p. 78.
8. Ibid., p. 192.
9. Pisor, *End of the Line*, pp. 63–70.
10. Ibid., p. 65.
11. Ibid., p. 67.
12. Prados, John and Ray W. Stubbe, *Valley of Decision: The Siege of Khe Sanh*, Houghton Mifflin 1991, pp. 262–264.
13. Elsayed, N. M. "Toxicology of Blast Overpressure," *Toxicology*, 121(1): 1–15, July 25, 1997.
14. Brush, Peter, "Home Is Where You Dig It (Observations on Life at Khe Sanh Combat Base)." *The Sixties Project, Vietnam Generation Journal* 4, 3–4, November 1992; www.lists.village.virginia.edu/sixties.html.

15. Pisor, *End of the Line*, p. 218.

16. Stubbe, Ray W., *Khe Sanh and The Mongol Prince*, unpublished manuscript, 2002, p. 21.

17. Prados and Stubbe, *Valley of Decision*, p. 410.

18. Ibid., p. 425.

19. Sward, Susan, "Immeasurable Losses," *San Francisco Chronicle*, April 27, 1995.

20. Francis B. Ahearn, Memorandum, Re: T.P. Mahoney, September 4, 2003.

21. U.S. Library of Congress, *Personnel Missing South East Asia (PMSEA), South Vietnam, pre-1975: Report of death; case of Lance Corporal Thomas P. Mahoney III 2375990/0311, USMC*, REFN0 1224-0-01.

22. U.S. Library of Congress, DOD/DPMO Research and Investigation Team Research Report 03-016; Vietnam Historical Reference to Battles at Hill 845 in Quang Tri Province, Case 1224-0-01.

23. Comments of K. J. Camp, Re: conversation with PFC Bruce Bird, February 7, 2003.

24. Lownds, David, Transcript of his speech made during a ceremony to inter unidentifiable remains from the Khe Sanh battlefield at Jefferson Barracks National Cemetery in St. Louis, Missouri, July 12, 1997; www.geocities.com/pentagon/4867/reuniontext.html.

25. Brush, Peter, "The Withdrawal from Khe Sanh." *Vietnam History*; www.vwam.com/vets/khesanh.html.

26. Letter of Captain Robert Black, August 5, 2004.

27. Stubbe, *Mongol Prince*, p. 5.

28. Ibid., p. 27.

29. Pisor, *End of the Line*, p. 127.

Appendix

```
                        COMPANY "B"
             1ST  Battalion, 1ST  Marines
             1ST  Marine Division (Rein) MC
             FPO, San Francisco, California

                                      12 July 1968

Mrs. Patricia Mahoney


Dear Mrs. Mahoney:

It is difficult for me to express the regrets and sorrow felt by the
Marines in the company and myself over the recent death of your son,
Lance Corporal Thomas P. Mahoney III, U. S. Marine Corps, on 6 July
1968, in Quang Tri Province, Republic of Vietnam.

As you know Thomas was assigned as a rifleman in our first platoon.
During the afternoon of 6 July 1968, the company was in defensive
position and was engaged by the enemy.  During the ensuing battle,
Thomas was mortally wounded by enemy rifle fire.

It may comfort you to know that a special mass will be said for Thomas
at our Sunday service, which will be attended by his many friends.

Thomas was a sincere hard working young man who impressed everyone
with his eager manner and courteous demeanor.  He took great pride in
doing every job well and constantly displayed those qualities of eager-
ness and self-reliance that gained him the respect of his seniors and
contemporaries alike.  Although I realize that words can do little to
console you at a time such as this, I hope the knowledge that we share
your sorrow will help alleviate the suffering caused by your great
loss.

Thomas' personal effects are being prepared for shipment and will be
forwarded to you in the near future.

If you feel that in any way I can be of assistance to you, please feel
free to write.

                              Sincerely yours,


                              R. A. BLACK, JR.
                    Captain, U. S. Marine Corps
                              Commanding
```

The President of the United States takes pleasure in presenting the PRESIDENTIAL UNIT CITATION to

**TWENTY-SIXTH MARINES (REINFORCED),
THIRD MARINE DIVISION (REINFORCED)**

for service as set forth in the following

CITATION:

For extraordinary heroism in action against North Vietnamese Army forces during the battle for Khe Sanh in the Republic of Vietnam from 20 January to 1 April 1968. Throughout this period, the 26th Marines (Reinforced) was assigned the mission of holding the vital Khe Sanh Combat Base and positions on Hills 881, 861-A, 558 and 950, which dominated strategic enemy approach routes into Northern I Corps. The 26th Marines was opposed by numerically superior forces - two North Vietnamese Army divisions, strongly reinforced with artillery, tank, anti-aircraft artillery and rocket units. The enemy, deployed to take advantage of short lines of communications, rugged mountainous terrain, jungle, and adverse weather conditions, was determined to destroy the Khe Sanh Combat Base in conjunction with large scale offensive operations in the two northern provinces of the Republic of Vietnam. The 26th Marines, occupying a small but critical area, was daily subjected to hundreds of rounds of intensive artillery, mortar and rocket fire. In addition, fierce ground attacks were conducted by the enemy in an effort to penetrate the friendly positions. Despite overwhelming odds, the 26th Marines remained resolute and determined, maintaining the integrity of its positions and inflicting heavy losses on the enemy. When monsoon weather greatly reduced air support and compounded the problems of aerial resupply, the men of the 26th Marines stood defiantly firm, sustained by their own professional esprit and high sense of duty. Through their indomitable will, staunch endurance, and resolute courage, the 26th Marines and supporting units held the Khe Sanh Combat Base. The actions of the 26th Marines contributed substantially to the failure of the Viet Cong and North Vietnamese Army winter/spring offensive. The enemy forces were denied the military and psychological victory they so desperately sought. By their gallant fighting spirit and their countless individual acts of heroism, the men of the 26th Marines (Reinforced) established a record of illustrious courage and determination in keeping with the highest traditions of the Marine Corps and the United States Naval Service.